A LIFE WELL LIVED

Margaret Gay Brooks

HER AUTOBIOGRAPHY

ryelands

First published in 2025

Copyright © Margaret Gay Brooks

All rights reserved. Apart from any fair dealing for the purpose of private study, research, criticism or review, as permitted under the Copyright, Designs and Patents Act, 1988, no part of this publication may be reproduced, stored in a retrieval system, or transmitted in any form or by any means, electronic, electrical, chemical, mechanical, optical, photocopying, recording or otherwise, without the prior written permission of the copyright owner. Enquiries should be addressed to the Publishers.

Every attempt has been made by the author and publisher to secure the appropriate permissions for materials reproduced in this book. If there has been any oversight we will be happy to rectify the situation and a written submission should be made to the Publishers.

A CIP catalogue record for this book is available from the British Library.

ISBN: 9 781906 551599

Ryelands
Halsgrove House, Ryelands Business Park,
Bagley Road, Wellington, Somerset.
TA21 9PZ
Tel: 01823 653777
email: sales@halsgrove.com

Part of the Halsgrove group of companies information on all Halsgrove titles is available at: www.halsgrove.com

Printed and bound in India by Parksons Graphics Ltd

Contents

Introduction		5
1.	Brockton	7
2.	North Hawkwell	13
3.	Over View	18
4.	School Days, the Happiest Days of Your Life!?	23
5.	School Years, at Sherborne School for Girls	32
6.	Holidays	35
7.	More North Hawkwell Tales	40
8.	My Equine Friends	44
9.	The Next Chapter	52
10.	The Next Step	57
11.	Ever Onwards	61
12.	Mendips and the Lake District	65
13.	Canada Here I Come	71
14.	Meeting John	80
15.	Beginning Married Life	93
16.	Our Next Move	99
17.	North North-West to Onoway	104
18.	Married Life and Farm Life	109
19.	Heading West!	114
20.	Puckle Road, Hurray!	118
21.	Further Tales from Puckle Road	124
22.	Bridget's Arrival	127

23.	Anchors Away	**130**
24.	Returning to England	**133**
25.	Meeting Norman, Spring 1986	**137**
26.	The Reclamation of Gunns Farm	**140**
27.	Jason and Martha	**144**
28.	The Changing Seasons	**147**
29.	The Beginning of the Struggle for Martha's Health	**149**
30.	Getting to Grips with a New Routine	**152**
31.	A Rack of Ruined Bread	**155**
32.	Is There no End to This?	**159**
33.	Daylight at the End of the Tunnel?	**164**
34.	Back, Yet Again to the Vets	**167**
35.	Convalescence: Re-establishing Our More Normal Routine	**170**
36.	The Merry-go-round Continues	**174**
37.	Happy New Year	**178**
38.	Our Favourite Pastime – Watching the Red Deer of Exmoor	**181**
39.	January with Further Ups and Downs	**185**
40.	Martha Back to Health	**188**
41.	Travel Across Exmoor – Exmoor my Playground	**191**
42.	Learning to Cope with Polymyalgia Rheumatica	**195**
43.	Festa, the Bengal Eagle Owl Takes up Residence	**200**

Epilogue   **206**

Introduction

Dedication: To my daughters Pamela and Bridget who, for years, have been urging me 'to write it all down'. I feel I have been on quite an emotional journey, mostly enjoyable, some heart rending although, in the main, worthwhile. Enjoy!

Notes made in 1982 in Canada. Today I let one of my house cleaning jobs go; the feeling of relief as I closed the door for the last time was immeasurable, just relief from pressure I must add. Not from the people or the house, both very pleasant. Now I am just left with my home, two teenage girls, two dogs, four cats, four horses, one house cleaning job and eighteen hours of riding instruction to give. Add the house cleaning to the riding lessons and for someone who is only meant to work part time my hours nearly total full time! No wonder my Ex says I am always farming the road allowance: the road allowance being the land left for roads across the prairies between the quarter, half or full sections of land, all going, basically, east to west or north to south with the odd bend to go around lakes and slews or to dip into valley bottoms; a grid system that is easy to follow. But not so on Vancouver Island where it is very much like Britain.

How did it all start? Maybe growing up in Britain during the war years had something to do with my restless spirit. Having a father who, in 1942 in the middle of a war, uprooted his family from a prosperous dairy farm in the Midlands; with the constant sound of enemy planes overhead on their way to bomb our cities, with sickness in the dairy herd maybe, who knows, to a quiet hill farm in Somerset. Overnight it seemed to me, at not yet quite five years old, from a large well-appointed Georgian farm house with all modern conveniences to a much smaller farm house with running water (out of a pipe in the wall outside the back door into a trough then away down the side of the little back yard) and a 'loo' actually flush type, the previous owners' only concession to modernization down an outside passage from the back door, stone flags on all the floors downstairs and oil lamps to see by. We grew to love it.

I remember, I remember, it is the stuff dreams are made of. It is easier to dream backwards than forwards. To dream to remember; the happy times, the frightening times, times when decisions were made that would, unknowingly, shape the course of life for years to come.

What Exmoor Means To Me

I love this land of green with combes so steep
With chortling rivers running deep.
Where purple crowns adorn the hills
And swirling veils of mist drift by.

The moorland rolling, fold on fold, to meet the sky
With wooded valleys leading to the sea.
Criss crossed with age old pony tracts, and standing stones
And sheltering beech that weathers many a gale.

A land where deer roam free, the sheep and ponies too
And buzzards glide with mewling cry.
Where kestrels soar as fox slinks by
And darkness cloaks the badgers nightly toil.

A solid land where values still stand true
And sturdy moorland churches ring out their Sunday peal.
A place of twisty country lanes and open views
With pubs that welcome walking boots - dogs too.

This is an ancient land, at times forbidding
More oft made soft by sun and showers.
Here is a place to rest the weary, ease the soul
A paradise indeed for those who care to seek.

Chapter 1
BROCKTON

I was born on September 1st, 1937, in Brockton House, Shifnal, Shropshire a large Georgian country house which was a working farm. I don't know the time but as I always used to be an early riser, I assume it was in the early hours of the morning. I was the eldest of three children although, in reality I was the second child and, although I had responsibility thrust upon me from an early age I felt my temperament was more suited to be a follower than a leader: Extraordinary really but home births were the norm then and after the experience Mother went through with her first born when everything went wrong and the whole process went on for hours and hours and the baby boy was born dead I can only think how brave she was. My grandmother, who was renowned for always calling in specialists, apparently was there and never suggested calling in anyone other than the local GP. After losing this first child one wonders if specialist help was on hand for the second birth. Whether it was or not I, obviously, survived. After losing the first baby Mother was kept in bed for many weeks and made to drink pints and pints of water every day, a habit she kept up all her life.

My mother. Monica Nellie Sugden. Nellie being her mother's first name. Her parents were fairly strict practicing Methodists, so Sunday activities were restricted to attending chapel, reading a book or going for walks. I wish I could describe my mother to you. Mother, she was just there, all I can do is put down some facts. She was the fourth child of five. Her grandparents had emigrated to Canada and her mother was born in Quebec City; she and her sisters returning to England after their parents died. Her mother and sisters were swindled out of most of their money either by a confidence trickster on the boat over or by a crooked solicitor once over here. Her father an insurance broker. She was competitive and a good tennis player, loved to sing and had a beautiful voice. She used to go for long walks at the weekends in the Peak District, hop onto a train, walk from one valley to another, hop onto a train again and so back home. She was very close to her younger brother, Jim, they were quite close in age. After school she was told, in no uncertain terms, to train as a secretary (I think she had other ideas!) so that is what she did.

My father, Robert Blakely Collier, an only child. His mother, Maud, my granny, was one of four girls and the only one to marry. They devoted themselves to 'Good Works' and through their church belonged to an organisation helping young girls employed in the many mills in the area. They also did amazing needlework. All Maud's linen for her marriage was worked by them into the most beautiful table cloths, sheets, pillow cases, tray cloths; all deemed necessary for a young couple setting up their home. (I still have a drawer full of this exquisite work, a testament to all their labours.) Maud was a formidable and very strong-willed lady who must be obeyed. At all costs. If my father, as a child, displeased her he was shut away, half way up the stairs, in a dark cupboard. He remembered his father begging him to say 'sorry' even if he did not know what he was apologising for.

My father's father Frank Collier, my Grandpa, was in clothes manufacturing. He was a very gentle man and well thought of in the manufacturing community of the Salford/Manchester area. He was honorary treasurer for The Shirt and Collar Manufacturers Federation and honorary secretary for The District Federation. We have the details for the complimentary retirement dinner given 'In Appreciation for Services Rendered to The District Federation for Mr Cameron, retiring and F Collier Esq, Hon Secretary, retiring. It is as follows.

Royal Whitstables (oysters) mock turtle soup. Fillet of sole vin blanc. Sweetbread Financiere, roast mutton-onion sauce-potatoes-sprouts. Cabinet pudding, coffee.

Quite a feast and with all the speeches quite an evening.

At thirteen my father was sent away to a boarding school, in Cambridge from whence he wrote letters home pleading to be taken away as he was so unhappy there, but to no avail. My father's religious upbringing was down to the Baptist Church which I find quite extraordinary for I have recently been to a celebration of life in a Baptist chapel and I just cannot see my rather austere grandparents being in such a congregation with the enthusiastic hand clapping and swaying to music that I witnessed at this service.

Regarding my religious upbringing. Mother a Methodist, Father a Baptist, where should I be placed? It was decided that they would join the Church of England and I was duly christened under the names Margaret Gay; it was decided not to name me after any relations to avoid favouritism in the families. Imagine their horror and my father's parents joy when, on returning from a holiday abroad they find their first grandchild named after his mother. No-one realised that Maud was a diminutive form of Margaret! So, to even things out Mother's maiden name, Sugden, was also given to me. Subsequently my sister was named after Mother – Monica Elizabeth – and my brother after Father – Robert Jonathan – each with the appendage Sugden for good measure. And no – no one ever explained why all three of us are called by our second Christian names.

After boarding school Father went to study agriculture at Harper Adams Agricultural College and thence to a year's student exchange to Ontario, Canada. The city of Hamilton has long since swallowed up the land where the farm was located. All the ploughing and harvesting was done with teams of horses. They always had a rifle under the seat to shoot the marauding wolves they used to see lurking at the forest edge. This adventure came to an abrupt end one day. After getting down from the seat of the harrows to adjust a piece of the machinery the horses moved and a sharp piece cut his leg nearly severing his Achilles tendon. He spent three months in hospital. He was the darling of the ward with his curly blondish hair and English accent. All the tender attentions of the nurses and one in particular who plied him with glasses of milk on request resulted in him leaving hospital with much gained weight, a limp which he never really lost and once home again in England, a strong desire to emigrate.

Family legend has it that once home from Canada he lost no time in seeking out my mother; they had known each other in their teens and Father must have been cherishing fond memories ever since otherwise why go looking for her? Mother came home one afternoon from work to find Father having a cup of tea with her mother. Apparently he went home afterwards and told his parents he had found the girl he was going to marry. Their romance blossomed and subsequently they became engaged. I hope he wrote a kind letter to that nurse in that hospital in Canada. On hearing Mother was going to marry a farmer, her brother-in-law Warwick Frost advised her never to learn to milk a cow, make bread or kill a chicken. I think he must have said it in jest but she successfully avoided these three chores all her life. My father taught me how to wring a chicken's neck but I did not enjoy doing it and avoided it if I could.

His parents were very much against his idea of emigrating and soon put a stop to this flighty idea (as they saw it) about emigrating anywhere. He was an only child, compromise was the name of the game. They bought Brockton, a dairy farm with a large Georgian house just south of the town of Telford in Shropshire with a long drive leading up to the front door and all the farm buildings behind, including a walled garden.

I am not sure how many were employed outside. The milking herd were Ayrshires. What a sight they made, all lined up in the shippen waiting their turn to go along to the milking parlour, the differing tones of brown shading into the white areas on their bodies, the soft warm expressions in their large brown eyes. The bulls were another matter altogether having very uncertain tempers (who would be kept chained up all the time except when serving a cow). Frankly they were dangerous and it was well drilled into everybody, especially me at my very young age, never to go anywhere near the bull pens. There were 75 or 85 cows in milk plus dry cows, cows in calf, young stock and the bull. There was a head herdsman, Scottish, who, in 1941 never noticed we had the abortion syndrome in the herd. Mother, walking in the fields one day came upon an aborted foetus and subsequently many others were found. This meant there was brucellosis in the herd, brought in by a cow Father had bought at a farm sale. This must have been so distressing; this beautiful herd of happy Ayrshires decimated by disease. Before this catastrophe though I believe the farm was a happy place to work. Father won the Clean Milk competition three years in a row, we still have the handsome silver cup. He always said that if the judges had realised he had already won it twice they would have awarded it to another farm. Winning it three times meant he got to keep the cup for ever.

In the house Mother had Mary Jasper, née Priest five and a half days a week. Mary lived on the other side of the main road which bordered the property on the east side (I think) in Pillar Box or Post Box Cottage as the post box was let into the garden wall. Before Mother and Father left they made sure Mary had a watertight lease on the cottage which had running water into the kitchen but no other indoor plumbing. I think Mary and, subsequently, her husband were afraid to ask for improvements in case it gave the landlord an excuse to turf them out. I remember hearing that there were efforts to get them out down the years, I expect they only paid a peppercorn rent. Mary died in the early '90s and, to the end of her days, she never had indoor sanitation. You had to go out of the back door, down a short flagged passage, very slippery when damp, and into a spotlessly clean shed with some sort of a toilet, certainly not the flush type we all take for granted these days. Mary had a lot to do with me as she doubled up as general help and nursery maid. There was also Mrs Churm, who came from Madeley, for the heavy scrubbing and laundry. And the house was full of Land Girls once the war started. There were miles of flagstone passages although Father knocked down a lot of miscellaneous sculleries etc. at the back.

Father was a very innovative man and he designed a very modern milking parlour and cow shed. The cows stood in stalls down either side of the alley and the dung was swept into this wide alleyway with a conveyer belt running down the middle behind the cows. The muck was carried by this conveyer belt to the outside and dropped into a pit which was easily accessible from the outside for spreading onto the fields. From their stalls the cows proceeded to the milking parlour and afterwards were released out into yards and thence to the fields. He also had the first grass drying plant in Shropshire and a cousin, Doris Bell wrote a murder mystery centred on this plant called *Murder at Wrekin Farm*. The Wrekin being the local hills. Doris's father was a doctor and he identified the facial palsy which affects the face. It causes one side of the face to droop, pulling the contour of that eye out of shape so that eye is constantly watering. It is a very painful condition now known as Bell's Palsy. My sister Liz contracted this whilst training to be a Nursery Nurse at a hospital in London. She spent some time at home to recover and, I believe, had some private treatment in Taunton which helped get over the paralysis so her face returned to nearly normal.

Although the eldest of three children I was really the second child due to the loss of the first. I always felt my temperament was better suited to being a second child; I always wanted someone to lead me, shelter and protect me. Instead I had to forge ahead, make my own way. I was very much treated as the oldest. I had responsibility thrust upon me at an early age, so much so that I accepted it as the norm and it is only in older life that I have begun to question that aspect of my childhood and subsequent life and wonder what influence this most certainly had on the decisions I was to make throughout my life. I was labelled "a responsible child" from an early age!

I believe I was a happy and secure child. At least in the early years. There are photos showing happy family groups on the lawn at Brockton with grandparents, aunts, uncles and cousins present, and ones of Father with me up on his shoulder and dogs running around. I suppose I would have been around eighteen months when the talk seriously turned towards WAR. I am convinced that very young children pick up tensions, vibrations, and unhappiness being expressed by those around them.

The war to a great extent passed me by though I must have been picking up the aforementioned vibes as any mention of troubles or war used to make me sick to my stomach. To quite an extent it did impinge on my subconscious. It obviously came our way to a certain extent. Father belonged to the Home Guard and was also a Special Constable, mounted division, in Somerset. The house was full of Land Girls for the milking and the milk rounds which were done with small vans. A lively group I believe and Mother kept up the friendships after the war. We must have had some air raid scares though as I remember being picked up out of bed in the middle of the night and carried down to shelter under the dining room table which was rather alarming.

The Air Ministry commandeered some of our flat fields and aeroplanes were stored there, away from the known airfields, for safety. Father, an uncle (I think Uncle Bob) home on leave, and I went up there one evening. I suppose I would have been four or thereabouts. We walked around them and under them and someone climbed onto a wing and all the time I wished Father and Uncle Bob would hurry up: I was sure we shouldn't be there at all even though Father owned the fields. What if someone came along and found us there! My insecurity and feelings of apprehension have to stem from the war years.

We had a beautiful carthorse called Turpin. I used to love being popped onto his broad back and, once, when I was on the dray, standing beside the carter, I was handed the reins with instructions not to move, whilst the carter got down to talk to Father. In reality I expect he was close enough to prevent a disaster What a proud moment, in charge of this enormous beast. I was turned to stone, I'm sure, not even a fly landing on my bare leg interrupted my concentration on keeping absolutely still. Who knows what forces I might unleash if I so much as twitched a rein. I can see myself now; I have such a clear image of this moment.

Mother always had a terrier but the favourite dog was Smithy, an Irish Wolfhound. His party trick was to stand on his hind legs and pick plums off the tree and eat them. I wonder what happened to the stones? He used to graciously allow me to take him for walks. What a gentle beast he was. The lead used to hang in a great loop from his collar to my hand as he stalked majestly behind me around the yard. Another gentle giant. He did something naughty one day and Father shut him up and when he went back to let him out he was dead. He had had a very poor start in life, had been almost starved. My parents bought him out of a farm sale; he was the last item to be sold (can you imagine?) and it was assumed his heart must have been weak from his early life. Father was very upset. But you did things like that in those days. We also had an Old English Sheepdog called Betsy.

There was a sort of magic to being ill when I was young. The large bedrooms had high ceilings and fireplaces. Lying awake, all cosy and warm, watching the firelight flickering on the ceiling and seeing the comforting shadowy outline of Mother or Mary sitting behind the screen between the bed and the fire. Maybe aware of them quietly moving around the room, offering a glass of water, smoothing a pillow, talking in low hushed tones. And the sweet smell of laundry airing on the 3 foot high brass fenders arranged around the fireplace. And kneeling beside the bed to say one's prayers each night.

Lying in bed, lazily watching Mary going backwards and forwards with large jugs of warm water for the tin bath set up in front of the open fire. Being carried over and set into the bath with Mary kneeling down, the better to wash me with a large sponge. Being lifted out to stand before the fire wrapped in a large fluffy towel and patted dry and left settled in Mary's chair beside the fire whilst my bed was made straight, all warm and cosy, wrapped in a cocoon of loving, healing care. Getting better with a return to solid food, the sweet taste of that first slice of fresh bread with a scrape of butter. Nursing the old fashioned way and how comforting it was. Kneeling beside the bed each night to say one's prayers. "Dear Father, who art in heaven, please bless Mummy and Daddy, Granny and Granpa. And help me to be a good little girl." Amen. Later my sister and brother were added.

Having mastoiditis was another story and I really do not remember much about it. I was obviously very ill as I was in hospital for three months. No penicillin in those days and I was operated on. Just one slip of the knife and I could have been a vegetable for the rest of my life I believe. Scary thought. I've only ever had partial hearing in that right ear which never bothered me until now I am losing it in my left, good ear.

Chapter 2
NORTH HAWKWELL

And so to North Hawkwell. Actually, Father bought three farms: North Hawkwell, North Combe and East Harwood, totalling some five hundred acres. We were to live at North Hawkwell which, although much needed to be done to it at least had a house and was reasonably accessible. North Combe with only a large barn and no house was out of the question and East Harwood had tenants in the house.

I admit I am a little confused here re the dates of the move. I thought we were there for my fifth birthday, September 1st. I certainly remember all the empty rooms and work dust everywhere. Looking back from now that must have come from the work being done in the house. Installing the cooker and the bathroom must have created lots of mess. I do remember that Mary was with us at this time and she left a half-eaten apple on a windowsill and the next day it was all brown on the outside and Mary still finished it. I did not like the idea at all. So we could well have stayed there over my birthday but not actually moved in. During this visit we were staying at West Harwood Farm with Mr and Mrs Daryl Stevens which is just slightly further down the valley and then up a steep lane. Apparently I spent hours following Mr Stevens as he went around doing his farmyard chores. He always wore a jute sack against the weather when it rained. I believe he was crippled with arthritis in later life. Also I remember being at table and chewing a piece of meat around and around in my mouth, getting up and going outside closely followed by one of the dogs who promptly ate what I spat out.

The confusion arose when I discovered details of the sale in Shropshire:
- Important Agricultural Dispersal Sale
- Blakeley Herd of Attested Ayrshires
- Founded 1930
- Wednesday 7th October 1942.

Maybe best just to say we left Shropshire in 1942 to move to Somerset. The dairy cattle had all been sold although there was still a lot to move. It all came down on the train, machinery, livestock, horses I assume and dogs, maybe, also, the Jersey milk cow, all unloaded at Dunster Station.

North Hawkwell. An Exmoor hill farm situated up a very steep drive on the lower slopes of Dunkery moor in the parish of Timberscombe. The boundary of our top fields lay against the moor at Spangate and our lower fields ran alongside Snowdrop Valley and the adjoining woods.

North Hawkwell had none of the things Mother was used to, Father too for that matter. There were no modern facilities: No telephone, no electricity, no indoor plumbing although there might have been a cold water tap in the kitchen. Father was on his 'Adventure'. Denied the chance to emigrate to Canada he was, nevertheless, doing a version of emigrating, just on home soil. He had been strongly advised by a friend to purchase and take with him an Esse cooker which would cook and heat the water. This was installed in the big, open, fireplace in the kitchen and the middle bedroom at the front was converted into a bathroom with a large, walk-in airing cupboard. Once, during lambing, Father could not find Mother anywhere. Eventually he located her, sound asleep, standing up in the airing cupboard with her arms draped across the hot water tank. I wonder how many times Mother was to offer up little prayers of thanks to that friend for his foresight in offering much needed advice.

The drive up to the farm was nothing but a steep rutted track that the car could not negotiate frontwards. It had to be backed up which cannot have done much good to the gear box. The day the grandparents came for their first Christmas with us it was raining. I went with Father when we drove to Dunster Station to pick them up in the car, having previously left a tractor and trailer, with tarpaulin, down at the bottom of the track and loaded them, and a protesting me, under the tarpaulin on the trailer and hauled us up the house that way. Once there it was up three steps into the front bit of garden leading to the front door set into a porch with seats on either side. This front door was rarely used. The post mistress, who, six days a week, walked from Timberscombe, the village 3 miles east, delivering post to all the dwellings on either side of the valley, left the post there and we would often find a parcel of venison there too.

The back door was the one most used. There was a small concrete yard and under a bit of sloping roof water dribbled out of a pipe in the back wall into a trough to run away down the open drain at the side of the yard. Here a scrub brush hung from a nail on a piece of string for everyone to scrub their boots before entering the kitchen. The opposite side of the yard was a roofed-in shed and a passage down to the flush 'loo'.

There were large stone flags throughout the ground floor. Those in the kitchen never seemed completely dry, especially after wash days. The laundry was put to soak in large tubs on the kitchen floor last thing before bed on a Sunday night. This was then scrubbed and wrung out on Monday and put through the mangle which was set up above a large galvanized barrel outside the back door. The squeezed water from the clothes was collected in this barrel which was then emptied into the drain that ran down the yard. Not always immediately. My sister Liz, aged about three, was, one day, found energetically swishing her kitten around in the bottom. There after mother always made sure she emptied the barrel after use. The newly bought Esse cooker installed in the inglenook fireplace provided a constant source of heat, did all the cooking and heated the hot water. On the opposite wall was a hatch into the dining room and the sink and draining board beside where I think the original back door opened. The window, with window seat, opened onto the little yard and we had a large wooden kitchen table there. A door at the back, left corner, led into the passage to the rest of the house. A little room on the right, a door opposite to the front hall and straight ahead to the larder with its stone slabs, a long trestle table and a small window in the west wall; very cold in here, excellent for keeping food cool though. Into the hall; immediately on the left the door into the dining room although a more factual description would be to call it the living room as we spent all our leisure time in there also. The stairs went up opposite the front door and a door on the right beside the front door led into the sitting room, rarely used except at Christmas and in the summer when the weather was warm. At other times it struck cold as you entered and every surface always seemed covered in dust, even after just being dusted!

At the top of the first stairs a door opened left into what was to become my bedroom. A long room with its window in the west wall overlooking the lane that ran down past the house; a right of way that avoids going through the farm yard. This room adjoined the stable behind and the rats running over the ceiling used to wake me up at night so Father supplied me with a long handled broom which I would use to knock on the ceiling to frighten them away. Mice, and cockroaches, were a constant problem too. Anyone going down to the kitchen in the dark with only a small torch to see by could not avoid crushing cockroaches under foot as one went through. I can still hear that distinctive crunch! There is a small landing here. I imagine this part of the house could have once been part of the stable behind as there is something resembling a hatch in the partition wall beside the door. From the top of these stairs you turned right up a short flight into a large bedroom over the kitchen where Mother and Father slept or you turned back on yourself up another flight of stairs leading to the two front bedrooms and the bathroom.

I remember I tripped once on my way to bed and dropped my oil lamp which spilt and the lit oil started to spread flames across the carpet. Father came running and stamped on the flames and put them out. Another time, after we had the generator, the lights went out whilst I was in the bathroom and I panicked. Not used to the erratic behaviour of generators my panic saw me hurtling down the stairs so fast I tore the sole completely off one of my sandals. Being at school at Nettlecombe Court was a pretty scary experience and I can only think memories of ghostly tales precipitated me down the stairs rather faster than usual.

Once outside again the yards are behind the house. One yard was divided into two by the end of one of the buildings; a bit of wall with the drinking trough going through so stock could drink from either yard and a gate. The first building, on the left, was the tool shed which also had a couple of comfortable old arm chairs for those eating their packed lunches. The dog kennels were here also – sawn in half beer barrels, propped up with red bricks to stop them rolling and filled with straw which usually ended up more outside than in. The working dogs were tied up here with long chains when not working. One learnt to one's cost to walk around them not over the chains as a dog getting up to greet you tripped you with the chain which was usually quite painful. Then came the stable with, originally, four tie stalls. Father took out one partition to create a large loose box on the right hand side. The floors were cobbled with a drain behind where the horses stood for the muck to collect.

Opposite the stables were traditional barns, divided into different sized spaces often by the use of wooden hurdles; very dark. What little light came through small windows set high usually coated with dust-covered cobwebs. The upper yard had a large two-storey barn built into the hillside so both floors were at ground level. Cow stalls on the ground floor facing south where the house cow was milked twice a day and, entered from the higher ground facing north, the upper storey where the shearing was done. Here also was the large Dutch barn where the main crop of hay and straw was stored.

As there was no electricity we used oil lamps or candles in the house and the wireless ran on batteries. During the winter the only light in the cow sheds was provided by hurricane lanterns which were hung from any handy nail in the beam over one's head. The soft warm glow from these lanterns spilling light in semi circles from the doorways onto the cobbles of the yard remains with me to this day.

Above this is the steep field we used to call The Running Field, because, as children we used to run down it. My father excavated a pit and constructed the sheep dip here. Just out of the top yard, up the lane on the left Mother had her poultry enclosure where she kept her flock of laying hens. No water laid on here, it all had to be carried from the yard. I know, because, as I grew older, in the holiday time the hens were my responsibility. Facing down the hill from here, at the back of the stable, is a linhay which housed the cider press which was used every autumn to make the next year's cider from the cider apples in the orchard. All the lorry drivers delivering whatever the farm needed were encouraged to help themselves to a refreshing mug of cider before leaving. Cider making went on for years until my brother also found cider rather refreshing and started to help himself!

This lane, going up to the fields behind the buildings was very steep and rutted with a sharp bend half way up which is where someone coming down on a tractor towing a fully loaded trailer of hay got the tractor wheels stuck in a deep rut , lost control and the trailer tipped over. The mind boggles. This was a wonderful area for blackberry picking. I used to enjoy this activity as I could pick from the back of my pony and anything involving the pony had to be enjoyable. Of course it was a contest as to who got to the best berries, me or the pony.

Opposite the back door is a steep bit of ground I called 'the plat.' There was a ground level upper storey to the barn in the lower yard where my pony Robin sometimes lived and Mother kept her geese here and hung out the laundry and had a strawberry plot and white rabbits in a hutch with wire netting run; maybe not all at the same time. The geese were the bane of my life. For some reason one spring holiday my pony had to live in this upper barn close to where the goose was sitting on eggs with the gander constantly on guard. I believe the stable was full of sheep. We never wore trousers back then. It was bare legs and skirts or frocks unless we were actually going riding when we wore jodphurs with wide flanges on the outside, above the knee. I was forever getting attacked by this gander, I would grit my teeth and try to walk quietly past the beastly, hissing thing without him noticing I was there. Even with his head tucked under one wing and, seemingly, asleep he would spring into action, grabbing my skirt in his beak and beating my bare legs with his wings which was not only painful but quite frightening. To add insult to injury, one day Robin stood on my foot whilst I was grooming him ready for a ride. I must have been in immense pain as I flew past the gander to run indoors to Mother. Once there I got short shift and sent to my room; there must have been a crisis on and Mother didn't have time for a weepy child. When all was quiet I crept downstairs and Mother apologised for not listening to me. Only a few years ago I went to my McTimoney Chiropractor for a massage and mentioned my foot. She said she had never come across such a mangled foot and worked on it and it is now fine. All those years and buying corrective insoles in Canada and it just needed tweaking.

Chapter 3
OVER VIEW

Looking back I feel things lurched from one crisis to another. We had a shepherd, Mr Crockford, a full-time farmworker Bill Coles and his brother Charlie who worked part time. Lambing time involved agricultural students in the house. By now Mother had two younger children, just fifteen months between them. She used to employ young, local, girls in the house but they always seemed to be going home for their days off and not returning. The students caused me a lot of hassle. They were for ever ambushing me by the water trough or on my way into the house and squirting me with the lambs' feeding bottles that they just happened to be cleaning as I was passing by. The laundry must have been a major chore and nappies too.

Haymaking always produced traumas too with the baler breaking down at a crucial stage. We could hear Father coming as he had all his shoes fitted with hob nails. You would hear him coming through the kitchen, along the passage to the foot of the stairs where he would swing on the newel post at the bottom and yell "Darling! The ------ baler's broken again." Whereupon Mother would make soothing noises and Father would tramp out again to arrange for it to be towed to Williton for repairs. The tension could be cut with a knife and the whole situation could have been prevented, I'm sure, if the thing had been properly serviced at the end of haymaking each year instead of being parked up and left somewhere out of the way and out in the open.

Another time we received information that one of the bulls (Father was now breeding Aberdeen Angus beef cattle) had got out of his field and taking his cows with him was heading towards the other bull, with only one five barred gate separating them. This would have splintered like match wood if they had caught sight of each other and decided to have a battle. All available help leapt into the Land Rover, somehow I scrambled in too, all clinging onto what ever came to hand as Father raced, at full throttle, up the rutty lane and over the bouncy fields. We got there in the nick of time and turned the maurading bull back to his own pasture. I thought it was terribly exciting, a viewpoint not shared by either my father or whoever else was there.

Another time involved moving cattle in deep snow. Again we must have been taken by surprise, this deep a snow over the Christmas period; no five day forecasts in those days. Bill's brother Charlie had the uncanny ability to smell impending snow on the wind, if that were the case he cannot have been around the day before to warn us of the storm to come that night. The snow was deep, my legs still quite short, the cattle were on the high ground and the wind was vicious.

The gateways were full of drifted snow, someone must have thought to bring a shovel. We battled our way up to the top land, me following in others' footsteps; not that easy even so, as they were all much taller than myself so took longer strides. The aim was to get these cattle down to East Harwood where most of the hay was stored. They were hungry and milling around complaining bitterly as we struggled to free the gates and start them on the journey down. Once moving, in that uncanny way of animals to sense a good thing they were easy to keep going. And, for me, the going was much easier following in the wake of the cattle. I remember, we were on the way home, Mr Crockford turning to me and asking if I was very cold and I replied not at all. I had youth on my side.

1947. I feel they were never quite ready for winter, never more so than when the snow hit that year. Tons of it. There was no wood cut for the fires and no-one had the time or the energy to get some in. This snow came so late in the season. The farmers were all lambing but no one had the indoor facilities there are now. Lambing was done outside in the fields. Lambs were dying like flies, being born and freezing to death if not found immediately. The only way Walter Crockford could get to us from Brockwell where he lived was to walk and a lot of that walking was actually over the top of the hedges. Absolutely horrendous conditions endured by anyone who had livestock. Weak, ailing lambs were a common sight in boxes by the Esse, or even in the bottom, cool oven and others were wrapped up and placed in holes in the dung heap with just their heads sticking out. The dung heap was warm and there they were fed until they had warmed up and could be returned to their mother.

We had sheep and the house cow initially plus a lovely bay gelding called Bay and three others, all greys, a gelding and two mares, all related; one mare was called Melody and the gelding was Sahib. They must have been all sold on, one of the mares was struck dead by lightning after it was sold, and that is all I remember about that trio. And the shepherding pony Jane. Plus cats, Mother loved cats; it was so distressing when they all contracted cat flu and gradually died. And a couple of dogs I think; there were always dogs around so there must have been one or two. And, again, very distressing when her first Golden Retriever, Choti, got hardpad and died. There was a new vaccine too but the vet never told Mother about it as he did not think she would like the source; something to do with calves feet? And, of course, if you have sheep, a sheep dog. I remember Shep, whether he came with the shepherd, Walter Crockford, or was one of ours I am not sure. He was followed by Jock, a most undisciplined dog with a lovely, warm character who just wanted to be loved; useless for work though. Mr Crockford always maintained he had been spoilt by us children as a puppy; he knew the exact length of the lash of a hunting crop and would circle just out of reach barking all the time. It was just a game to him. Mr Crockford bought a longer lash; he only caught Jock once with it, Jock's circles just became that much larger!

There was Jasper, a spaniel, who was, theoretically, my dog. He had a nasty skin condition which would not get better. I was told he had been returned to the breeder. Hindsight tells me he was put down. Likewise a terrier of Mother's who would get out and go sheep worrying. I was told he had been found a new home in Brompton Regis. I remember once going there and craning my neck out of the window hoping to get a glimpse if him. Now I realise he too must have been shot.

All the sheep work was done from the back of a pony and, after I could ride, I spent many happy hours riding out with Mr Crockford, as he did the daily check or moved them onto fresh pastures. I used to love watching the young lambs of an evening, playing on the banks of the water leats that ran across the meadows bringing fresh water to encourage the growth of new grass each spring. They would hop and skip and run up and down and head butt each other. Father hated to see this as he said they got overheated and would then get chilled and develop pneumonia. It is said sheep should never hear the church bells twice from the same field. Maybe this saying relates to the fact that after a short while in one field sheep will start to look for a way to escape to pastures new. Mr Crockford wore breeches with gaiters and hob-nailed boots and a jute sack in wet weather. We grew mangles (a kind of beet) for the sheep which were stored in a cave made of straw in the field above where the sheep were to be fed in the winter. This made for easy feeding as the mangles were either thrown or kicked over the hedge into this lower field. I loved kicking them, I became quite accurate at it, a useful skill I was to use years later in my working life with horses: A well aimed high kick to the rib cage will soon sort out the most obstreperous of arguing horses.

There was a nasty incident in a field of standing corn one night. According to The War Agricultural Committee regulations we were growing grain, oats most likely or wheat on our hill farm. These farms are not suitable for growing grain but orders were orders. On top of the normal, difficult, weather conditions we had to contend with it was proving impossible to keep out the deer. They would come in under the cover of darkness, eat the ripening seed heads then lie down for the day in the middle of the field, creating large squashed areas that were ruining the crop. Father organised a shooting party in the hope of killing the ring leader and frightening away the rest. And I went along too. The shooters were placed around the top edge of the field and someone was sent in to rouse up the deer. This particular evening a large stag was lying up in the middle of the field, quite hidden until driven to his feet. Whether someone was in hurry with their shot or the light was fading making a sure shot more difficult was never discovered but instead of killing the stag the bullet took the tip off his highest antler and came ricocheting back through the ears of grain, you could hear it coming and passed, too close for comfort, between myself and Father. There was a deadly hush, I couldn't understand what had happened, I just suddenly found the atmosphere frightening. Father was very shaken. " Enough of this," he said, "it's not worth the risk" and put an immediate ban on any more shooting. He decided if the War Ag. Committee continued to insist that he grew grain on such an unsuitable farm they could put up with the low yield caused by the weather and the damage from the deer. This large stag was easily identified until the following spring, when the old antlers drop, by the missing tip of the top antler.

There is no doubt the deer were an absolute menace and did a lot of damage making great tracks over the hedges and eating too much grass, needed for the farm stock, as well as damaging the harvest. A certain amount of deer control was carried out. Father did not like this method of reducing numbers but he went along with it as an alternative to the aforementioned incident. If I remember rightly the deer were driven up Bincombe to where a line of guns was waiting on the edge of the open moor. I was never taken along on one of these for which I am thankful as Father found them distasteful; he thought they were unsportsmanlike affairs, rather akin to shooting rabbits, not worthy of the deer, and always worried about wounded deer not being tracked down and finished off properly.

I do know we ate a lot of venison; we would often find parcels of it in the front porch. Mother roasted it in a flour and water paste which set hard around the meat, sealing in all the juices, resulting in tender very flavoursome joints of meat. This crust made marvellous scraps for the dogs. Mother made the most delicious potted meat from the left-over roasts which was put into little jars and sealed with melted margarine and used to keep very well. I wish I had that recipe now, best eaten at picnics spread on a hunk of fresh bread.

Ours was a busy working farm. There was no time for entertaining children, we made our own activities and if we ran out of ideas and complained of being 'bored' we were soon found something to do, not always to our liking. In the main we learnt to keep quiet and occupy ourselves once our assigned chores were finished. Occasionally when maybe we were housebound through a prolonged period of rain, Mother would make up a mixture of cream with added Ovaltine crystals and drinking chocolate mixed to a thick consistency and put into individual egg cups. Armed with the smallest teaspoons she had we would sit on the edge of the long kitchen table with our legs swinging as we spooned up the delicious mixture. The winner was the one who made theirs last the longest. Inspirational!

Whether through uttering the "forbidden" word or just to give me something to do or to get my head out of the current favourite book remains a mystery, nevertheless it used to be suggested to me that I might like, seeing as those 'pesky deer' were 'in' again to do something about it. So I would saddle up Robin and ride up to the top fields to find and chase away any deer that were peacefully snacking on Father's lush, green, pastures. I'd gallop flat out towards them, cracking my hunting crop and yelling and the hinds would melt away, anything for an easy life, but the stags were a different matter, much harder to push out. We had a large area of huge gorse bushes and the stag would head for there with me galloping along behind, Around the outside track we would go then I'd wheel Robin and gallop the other way and meet the stag face to face whereupon he would jump into the middle of the gorse. We would stand and stare at each other, stag's sides heaving, pony's sides heaving until, knowing I could not shift him, I'd head for home and supper. Great fun.

We also had the odd pig around which was duly slaughtered. This always had to take place once the post mistress had delivered the post in case we were slaughtering more than our allowance. Mother tried to keep us away from the window as the pig was actually slaughtered but this was a difficult task as the slaughtering took place in the little back yard with its good drainage and close proximity to the hot water needed to facilitate the removal of all the bristles once it was dead. Father would look up and see three little faces peering out of his bedroom window; it would be another case of "Darling, will you please remove the children from the window". The pig was cured and hung in the kitchen and the larder, and divided amongst those that worked for us.

The house cow was a Jersey who gave us gallons of very rich milk. She was milked twice a day. Mother used to set tall glasses of milk for us children in the larder where, over time, the cream would rise to the top of the glass. This was the only way I would drink it, warm milk straight from the cow I found quite revolting. One drank the milk first from below the cream, ending up with a white moustache, and the cream last; this must be where my love of cream came from. The bulk of the milk was poured into large, shallow bowls and left to rise on the cool slabs in the larder. Some bowls were then set on the Esse for the milk to slowly heat up and the cream to clot on the top. Fresh clotted cream with Golden Syrup on new white bread has to be one of life's most decadent pleasures. We made our own butter too: the fresh cream was skimmed from the milk and placed into the butter churn. This could be very rewarding if the butter 'came' quickly but hard work if, on warm days, the cream just sloshed around and around whilst we kept turning the handle, anxiously waiting to hear the first clunk as a lump of formed fat hit the sides of the churn. The residual liquid, the butter milk, was fed to the pig as was any surplus skimmed milk. Milk straight from the cow is the right temperature for making junket which, to this day I cannot abide; the slippery feel of the set milk on my tongue was quite abhorrent to me. On the other hand Mother's rice puddings were absolutely delicious. Hours in the bottom oven of the Esse produced this very creamy, slightly pink pudding with a crispy top. Nothing like the stodgy rice puddings we were fed at school.

Mother had her flock of laying hens and also used to rear table birds; cockerels that were caponised with a pellet under the skin of their necks to stop them fighting (chemical sterilization) and help them to fatten better. Cider was made in the autumn. I only remember watching this once, it must have been before I was sent off to school. I remember the men turning the wheel and the juice, all frothy, coming down the sluice to be collected and transferred into oak barrels.

Chapter 4
SCHOOL DAYS, THE HAPPIEST DAYS OF YOUR LIFE!?

Boarding schools. For all the years I spent in boarding school, desperately home sick for most of the time, I have to give credit for where credit is due. Going to boarding school was a rude awakening; it thrust me out of the familiar, gone was the comforting daily routine of family life, the regular familiar stable guidelines that one, without realising, followed each day. Instead all was strange. Boarding school though gave me the grounding to go out and survive the challenges that my life was to throw at me down the years.

After being in hospital for three months following a mastoid operation and then the move to North Hawkwell my schooling was on hold. The village school was not considered an option as this was situated in Wheddon Cross, some 2 miles away and one had to walk to get there. Two miles does not sound too arduous but it was down into the valley and up the other side through tracks in the woods, very muddy in winter time, and there was no one from our side of the valley going there to keep me company. My sister Liz (five and a half years younger) and my brother Jonny (six and three quarter years younger) both went to the village school for a time. Mrs Jolly was the headmistress. And they went by taxi! My brother had been very ill; it now transpires that he actually had had polio and was considered delicate. This taxi also picked up the children from West Harwood and maybe, children from Bench Cottage also. It was not unknown for Jonny to rush indoors after being dropped off at the end of the school day, grab a jacket and his wellingtons, run down the steep field, often in time to wave to the taxi as it went past and so up the steep lane to West Harwood to play. This right after the taxi ride home because he was meant to be delicate!

There was talk about 'going away to school' but I had no concept of what that really meant. I wonder how Mother felt? Was I going because it was the 'right' thing to do? Was she worried or apprehensive for me, did she ever question the decision. Did she just think that with a new baby on the way and no way for anyone to get me up to Wheddon Cross the question of the local school was just out of the question. Did they ever think if it was right for me? I believe there was a school in Minehead, 10 miles away, that was being considered, either on a daily basis or as a weekly boarder. I imagine as petrol rationing was still in force it would have been the latter option. This closed, so that option was out. It was decided to send me to Nettlecombe Court, a PNEU school (Parents National Education Union), situated up a remote valley behind Monksilver. The aim of PNEU schools was to provide a broad, balanced, creative and challenging curriculum both inside and outside the class room. The moto might well be " I am, I can, I ought, I will." I went in 1943 and was there for seven and a half years.

If I had not gone away to school how different my life would have been. I was sent out into the world at six years of age, to be a full time boarder at a girls prep school. I know, an enclosed, almost cloistered one but still out. Being the sort of child I was these frequent pushes outwards, first by my parents then circumstances, were very necessary for my development. Left to myself I would have stayed forever 'at home', timid, quiet, retiring, surrounded by dogs and horses. Thinking back, although we were bought up on a farm we were never encouraged to think about farming as a career. I expect the idea never entered our parents heads, or we were firmly steered away from the very idea.

Nettlecombe Court. A fine Tudor manor house, once the home of the Raleighs and the Trevelyans. A many gabled red sandstone mansion dated 1599 on the porch. The south front had buttresses suggesting there was an earlier house here and the date 1599 relates to a re-modelling. A medieval manor house that just reeks of history. Nettlecombe was granted by the king to Hugh de Raleigh in c1160. It is known that a John de Raleigh was pardoned in 1347 for leaving the overseas army without permission. He was later Sheriff of Somerset. The Trevelyans came on the scene at Nettlecombe when John married a Raleigh heiress who inherited in 1481. I believe the Trevelyans originated in Cornwall. Judge Jefferies was there, in rumour if not in fact. There are three circular rooms, one above the other, each with two doors. The lowest of the three is located on the ground floor and is called The Pardon Room. Here prisoners were bought before Judge Jefferies and, supposedly, pardoned but on passing out through the second door were summarily executed. There was lots of speculation about secret passage ways and 'the lady in grey' (a familiar ghostly figure of legend in many old houses). The hall, with its tall windows, large expanse of polished wooden floor and the seventeenth century plaster ceiling and minstrels' gallery at one end, is quite a feature of the house. There is a large overmantel with a coat of arms above the fireplace and between the windows and around the other walls heads of long dead stags and old family portraits jostled for space. Large rooms, high ceilings, lots of ghost stories and bitterly cold. This was Nettlecombe Court, where I was to start my school days. Hardly an ideal setting for a prep school for little girls.

So to boarding school aged six years of age. School was very frightening and perplexing. So many Do's and Don'ts. A continual minefield for the timid child always fearful of doing the wrong thing. Trying to tread carefully and heed the directions of those in authority often produced a zombie-like child who would be described as quiet and biddable. This very effort putting her at odds with her peers. Longing to join in, not sure how to break down the barrier between herself and her more boisterous class mates, envious of the way they could giggle and laugh off the trouble their high spirits inevitably landed them in. How easily the label 'teacher's pet' could be stuck on such a child and how difficult to dislodge. I was such a child, fearful in the real meaning of the word. Always afraid of doing or saying the wrong thing.

The Headmistress and owner of the school was a comfortable-looking middle-aged lady called Miss Aspinall. She had evacuated her school from the London area at the beginning of WW2, first to Simonsbath then to Nettlecombe. We called her 'Auntie'. Miss Aspinall had a rule for parents of new girls. "No visits for at least a month" to allow the new pupils to 'settle' in. I do not remember a single thing about that month. I should think this experience so relatively soon after the three months in hospital must have numbed my mind to anything except surviving. My memory is indeed rather sketchy about much of my time there on a day-to-day basis. Certain instances do stand out though and I hope to relay them here. One afternoon, after the required settling in period had passed, I was taken down to the drawing room. From the doorway, across a vast expanse of carpet, I saw my parents standing in front of the fireplace. I was absolutely rent with emotion. I believe I thought I would never see them again. I threw myself across the room at Mother in a most unusual display of grief mixed with relief, awash with tears and sobbing. How embarrassing it must have been. Subsequently I spent my entire life at school determined not to cry. I doubt I ever fully recovered from that initial sense of bereavement; each leave taking at the beginning of every term was agony. And, never once, after that initial bout of crying did I ever allow myself to cry again. Until years and years later, in Canada, where, if under great stress I realised I needed to cry I would go to the local library and borrow Rumer Godden's book, *China Court*. Reading that book, in bed at night after the kids were asleep would release whatever was building up in my head as it always reduces me to stress-relieving tears which are so cathartic. I love that book which would have to go with me if I was ever on Desert Island Discs!

Although, over the years, I learnt to control my feelings I was always churned up inside and silent on these thrice yearly drives to school and wished Father wouldn't drive so fast. In complete contrast were the homeward journeys at the end of each term during which I would talk to Father non-stop, my liberated self overcoming my more usual reticence in his presence.

Thus began a series of afternoon visits, one in the middle of each term, which usually involved going to tea at The Dragon House Hotel in nearby Bilbrook. I was never taken home on these afternoons. Just recently, having returned to the area, I realised, with something of a shock, just how close Nettlecombe Court was to home. So I took a drive. Down from North Hawkwell, left at the bottom of the drive and along the lane to Steart Bridge. Turned right here, over the bridge and uphill all the way to Wheddon Cross. Left here at the cross roads and uphill again to Heathpolt Cross. Here the road levels out somewhat, gentle curves and undulating gradients following the route the drovers took in olden times, where possible keeping to the high ground to make it easier for their herds of animals.

A lovely road, full of history; marching armies, drovers herding flocks of sheep or herds of cattle, weary miners toiling home; a road to set the imagination tingling.

Left at Raleigh's Cross, now down, down, down, a first glimpse of Nettlecombe Court on the right, still down, right at Yarde Cross, right again in Monksilver and up the valley to Nettlecombe. Or, if the weather was dry, we took the farm track down the fields, thereby cutting off a huge corner to come out by the stable block, 25 minutes door to door! Or even less if Father was in a bit of a hurry.

Going back each term was painful. So sunk in misery would I become at the beginning of each term that Miss Aspinall, in an effort to cheer me up, would offer me the first ride on the ponies which were used for our lessons. Maybe petrol rationing had something to do with the fact that I was never taken home during the school term, or Mother just could not face the misery of taking me back after an outing. Certainly becoming a weekly boarder was firmly squashed the only time I mentioned it. So a silent, white-faced little girl with her arms hugging her tummy was deposited at the imposing entrance three times a year for the terms and, maybe, three times a year after an afternoon outing.

In front of the house there is a large circular gravel drive bordering an area of rough grass where we were given our riding lessons. On a slight slope downwards and, beyond that, an area of rough grass going up to meet the park railings that bordered the farmland. Here we used to be let loose to play. In those days I had a mass of curly hair which the person in charge of us, the Matron or a nursemaid, loved to turn into long ringlets and tie with green ribbons. This prolonged attention I received whilst they played with my hair swiftly earned me the title of teachers pet. These ribbons used to slide off which was OK whilst we were inside; easy to find on the polished floors but a nightmare once playing outside. I'm sure I spent more time looking for lost green ribbons in the long green grass than actually playing with the other children.

The school used to present a pageant or nativity play at the end of the autumn term to entertain our parents before we were whisked home for the Christmas holidays. I only remember one of these; maybe the effort to stage it and the end results being rather disappointing were more than the staff could face year after year. Or maybe I was, inadvertently, the final straw. Of course we were all given a part to play. I presented quite a problem. I was completely overcome with stage fright and could neither be persuaded to sing or even walk across the makeshift stage as a wise man bearing gifts. In the end, not to be beaten, they cast me as a picture of Mary. I was arranged, sitting on a cushion inside a frame, cradling a doll (how I hate dolls) and instructed not to move. I was frozen in place, utterly embarrassed, feeling all those eyes boring into this living picture.

I expect it was during these early years of my schooling that I developed the knack of melting into the background. I was a very biddable child and, when noticed, could be relied on to do exactly as I was instructed. These traits of my character coupled with my tendency to keep myself to myself did not endear me to my fellow classmates. As my reading improved I tended to while away the lonely hours of playtime deep in a book so the label of 'bookworm' was added to 'teacher's pet'. Even though I never told tales I was never quite trusted by my peers. All I ever wanted was to be 'one of the crowd' but the key to popularity seemed to pass me by so I walked this rather lonely road.

There must have been something in my character though that appealed to my fellow pupils. Maybe, even then they subconsciously recognised what a reliable and responsible person I was to develop into as I matured. I was always the one woken up to fetch Matron if anyone was ill during the night. We slept in dormitories, two lines of beds, maybe six or eight to a room. In the middle of the night there would be a frightened little voice calling out" Gay, I don't feel well, will you get Matron." Always me. Grope for my slippers, grab my dressing gown and set off. A frightening journey, past the minstrels' Gallery with its creaks and groans, feeling my way down one set of stairs and up the other to knock on Matron's door. Did I have a torch or was this all in the dark?

The school was never very warm. Our main class room was quite large and in two halves. It had four large windows facing south and, on sunny days, there was usually a stampede to grab a window seat and have a warm up before class actually started. This room was heated in very cold weather by a single bar electric fire which faced the larger half; the unlucky people in the back half had no direct heat at all.

We ate in a downstairs room off the kitchen, sitting on benches at long trestle tables. I think this room is partly underground as the back wall was living rock. This was always slimy with water trickling down it and wet, as a consequence of which the floor of stone flags was also wet all the time. We ate tripe I think, in hindsight it was because it was extremely cheap. I don't know what they did with it but it used to arrive on our plates in slabs floating in a watery, green, liquid. Quite, quite revolting, somehow swallowed as we were always so hungry as young people usually are. We weren't starved, we ate lots of bread.

Chilblains, colds and ear aches occupied our minds and bodies throughout most of the winter terms. We had chilblains on our fingers and toes, great red, very sore, itchy, swellings. The queue for chilblain treatment alone stretched half way down the staircase each morning. Once some awful affliction hit us; you were never told what was wrong with you in those days, we were just encased in a sticky plaster bandage all around our midriffs and kept in bed. The constriction and the itching nearly drove us mad. Most likely it was only fear of the unknown thing we had that kept us under control at all. And when it came to removing it, well! They didn't take a pair of scissors and slit it down one side and remove it in one piece, no, we had to stand in the middle of an open space and the bandage was unwound from our bodies roll by roll. I do believe they were trying to be kind and not hurt us by doing it this way. Try pulling an ordinary plaster off a piece of hairy skin and feel the agony as you slowly pull it away and then magnify that awfully painful feeling a hundred times and you have an idea of how much pain we endured. We soon forgot the itching in the exquisite relief and freedom of movement again.

Why do I have memories of being ill? I was ill in bed one time, all by myself. I was in the middle bed on the right hand side of the dormitory. At teatime I was given one biscuit, a digestive. To while away the time and make the biscuit last longer I broke it up into many tiny pieces. I had just started to savour each tiny morsel when one of my classmates came in and saw what I had done and ran to tell the teacher. The teacher swept in, caught up my plate, lectured me on 'playing' with my food and marched out leaving me hungry, bored again and suffering a deep sense of grievance at the unfairness of life. After all, I never told tales on anyone.

Then, in the atrocious snows of 1947, most of the school came down with something, measles I believe and were confined to bed and the food ran out. Dormitories of convalescent children, desperately hungry, clamouring for food, must have taken some putting up with. I hate Bread and Milk with a passion, The feel of it on my tongue is quite repulsive. Then along came Miss Aspinall with bowls of the stuff and we all, including me, just wolfed it down. A little later on the next door dormitory housing the older girls having refused the Bread and Milk, were given something much nicer! My dormitory were quite upset and, for me, yet again, the unfairness of it all really hit home.

Bath times. We bathed once a week. We were allowed two inches of water and given ten minutes of time! There was more than one bathroom. The one I liked most was situated in the middle room of the tower of three. The bath was raised so one went up two or three steps then down into the bath, the like of which I had never seen before or, for that matter, since. Lavatories. I am not sure how many lavatories there were but I well remember one of them. This was in a large cupboard in the middle of a long internal passage with the light switch on the outside. Older girls thought it a great joke to switch off this light when us littler ones were in residence leaving us in complete and utter darkness. Then, having groped our way out of the lavatory we would find they had also turned off the passage light. And it was no good complaining to Matron as, next time, they might think up some nastier trick to play on us. Another time we were told the lavatory nearest to our class room had been disinfected and we were not to use it. No suggestions which other to use and we were never told when we could use it again. In desperation when I was on the point of wetting my pants I slipped into it and sat in the dark, in fear and trembling in case I was doing the wrong thing.

The classrooms were fitted out with long tables and chairs. We sat on either side of these tables, four to a side and one at each end. Our French and Scripture teacher - I'll call her Miss Trent as I do not remember anyone's names from that period of my life - had lived abroad for many years and the parts of her we could see were yellow; from the tips of her nicotine stained fingers up to her scraggy neck and deeply lined face and the top of her head with its thin titian dyed hair. She tended to wear yellowish jumpers with amber beads and thick, autumn-coloured tweed skirts. She was, just, yellow! If things were not going to her satisfaction she would walk past us walloping us on our heads with the text book, muttering 'imbecile, imbecile'. We really did not mind the French grammar being used in this fashion but felt quite incensed if she used the bible during a scripture lesson. Looking back I think she was a brilliant teacher and the others must have been also.

Miss Trent used to take us for extra reading. Her command of our language and the interest she awakened in us for the written word was quite remarkable. We would gather in her bed-sitting room and, just avoiding gagging on the tobacco fumes, would take it in turns to read passages from the chosen book. One time I got into a muddle over the punctuation in the piece I was reading. 'Read it again, Gay, read it again' until I couldn't tell the wood from the trees. The passage was handed to someone else who immediately read it correctly. I felt hot and cold all over that I hadn't seen it properly until I looked up and glimpsed an understanding look in Miss Trent's eyes. I came out of there thinking 'it's alright to make mistakes if you have been genuinely trying to get it right'.

The hall. This was very simply furnished, a large rug before the fireplace, a couple of arm chairs and a grand piano with a lamp beside the fire place and another for the piano. Events of importance took place in the hall; ballet and music lessons with their attendant exams and the Christmas Pageant. For ballet we lined up along the back wall facing the piano and endlessly practiced our foot positions and holding the arm positions absolutely still and the exams were conducted like a group lesson. Not so the piano examinations. These were awe inspiring, to put it mildly. First the long walk down the hall to meet the examiner standing waiting beside the piano, with a polite handshake. Then the scales followed by the much practiced set piece and, last of all, and the most daunting, the singing part. All the hours of lonely practice must have paid off as I did pass grade one and two. I never remember a piano at home although the Grandparents had one but not near enough for me to practice so now I doubt I could even remember the scales.

Here, in the hall, we used to gather on a winters evening trying to be comfortable sitting on the rug with our knitting whilst Miss Aspinall read to us by the light of the single lamp. I think I was about ten years old when these winter evening sessions began, around the time we started knitting knee socks in our school colour of purple, with four needles. The portraits stared down at us, no doubt in disapproval of our bare knees, the shadows danced from the fire light and the minstrels 'gallery from one end emitted it's usual creaks and groans as Miss Aspinal read Sir Walter Scott to us. At bedtime we used to race past the door into the minstrels' gallery arriving in our dormitories with pounding hearts and quite breathless.

I expect it was after one of these scary sessions that the big girls decided on yet another prank to play on me. My bed that term was in the middle with a large white wardrobe between my bed and the next one. I woke up early one morning to see a hand dangling from the top of the wardrobe on my side. I was terrified. So often we went to sleep with ghost stories ringing in our ears from the older children and here was something right over my head. I buried my head under the bed cloths and must have gone back to sleep. When I woke up at the proper time I peeped out and there was nothing there and, as I never mentioned the apparition to anyone, I was none the wiser.

Riding. The first riding instructor there was a man. He was very much of the old school. We used to go around and around the grass area in front of the house with large maple leaves under our knees and admonished to 'grip tight.' I just remember how tiring this was but it was to stand me in good stead once I had my pony Robin at home. After this we had a lovely lady who did more fun things with us. We went out for rides, we learnt to jump and, one memorable morning, we got up really early. This must have been the year before I left. It was the summer term and the weather must have been hot. We were left food in the kitchen, summer pudding which I had never had but absolutely adore now and glasses of milk. Off we went into one of the lower meadows and we were to learn how to do 'flying changes'. This is done at the canter on a figure of eight pattern, getting the pony to change from one leading leg to the other. Quite difficult, especially on untrained ponies. One or two of the more agile ponies picked it up quite quickly, a bit like training a circus horse. Others were a little more difficult, I was on one of those so I got lots more attention and it was such fun. The whole morning had an, almost, magic feel to it.

We did spend a lot of time unsupervised. We were in the stables, maybe cleaning tack, mucking out, learning how to hog manes the old fashioned way, with hand sheers, no electric clippers then for us. I remember being given a leg up on to a pony and being handed the shears so I could cut along the crest of the neck from the withers towards the ears for as far as I could reach. Such a lovely feeling sitting on the pony bareback. We knew the gardens well too as we used to have lessons there in hot weather, lying on slopes of grass under the rather magnificent trees. On the way back from the stables we would detour through the gardens There was one particular tree, it was a sort of fir and its branches swept to the ground, rather like a weeping willow but much more substantial. The girls used to climb up the trunk, then out to the edge of the weeping branches and cascade down the outside to the ground. Again and again. I only ever did it once, in response to goading from the others. It was a scary experience and I left them to it.

The parkland outside the railings had been neglected for years and the slopes were covered in bracken. We were taken out there to play in the summer terms. We used to make tunnels in the bracken and dens to lie in; maybe Lyme disease had not been detected back then. And never a word about the possibility of adders lurking in the undergrowth either!

I remember fireworks one winter's evening. We were taken out to the enclosed lawn that we never used, to stand behind the railings and watch this firework display. I remember being cold. Looking back it must have been our celebration of the end of the war. Also I remember the whole school being taken to the cinema in Minehead to see the film *Lassie*. And not knowing what I was going there for and to watch this frightening tale not knowing it was a made up story. Oh dear. To this day I never go to animal films, certainly not *Lassie Come Home* when that came out. Maybe for this outing I had to phone home for permission. Another thing I did not understand, how to use a telephone. Phoning home must have meant we now had a phone at North Hawkwell. So I was pointed to the phone in the study and told to lift the receiver and left by myself. Of course I did as I was told fully expecting my mother to be there. Of course she wasn't I had got through to the exchange. "I want to speak to Mummy, I want Mummy". It was awful. I ran out of the study and I think someone helped me but it was years before I was comfortable using the phone.

In my last year there I sat the entrance exams for Sherborne School for Girls and passed them. I was to leave Nettlecombe at the end of the Easter term and start at Sherborne at the beginning of the summer term. I was the last girl to be picked up at the end of term. Everyone had left and the staff were busy stripping beds and generally having a good clean up. I wandered along the top passage from where I could watch for Father if he took the short cut down the field past the stables. I became aware of a presence and looking up I saw her. The Lady in Grey watching me from the corner by the door. We looked at each other and then she faded into the woodwork. To this day I believe she was guarding me throughout my stay there, giving me courage on my night-time jaunts to fetch Matron and generally being a watchful presence and had revealed herself as I was leaving, to come and say goodbye.

Chapter 5
SCHOOL YEARS, AT SHERBORNE SCHOOL FOR GIRLS

Although I did not question it at the time but it was very odd to leave one school in the middle of the school year and be sent to a completely different one. Many years later I heard a rumour that Miss Aspinall's school had gone bankrupt which would explain the abrupt change. This rather famous school is in Sherborne which is just over the boundary into Dorset. At that time there were eight red brick houses and the main school building with lots of playing fields, tennis courts and a swimming pool. I believe it is much enlarged now. Each house had fifty girls living in it with a House Mistress and a Matron.

I was assigned to Thurston, one of the farthest from the main school buildings. Our Housemistress was Miss Williams from Southern Ireland and Miss Groves the Matron from Northern Ireland. Miss Williams had played hockey for Ireland and she was a martinet on the side lines at interhouse games of hockey if we did not run fast enough or missed the ball. Occasionally she and Miss Groves would exchange friendly banter as to the merits of North versus South Ireland. To listen to them you would not know they were Irish as neither had a distinctive accent. In fact we were not allowed accents at Sherborne; any girl arriving with one was ragged unmercifully until she forced herself to assume the 'Sherborne sound'. We slept in dormitories but each had an individual cubicle with bed and dressing table and stool and a narrow wardrobe. The partitions stopped short of the ceiling, so even if one did not have a window there was still plenty of light. There was a dining room on the first floor where we ate all our meals and, downstairs, a large common room with many shelves of books. Lavatories and wash basins and, I imagine the kitchen and larders and laundry rooms occupied the rest of the ground floor.

We had brownish skirt and jacket suits for wearing to Sherborne Abbey for Sunday services, four hundred girls in crocodile, and special occasions in the school assembly hall. For every day we wore green tunics, called jibbahs, over our regulation blouses with knee socks in winter and ankle socks in the summer.

We played tennis and cricket. I was as broad as I was tall in those days, a stocky five foot two inches and always the wicket keeper; maybe I couldn't run very fast and being quite broad and being behind the wicket was deemed a suitable position for me. Hockey was not enjoyable as, again, I was not very fast and got no joy in rushing around with the stick. Lacrosse was the only one I enjoyed. Although, again, not fast I mastered the technique of cradling the ball and passing it on. As far as I was concerned we did not play enough lacrosse. The swimming pool was outside so we only swam in the summer term. I did learn to swim after a fashion but never mastered the correct breathing technique, and started diving lessons but it was not a favourite pastime for me. One summer term was a bit of a washout as many of us got verrucas, which are catching, on the soles of our feet. Last but not least, netball, which again I enjoyed as I liked the precision of netting the ball.

We got plenty of exercise as we walked to school two or three times a day. And we were never to walk alone. A group must always catch up to a lone walker and include them in what ever they happened to be discussing. And talking of conversation, Miss Williams used to take groups of us for just that, polite conversation in her drawing room. And we were all meant to participate. The first one I attended was very embarrassing as I became completely tongue tied and could not think of a thing to say. So we all sat in silence, the longest silence you could imagine as I struggled to find my tongue. I do not remember the outcome, maybe someone to help me out actually said something to me.

Arriving at a new school in the middle of the year is not to be recommended. Everyone has formed friendships during the previous term and are settled too into their classes and know the routines. Each subject was divided into three of four levels according to the pupil's ability. As a result of passing my entrance exams quite well I was put into the second highest group in all my subjects. And slid, quite swiftly to the lowest group. This is where, now, I recognise that the teaching at Nettlecombe Court must have been of a very high standard. My new maths teacher was Miss Williams and I found her method of teaching quite incomprehensible. Before I slid out of her class to join the lowest class I was assigned 1000 lines which I never even attempted to do. No point. My English teacher was inspirational and encouraged us all to use our house libraries as much as possible. Here I discovered Rudyard Kipling and other exciting authors so that was good. My geography teacher was also excellent, I found her lessons very interesting.

My introduction to Sherborne was not helped by developing appendicitis in my first term and having to have it out. Having been advised not to laugh afterwards because it was so painful, the friendliest nurse seemed to take a delight in teasing me, I'm sure just to watch my efforts in trying to not to laugh. After a few days in the sanatorium I was sent home to complete my convalescence. After a happy, happy, ten days at home, largely spent playing with the new sheep dog, Jock, racing around the lawn, having tugs of war with an old rope (not a good idea when you have just had your appendix out) I was taken back for the second half of term.

Upon returning to school after the summer holidays I found I was being kept down to start the year again which meant I was amongst the new intake who were all a year younger than myself. The years came and went, really nothing of note to record until we got to 'O' levels. Here things became a little unstuck. I took five subjects. The two English; grammar and English literature, domestic science, history, geography and scripture. The powers that be, my teachers I imagine, decided I would not pass any 'O' levels so persuaded my parents to enrol me again for the autumn term to retake the exams just before Christmas. Well, if not brilliantly I passed them all.

By enrolling me for the autumn term they were, obviously, playing safe. I expect the fees were paid in advance. I had no need to go back for that term, but back I was sent. Maybe the school would not give a rebate, maybe the parents did not want me around, maybe the school offered career counselling: be a nurse, be a secretary, become an almoner. I floated around in Remove until the end of the Christmas term. To say I felt in limbo is to put it mildly. Never a very brave person at the best of times, needing the guidelines of a system to give me direction, I really felt quite lost. The school did not know what to do with me. I did not fit the system at all, I was without a curriculum. Apparently I flatly refused to consider university though Mother swore blind many years later that it had been suggested to me that I could most likely make it into one of the minor universities that did not require Latin. I just do not remember. I do remember though some sticky interviews with my Housemistress and the Head, Dame Diana Reader Harris, although not a dame whilst I was there. That was to come later. I remember a career in the WRNS was broached and hospital almoner. And my eldest uncle considered all girls should become secretaries. All their efforts doomed to failure as all I did know was that I wanted out, out into the open air preferably galloping off into the sunset though it took a while for this hidden side to my character to penetrate their subconscious and, by then, it was too late. I escaped. I discovered the school library. Now I knew it was there, I might even have used it during my studies but never as a place to hide in. Here was I with all these blank spaces in my schedule, places that were meant to be filled with work for retaking those exams. After a couple of weeks my obviously bored wanderings through the school caught the attention of my Housemistress and she made me wardrobe mistress and general dogsbody to a very ambitious production of *St Joan* we were putting on at the end of term. I spent many hours assisting with the production of a large stained-glass window using stiff coloured plastic for the backdrop. It was very fragile and had been very satisfying to work on. This introduced me to using the library as a reference tool (which is what libraries are all about) researching all I could about Joan of Arc. During my wanderings along the shelves I discovered travel books. I read every Alan Moorhead book the library possessed and then moved on to Canadiana. Everything from mining to ranching to the early explorers; I devoured them all. I used to lose myself for hours at a time. I rode the range, I picked fruit in the Okanagan, I travelled the Canadian Pacific railways. As far as the school staff were concerned their worry what to do with me was over. As long as they saw me looking busy, frowning as I walked the corridors, weighed down with books, well, I must be achieving something so why worry. They had hundreds of better prospects to look after. So the term passed quite quickly as the seeds of unrest and wanderlust slowly matured. The big question of what I was going to do next was shelved by those in authority and I left as I had arrived, quietly and without fuss.

Chapter 6
HOLIDAYS

Holidays at North Hawkwell were really like being on holiday all the time. Mother feeling sorry for me being away at school, confined to the class room when I would have much preferred being outside all the time, gave me her outside chores to do. Life at home in the holidays was sheer paradise as I understood it. Once the hens were fed and watered and let out of their houses I was free; to ride the woods, the moors and the farm, to go for long walks or read the current favourite book. The hours I spent in my bedroom reading were limitless; the sloping ceiling, the little window looking out onto the lane outside and the closed up hatchway originally used for dropping hay through when the back of the house formed part of the stables next door produced the ideal atmosphere for reading and dreaming.

I remember reading a book once where the heroine spent hours up an old apple tree reading her book. I thought this sounded very romantic and took a book, one sunny day, down to the orchard and climbed an apple tree and settled down to read. I didn't stay there very long, no matter which way I sat in the fork there was a knob of hard wood sticking in somewhere. Lying on a rug under the tree was no more satisfactor. Creepy crawlies would crawl over my legs, maggots and other things would drop from the branches and lumps of soil were busy sticking into me from under the rug, putting me very much in mind of the tale of The Princess and The Pea. I forget how many mattresses ended up under her before she ceased to feel the presence of the pea. I didn't think Mother would approve of me taking my mattress outside so I returned to the comfort of my room.

Then Mother would be calling up the stairs "what are you doing up there, why aren't you outside in this lovely sunshine." And, much more welcome, "please come and help me make the tea and we will take it for a picnic." We seldom went far afield. Webber's Post was a great favourite. Where the car park is today were private little glades of close cropped grass amongst the pine trees whose resinous scent enveloped us as we ate our picnic with, usually, a cool breeze whispering in their tops.

Another favourite were the fields at Span Gate. The fields in those days had gorse bushes in abundance; a great place for hide and seek and other imaginary adventures, and we would find a dell in amongst these for our picnic. Sometimes we just went into the hayfields or the harvest fields once the corn had been cut and bound into sheaves and would play amongst the stooks or the loose hay depending which field we were in. The hay fields were our favoured choice as, when tired, we would lie and drink in the sweet smell of the drying hay and liked to pick a long piece of grass to tickle Father's nose with when he dozed off.

In July the whortleberries were ripe. Another excuse for a picnic. Our preferred place was the road above Cloutsham Farm. It was easy picking here as the bushes grew on the banks beside the road. They are little and fiddly to pick, well worth the effort though, just to enjoy their unique flavour. Whortleberry pie and clotted cream, an Exmoor summer dish fit for a Queen.

The sun always seemed to be shining in those summer holidays of yesteryear. The shepherd bought in a dead adder once for us to see and learn about. We were shown its markings and told never to touch one. If we thought it was a dead adder we had found we could pick it up over a long stick to carry it home for identification; dead ones must never be touched until after sunset as they were not considered dead until the sun had gone down.

Snakes never waited around to show themselves to me. My heavy footfalls and tuneless singing driving any self respecting snake to seek cover until the disturbance of my passing had faded. In the woods if out looking for deer I could be as quiet as any Indian scout. I loved going out on foot to see what I could find, summer or winter, especially after a snowfall as the tracks are so easy to follow then. Although not often seen a sharp acrid smell lingering on the air spoke of the passing of a fox. Many a time I was asked to take visitors out to look for deer. Here I was completely in charge, a heady feeling. Off on a summer's evening, moving quietly, no chatting or giggling allowed. This was serious business. Successful every time whether we would peer over a hedge into the field below or venture into North Hawkwell wood or further afield into Bincombe or Manley Combe.

Visitors; lots of visitors. Mother was the second youngest of five children. Uncle Jim was the youngest of the five Sugdens and the closest in age to Mother. From the tales I've heard they grew up more as twins than ordinary brother and sister and he was obviously her favourite.. He came down to us shortly after being demobbed from the army after the Second World War and we hung out all the flags across the front of the house and there was great excitement waiting to welcome him home. During the war, he was in the signal corps and received a "Mention in Dispatches". He was also demoted once as he fell asleep at the wheel of the large transport lorry he was driving and he and it ended up upside down in a ditch. He caused great confusion by marrying his eldest sister's step daughter Helen. I and my sister were bridesmaids at their wedding which I did not enjoy very much because of being part of the procession up the aisle. Whilst up at the altar rail we all knelt down for prayers and when we came to rise I found myself being pulled over backwards. Luckily the Best Man saw what was happening and helped me to lie back on the floor so they could free the heel of my shoe which was caught in the hem of my dress. I was very thankful when we were allowed to join our parents in the anonymity of their pew.

Mother's father came a few times, always whilst I was away at school. On Sundays he walked the 3 miles to the Methodist chapel in Timberscombe. He didn't believe in the car being taken out on Sundays and always refused the offer of a lift. It wasn't until many years afterwards that Mother discovered a Mrs Huxtable was taking him in after the service to give him a cup of tea before the long walk home. She thought he looked too frail to be walking such a distance. I wonder if he explained to Mrs Huxtable why he walked instead of being driven.

Mother's older brother, Uncle Bob, loved coming to Exmoor but there was a problem over the timing of his visits. No matter where he went for his holidays it was sure to rain. He was the greatest jinx on holiday weather ever known. From the lush green of Exmoor to the sands of the Sahara it was sure to rain if he was there. Father would not let him anywhere near the place during hay making or harvest time. Although there are other times of the year when torrential rain day after day is not too welcome, having put his foot down over the hay making times he had to give in gracefully at least once a year. Once here, I understand, Father thoroughly enjoyed Uncle Bob's company.

Auntie Kay, the middle sister, came once with her daughter, my cousin, Ruth. They were there at the time of the Lynmouth flood disaster. We were up in the top fields with Father and, looking west, saw this dense black mass hanging in the sky. Father said someone's copping it. The black mass was the cloud burst that caused so much terrible damage to the town with considerable loss of life. On a lighter note, I used to take Ruth down to the level meadow beside the River Avill for riding lessons on Robin. How effective these were can be judged by the fact that Ruth never really took up riding as a leisure activity

Then there was Auntie Maimie, Mother's eldest sister. Auntie Maimie was married to Uncle Stephen (Spackman), a clergyman in the Church of England. Uncle Stephen emigrated to Canada as a young man with his first wife to be the teacher at the Indian School up the north coast of Vancouver Island at Alert Bay. They had two daughters, Shirley and Helen and a son, David. After his wife died he, and the children, came back to England and he became vicar of Marple. Auntie Maimie had spent some years in New Zealand and then returned home. She and Stephen met going about their various parish duties, romance blossomed and the aforementioned wedding took place.

Auntie Maimie was a frequent summer visitor. She would come down on the train from Marple with her daughter Susan who was two years younger than me. Susan remembers coming down when she was very young and we had not long been at North Hawkwell. They came by taxi from Dunster Station to the bottom of the drive where they were dropped off. She must have been only four at the time, making me six – I came running down the drive to meet them. I must have been watching for them from the garden. One year Uncle Stephen came too and quite ruined the usual happy go lucky atmosphere that prevailed when they were with us. For some reason he asked to be taken to the top of North Hill, maybe even as far along the top as Selworthy Beacon. Maybe he felt in need of a long walk, maybe he had a sermon to compose; down the years the reason for this long walk has been forgotten. The distance from Selworthy Beacon to Minehead is somewhere between 5 and 7 miles and the last 2 miles are down hill. And Uncle Stephen was wearing open toed sandals. He could barely walk for the rest of the holiday, he sat around complaining, commandeered Father's armchair which nobody else ever sat in and vetoed any activity that involved walking. He expected life to revolve around him and his injured feet.

One year Auntie Maimie and Susan came bringing their young Corgi dog, Taffy, with them. On arrival we all trooped into the dining room where the cats must have been snoozing. Taffy took one look and leapt joyously forward snatching the lead from Susan's hand. Cats went in all directions. One shinned up the Welsh dresser scattering plates in all directions, another ran up the curtains and hung, swinging, from the rail hissing and swearing whilst the third ran between my legs and into the safety of the outdoors. Taffy ran around and around the table making extravagant leaps in the air below each cat, barking hysterically all the while. That holiday was spent trying to keep Taffy well away from the cats to avoid more confrontations. The cats were in such a state of frazzled nerves they scratched first and asked questions afterwards. I was busy in the stables one day assuring one that the nasty thing was tied up and it was safe to come down off that high beam and it did just that, landing on my upturned face. I've never stood directly beneath a cat since.

Susan had a horse at home, a chestnut mare called Colleen who couldn't come on holiday with them so she rode one of ours. I think she rode Jane although I cannot be sure. I only really remember three incidents. The first one was me behaving badly. We were out riding and on our way home through the fields above North Hawkwell. We had come through the gate and, for some reason, maybe I was in a hurry to get home, I clapped heels to Robin's sides and, without warning Susan, I galloped off. There was a yell behind me and I turned around to see Susan lying on the ground and Jane galloping for home. Now I faced a dilemma. Should I gallop after Jane, catch her and return to Susan or should I ride back to see if Susan was OK? The next gate would stop Jane so I rode back to Susan who was, by now, sitting up and seemed OK although a bit shaken. Jane, meanwhile, finding herself all alone came trotting back to see what was going on. Susan re-mounted and we rode sedately home.

Another time that stands out in my memory was some sort of a paperchase or mock hunt organised by the Devon and Somerset Pony Club during the summer holidays We were to meet at Alderman's Barrow which is a Bronze Age burial mound high up on the moors above Exford. We set off in pouring rain, up Snowdrop Valley into Bincombe, over Hatchams to Dunkery Hill Gate thence along moorland tracks, avoiding boggy ground, to arrive at our destination. We were met by Mother and Susan's mum, Auntie Maimie. I was divested of my wet mackintosh and put into a dry one whereupon Auntie Maimie grabbed my discarded mackintosh and put Susan into it; it being, apparently, more able to withstand the appalling rain than what she was wearing. They bred us tough in those days. A more boring day I had yet come across. The rain and wind made it virtually impossible to hear what the organisers were saying, we seemed to trot aimlessly along narrow moorland tracks (as if we had not had enough of those on the way over) nose to tail until, around two o'clock, the huntsman blew home on his horn and the agony was over, except, of course, we still had to face the long ride home.

The third instance involved a gymkhana being held in a field on the west side of Minehead, on the lower slopes of Grabbist which is the hill between Minehead and Timberscombe. I rode Robin, but cannot remember who Susan rode. We rode from North Hawkwell to Timberscombe and then up over Hooy (pronounced ouy), the rutted lane leading up and over the hill. Once there we entered various classes; looking back I don't believe I actually really knew what I was doing. I rode, therefore I should take part in these events As usual I entered the jumping and, as usual, Robin refused to go over a single obstacle. Why no one suggested some jumping lessons might be a good idea is beyond my comprehension.

At the end of the afternoon Susan and I set off for home. Having ridden over Grabbist we either went via Timberscombe or Wootton Courtenay. Either way we arrived at Waydown. I suspect we went the Timberscombe way, how else did we arrive at Waydown? In my mind I must have seen the map and, ever one for going in straight lines worked out that from Timberscombe the straightest line was up Waydown and through East Harwood. Here was where I made the biggest error. I should have then gone through West Harwood, hence into Snowdrop Valley and up the lane home. Instead I opted, in the gathering gloom, to go up over the fields and then drop down to home from the highest point of the farm. Susan, who did not have a clue where we were must have been almost dropping with fatigue. I, who loved riding in the dusk, was not feeling any desire to rush home. Reality hit when the Land Rover, being driven at great speed, came up behind us, screeched to a halt and Father leapt out. I don't remember exactly what was said but the rosy dream-like state I was in was completely shattered! He had driven down the valley to Timberscombe then to Wootton Courtenay then, beginning to be a bit more than rather concerned up Waydown onto the farm which is where he eventually found us. Oh dear.

Chapter 7
MORE NORTH HAWKWELL TALES

Father rode until the advent of the Land Rover. He then hung up his saddle and used the Land Rover as a horse. The first evening of the day it arrived, to challenge its capabilities, he took it up Draper's Way; one of the ancient routes used by traders with their pack horse trains since time immemorial. Draper's Way is very steep and, in those days, was just a rough track with great slabs of rock, quite a challenge to drive, much as Putham Lane still is today. He played up there for hours. Poor Mother, what must she have been imagining. It is lucky she did not know what he was to do with us later on in his ownership of the Land Rover on the steep fields behind North Combe. He was determined to drive it up this particular formidable slope which could cause you, if riding a pony up it, to cling onto the mane to stop yourself sliding off the back of the saddle. We never rode straight up this slope, we always tacked up it pretending we were a sailing ship. The front end of the Land Rover began to rear up so he stopped and got the three of us to climb onto the bonnet and, hanging on for dear life, up we went. It was scary.

On the other hand we loved it when he went into racing mode. He would drive the Land Rover in a crazy fashion all over the flatter fields, putting on spurts of speed with sudden turns and stops; we'd all be sliding around in the back, laughing our heads off. Ironically he never taught me to drive, never explained things. From an early age I would go with him when feeding stock. He would put me behind the wheel, put the Land Rover into first gear, walk around the back to throw out the hay whilst I steered! With no understanding of what I was doing! I doubt my legs could even reach the pedals. Maybe for the best as one can hardly get into trouble in first gear in a Land Rover and unable to reach the pedals.

One day I was with Father coming home up Snowdrop Valley. We had been to East Harwood for a load of hay. The canvas cover was not on the back so Father could really pile up the bales and then he tossed the sheep dog on top of the load. Half way up the valley there is a slight bend to the right, very slight, as you drive past Steart Bridge which spans the little River Avill. No matter that this is a narrow road, virtually single track, Father was, as usual, cracking on. I think he had quite forgotten the dog clinging onto the top of the load. Out of the corner of my eye I saw this object fly past to land in the river; it was the dog. Quite undeterred Father yanked the dog out of the river and tossed him back to the top of the load. If my memory serves me right we continued our journey home at a more sedate pace and the dog seemed unfazed by his one and only attempt at flying.

Christmas followed very much a routine in the early years. Granny and Granpa always came. On Christmas Eve Granpa and I would be dispatched to the sitting room to listen to the service of lessons and carols from King's College, Cambridge. We could neither of us sing a note in tune so listening to us singing along with that glorious choir must have been agony to anyone with an ear for music. This was followed by decorating the tree and hanging the paper chains we had been laboriously making for days beforehand and hanging up Father's socks for Father Christmas. These socks, found mysteriously hanging on the end of our beds, were opened on Christmas morning. They always contained something to eat in the toe and one or more activity toys to keep us occupied whilst Mother was cooking the dinner. Once I was looking after the hens for Mother in the holidays, aged around eight or nine, I also began going with Father to feed the animals as the men did not come on Christmas Day. Lunch was always at one o'clock sharp so to be finished and the washing up done by three o'clock, in time to listen to the King's speech. We always stood for the playing of the National Anthem.

My family learnt very early on to give me dolls was a waste of time and money. My lacklustre thanks said it all. Anything to do with horses was greeted with great enthusiasm, nothing else really appealed. After listening to the speech we opened our presents. Then there was a breathing space whilst the animals were seen to again and the sitting room tidied ready for tea around the fire. After tea came the Christmas tree. This was decorated with little gifts and real candles which usually refused to remain upright in their holders on the supple branches. The electric light was switched off. We all held our breaths as Father lit them using a long taper and keeping them alight long enough to appreciate just how pretty the tree looked was quite a feat. Once lit Father hovered over them, not exactly with a fire extinquisher, although I think there was a bucket of water standing by, but with the intent to snub them out as quickly as we allowed, always too soon in our opinion.

Opening the little presents off the tree was followed, in swift order by bed. Once I became a parent myself I could well imagine the heartfelt sighs of relief as peace descended on the sitting room after a day spent in frantic activity keeping the children thoroughly entertained with a seemingly, endless succession of surprises.

New Year's Day was spent at the grandparents' in Minehead. We would drive into town after all the farm stock were seen to, arriving in time for lunch. The front door opened directly into the dining room and we were greeted by the lovely smell of beeswax polish on all the furniture and the shining table laid with gleaming silverware. After lunch we were taken for a good walk up Hopcott Combe to run off some energy and work up an appetite for tea. The centrepiece of the tea table was an enormous fruit cake iced all over and well decorated with nuts and fondants. This cake was made with three layers, the lower and top were traditional fruitcake mixture with the middle layer being almond paste. All in all enough richness and sugar to satisfy the sweetest tooth. We had crackers to pull after tea and wore silly paper hats until time to go home.

Birthdays, on the other hand, were quieter affairs. One particular one stands out in my memory. I can only assume it was my birthday, most likely my sixth or seventh as I was wearing a white organdie frock. Very smart. To keep me busy whilst waiting for the Grandparents to arrive I was let loose with a pair of scissors to dead head the roses in the front garden. I found by picking up a fold of the skirt of the frock between my fingers I could cut into it and make interestingly shaped holes. For the first and only time I can remember I had the back of a hairbrush on a tender part of my anatomy for this misdemeanour. The next time I wore this frock it was covered with flower embroidery where all the holes had been. Someone must have worked hard to repair the damage.

I usually opted for a picnic for my birthday treat. Even my 21st was spent having a picnic, just Mother, Father and myself in a favourite spot by Weir Water. You can only get to my special place now by climbing a stile I believe. I haven't been back. Father gave me a picture he had painted of the lane where it goes up beside the house below my bedroom window. I almost cried. That picture goes everywhere with me. It has been packed and unpacked so many times that the gilt on the frame is beginning to chip off and I am sure it needs a good clean.

One year, I think when I turned ten my grandparents gave me a dainty wristwatch and a tin of home made ginger biscuits. The watch was a great disappointment as it would not go on me but the ginger biscuits went down a treat. I went through a succession of 'ladies' watches which never worked until, one day, I put on an old watch of Father's and it kept going. Long before it was the fashion to wear a big watch I was wearing one that covered my wrist and required a specially made strap as I have such small wrists.

Although, officially, North Hawkwell is in Timberscombe parish we always attended St John's church in Cutcombe, the little hamlet half a mile east of Wheddon Cross. This church dates back to Norman times and had, until fairly recently, faint colour and outlines of murals high up on the south wall. Sometime after we joined the congregation father became Vicar's warden. In those days there were two wardens to a Church of England parish, People's warden and Vicar's warden. Our vicar was Mr Jenhora and a niece of his was his housekeeper. After evensong we used to go into the Vicarage for a light supper. One winter's night Mother left something in the church and I said I would go and fetch it and Mother asked the unthinkable 'aren't you afraid of the dark?' which was such a silly thing to say. Up to then I had never even thought about the dark as being something to be afraid of.

Winter evensong services were not well attended. The vicar, a couple of Webbers in the choir and a handful of parishioners to lift their voices into the echoing heights of the roof. The church was so cold. There was some sort of free-standing pot-bellied stove at the west end of the aisle in front of the wooden doors leading to the bell chamber so one received a brief feeling of warmth as one went past; the further up the aisle one went the colder it became. We were always in the front, left-hand pew. Mother took a rug to place on her lap and drape over her legs and although always vigorously denied, had been known to also have a hot water bottle concealed under the rug. Once I could read I used to while away the time reading the wording on the memorial tablet on the north wall. This tablet, to Mr Norman of Lincoln's Inn Fields has inspired me through the years, it is so beautifully worded.

After the service had ended those there used to gather around the stove for a brief warm up before venturing out into the cold. Not being interested in adult conversation I used to wander off in search of other interesting tablets to read. The small, framed, poem that used to hang on the first pillar as one went in used to draw me back again and again. Titled "To Wayfarers" it begins 'Friends, we bid you Welcome to this Ancient house of God' and goes on for some twenty lines. A simple stanza that went a long way to encourage and include all those who pushed open the heavy door to venture into this rather dark and gloomy interior. A lasting testimony to the enduring presence of God.

Chapter 8
MY EQUINE FRIENDS

I had some riding lessons when I was four. Although there were riding horses at Brockton they weren't suitable for me so I was taken to a little riding school nearby for lessons. This had an oval track surrounded by trees and I used to walk and trot around here in a very controlled, safe, environment. After the lesson the riding mistress would put her little terrier onto the pony for a canter around. Always a worrier even then and I am sure this was done for my enjoyment but I was always on tenterhooks in case the dog fell off. Of course it never did and jumped down quite safely each time after this little exhibition.

Once settled at North Hawkwell a pony was acquired for me. This was Jan, a small, Shetland-type chestnut gelding. Jan's previous rider had outgrown him. This was not a good choice for me as he was used to being ridden and mastered on a regular basis but, with us, he was not ridden regularly and soon got the upper hand as I was such a novice and really could not ride at all. My final ride on Jan was a bit of a disaster. We had gone for a family walk up past the sawmills (what is now known as Snowdrop Valley), me on Jan and my sister in the pram. As we turned for home Jan took off towards home and I could not stop him. I tried turning him towards the steep bank on the right-hand side of the lane and he went up it. I pulled on the reins as I was sliding off the back of the felt saddle, Jan lost his balance and came over sideways. I hit the ground with one foot still in the stirrup and was dragged behind him. Luckily the gate between us and home was closed and he waited there for everyone to catch up. At some point I said what came easiest. Jan reared, but this was not strictly true as me, pulling on the reins, most likely caused the mishap.

No hard hats in those days. I was wearing a silly little soft cap with a peak. I came to lying in my bed at home with the doctor leaning over me. The walk home must have been a rather anxious one, a good fifteen or twenty minutes from where I fell, Father carrying an unconscious child, and leading the pony, Mother struggling up the steep drive pushing the pram. Did they have the telephone by then or did Father drive the 6 miles to get the Doctor from Dunster? Who knows.

For a while, after the Jan debacle, nothing much was done about riding at home. I was having a weekly riding lesson at school but, I suspect, my constantly trotting or cantering on my two feet around home pretending I was a horse got the message across that I really, really wanted a pony. Came the golden day, when Father said he would run the ponies down from the top ground and I could choose one. The fact that they were all unbroken two or three year olds was of no consequence. I wanted a pony, he had ponies, put the two together – what could be easier.

Father was well built and almost six feet tall, what did he want with ponies? He had become a devotee of the Brendon and Bampton pony sales held every autumn after the ponies were rounded up off the moors, the foals weaned and the surplus sold. Although going with the firm resolve not to buy, in my imagination I can see Mother at the gate waving him off and stating, categorically "no more ponies". Once there he could be overcome with compassion and he gradually acquired a few young ponies which were turned away with his young horses until such time as a use could be found for them. Pixie, the last one he ever bought at the sales, was a case in point. Obviously a very late foal, much too young to be weaned she was, nevertheless, offered, as a weanling, for sale. Father bought her, I expect he paid a couple of bob. Too exhausted and frightened to be thrust into a cattle lorry coming our way father took the front seat out of the car, blindfolded the pony and lifted her into the resulting space. All went well until they reached Porlock Hill which is very steep. The pony, no longer able to keep her feet slid forwards onto the dash board, her scrambling feet threatening the safety of herself and Father, but, in their own fashion, they arrived safely at the bottom. At Cutcombe Auction the following day a local 'wag' wandered up to Father: "have you heard about the man who drove down Porlock Hill one handed yesterday embracing a pony passenger with the other?" Pixie was bottle fed for three months and, eventually, became a good little (properly broken in) pony for my sister.

It must have been holiday time and I think I was seven or eight when that golden day arrived. Father rode up to fetch down his pony herd. I was perched securely, out of the way, behind a hurdle in the cow shed doorway. I could hear the yells getting closer, then the muffled hoofbeats of the unshod herd contrasting with the sharper sound of the shod horse Father was riding. All was pandemonium. They swept into the yard; Bill's hob nailed boots clattering on the cobbles as he rushed to shut the gate on the seething, heaving herd. They swirled around the yard seeking a way out through rolling, anxious eyes, heads up, nostrils flaring, ribs heaving from the exertion and the excitement of the gallop down from the top fields. Gradually all calmed down, the knowing ones going for a drink from the trough or picking at wisps of hay lying around. Using Jane, the shepherding pony, as a lure, the ponies were encouraged into the loose box in the stable. When the ponies were safely inside Jane was led out and, with the remainder of the bunch, young horses growing on, were let away up the lane to find their own field in their own time. Then, and then only, was I allowed out from behind the barricade to begin the exciting business of choosing My Pony.

One's hand hovering over the sweet jar was as nothing compared to the choice I was now being offered. How could one possibly know? I dithered and could not make up my mind. Father became impatient. A couple of years previously Jane had had a foal so I opted for that one. I could sense Father was not too happy with this choice but went along with it. A saddle and bridle were produced. The saddle, a large military type better suited to a large horse, was, maybe, the only one available, and the bridle, a Pelham with two reins and a curb chain for a small child and an unbroken pony!?

Two men caught the pony which was haltered and encouraged, with alarming plunges from side to side, from the stable into the yard. This pony, like all of them, was virtually unhandled but never mind, Father, as usual, was in a bit of a hurry. Here she was saddled and bridled and I was immediately put on top. She refused to move! Small wonder. Father was obviously becoming more and more impatient. "This one's no good" says Father, "fetch out another one". We were back to square one. This time Father made the decision and they pulled out a blue roan gelding. The same procedure was followed; bridle, saddle and me. This time though the pony moved, admittedly in fits and starts but around the yard we went then down to the front of the house where loud shouts of "Darling, Darling" brought Mother to an upstairs window.

Thus began a long association with Robin, a blue roan gelding about 14 hands high and, at the most, three years old but more likely only two; my faithful friend and companion through many adventures for many a long year.

Bill Coles was mainly responsible for my early rides on Robin. He was a great horseman, nothing could shift him and I like to think he passed on to me something of his limpet-like properties on top of plunging horses. Robin and I learnt together from our lessons with Bill, most often after he had finished work. The lack of proper mouthing of the bit was to be a problem for Robin and me for many years.

After Robin and I got going a bit Father took to leading us off another horse. These were usually rather nerve-wracking and fraught occasions; every gate presented problems as they never opened easily and Father's horses were always so impatient. I wasn't very good in the beginning at manoeuvring my pony around a gate whilst still attached by the leading rein to Father sitting on an extremely bouncy horse whose main idea was to charge through the gate and get galloping on. Robin would dig in his toes, I would kick like mad, Father would yell for me to hurry up. Somehow we always managed to emerge on the correct side of the gate. Robin, who remember was never properly broken in, would, at some stage, be completely overcome by the feelings of tension all around and indulge in a good bucking spree. This was bearable whilst I was still on the leading rein as I managed to stay on top and Father would pull his head up so he had to stop bucking. (They can only buck if their heads are towards the ground.)

Once I was considered competent and let off the rein things took a different turn. Robin would canter very nicely until another horse started to catch him up, then he would increase his speed but, on hearing the horse still coming up behind, he would put on the brakes and buck. Father coming along behind would find me crawling out from between Robin's hind legs or, worse still, from some handy gorse bush that Robin was nonchalantly nibbling at. Riding with Bill was a kinder experience all together, although he liked his bit of fun on a horse too.

Bill was often allowed to ride Father's horse, Bay, back to his home at the end of a day's work, quite often after he had given me a lesson. "Now Bill, mind, no galloping and getting him all sweated up." "No Sir" from Bill. If we had nothing better to do we would stand and watch Bill riding sedately down the drive and turn left at the bottom. Wait another few minutes and we would be rewarded by the sound of galloping hooves as Bill and Bay made short work of the lane leading up to West Harwood Farm. If he walked his horse across the next few fields he might arrive at his place with a relatively cool horse but we never placed bets on it. Despite this we knew the horse was in safe hands with Bill.

Years later, whilst home for a short holiday Bill offered me a day's hunting on a horse of his at a meet near to his farm. I gladly accepted. The horse was I believe a dark brown mare. The meet was in Brompton Regis, just a short ride from his farm. Not long enough to settle her down. The day was full of surprises. The mare was very fidgety and lively, given to alarming plunges forward regardless of the terrain. A fellow hunter who lived nearby offered me the loan of a better girth as he thought the old screwed up string one was causing the problem. I declined his kind offer. I didn't think a different girth would make much difference – the mare was just a little wound up. We survived the day, up and down the wooded slopes of the Haddeo valley and across the open spaces of Haddon Hill but I can't say it was one of my more enjoyable days.

The following week I saw the mare advertised in the local paper the *Free Press*. "Such and such a horse for sale. Hunted by a Lady." For Bill to have put "Hunted by a limpet" would have been a more accurate description as I am sure only his instructions in my early years of riding kept me on top of his young mare at all.

Because I was away at school Robin lived with the gang of assorted horses and ponies during the term time although these were gradually whittled down and sold on until we just had Bay and our ponies. These were bought down nearer the yard for the school holidays. One year he must have been in the same field as some sheep as he came in covered with sheep ticks. Well, not exactly covered, I counted twenty-five that first morning to be painstakingly removed by the correct twist to the right so the head came away as well as the body, otherwise infections would set in. That summer the ponies had to be checked every day before grooming could commence. I don't remember that again, or not to that extent.

There were three golden rules for when we were riding. The first rule was the pony had to wear its headcollar either under or over the bridle. The lead rope was in a loop around its neck and tied with the cavalry knot which is very smart and will not slip. This was so we were able to tie up the pony if we came across a sheep in trouble; caught up in brambles or, as can often happen close to shearing time, on its back and unable to right itself. The fleece becomes heavy and itchy and they roll onto their back to try to scratch and cannot get back up and will die if left like that. Sheep are very fatalistic, sometimes a loud yell will get them to struggle a bit harder and get up by themselves but most times it is a case of manually heaving them to their feet and holding them for a couple of minutes until their circulation returns to normal and they are steady on their feet.

Second rule: always carry a hunting crop. The crop handle is good for opening gates, whilst cracking the crop to make a loud noise is always useful around stock and I found this very difficult to master off a small pony. One day, deciding I needed height I climbed up the stack of hay in the Dutch barn and stood on the edge to practice. In those days the hay was forked onto trailers which were towed behind tractors from the field to the barn. Here it was, again, manually forked from the trailer into the stack and all available people would tramp around on the hay so it became a dense mass of sweet smelling winter feed for the stock – cattle, sheep and horses and it was even used to line the laying boxes for the flock of hens. This stack would be cut as wanted into huge slabs with a hay knife, a very sharp, triangular blade with a two-handed handle at the wedge end that was used to cut into the stack from above and took some strength to use. The advent of the baler arrived before I became strong enough to use this knife.

So here I am, teetering on the edge when one of the agriculture students came by; the tall one who was very impatient to finish his training and then he was off to Australia. He told wonderful tales of what he would be doing and how exciting it was all going to be. He was going to be working on some big sheep station and was looking forward to spending hours in the saddle tending the stock. This day I was standing as high as I could go, valiantly trying to master my crop to achieve that sharp cracking sound I desired (the theory being the higher you go the easier it will be). He asked me what would happen if I fell from such a height. Well, I didn't know, I hadn't thought about it but I remember I used to feel a little nervous up there. To get a satisfactory crack I had to stand right on the edge. It must have meant a lot to me to get the crop cracking as I have never had a good head for heights.

He thought what I was doing was dangerous and he had better teach me how to land safely if I fell off. He taught me how to stand on the very edge of the hay, jump down, land on my feet and forward roll into a stand. I must have had great trust in him as it was scary standing right there preparing to launch myself into space. I did it correctly the first time, loved it and kept up the practice for many years just for the fun of it and the slight adrenaline rush I got each time. I used to show off to my parents sometimes with Robin, standing on his back, sliding off over his tail, generally taking liberties with his good nature. However, some inner instinct suggested that I should not show this accomplishment to my parents.

Third rule: always carry a hoof pick to get stones out of pony's feet; these can get lodged under the shoes and are difficult to get out. Someone gave me a knife with a marline spike attached, although heavy in my pocket I found the spike better for removing stones than the hoof pick, more leverage. I still have it today.

I used to ride out regularly with Walter Crockford, the shepherd. One wet morning, riding up the back lane wearing my riding mac, I felt something moving on my arm. Riding macs have elastic cuffs to stop the rain going up ones arm so, what ever it was could not get out. I threw myself off Robin, tore off my mac and a cockroach fell out and scurried away into the long grass. Ugh. As we were always going to do something with sheep we had the dogs with us. Jock the loveable was the despair of Walter. He used to circle us, always barking. Walter would try to flick him with the lash of his hunting crop but Jock knew just how long the reach was and always kept just out of reach. Walter tried getting longer lashes, just one flick from the longer one and Jock would then keep out of its reach.

I joined the Devon and Somerset Staghounds Pony Club. We had indoor lectures during the winter and outdoor riding meets, called rallies, during spring and summer holidays. Getting to these, for me, involved quite long rides over the moor. I remember Father giving me directions. Ride to the top of the farm, at Spangate, go onto the moor. I was to then head (here a wave of the hand to indicate direction) towards Annicombe. In those days there were two crossing of Annicombe, an upper and a lower one and I was to go by the upper one which, I believe, is now completely overgrown and unridable. The track over the moor was very faint, more of a deer rack, not much used and the crossing was not visible until one was close to the edge of the combe. I always found it more by good luck than good judgement. Dropping into the combe the track was more defined although still very narrow, wending its way to the bottom, over the stream and a zig zag climb back to the open moor. Then head over the shoulder of the moor to Webber's Post and so on until, eventually, two hours later and having seen not a living soul except sheep and, if lucky, deer I would arrive at Porlock or Holnicote for the Pony Club rally. Here we would have a couple of hours of lessons and mounted games before beginning the long ride home. Why was I sent that way? It would have been so much easier to go straight up the track from Spangate to the road that runs over Dunkery and down that road to Webber's Post. Maybe he was worried about us meeting cars that way as Robin was not happy in traffic and it was deemed safer for us to be out in the vast expanses of open moorland. Who knows. The most important rule that was stressed time and again: if the fog comes down loosen the reins so the pony has a free head and it will bring you home. And how true that is although, in my case, it was not fog that was to put this theory to the test.

I was attending a day long rally at Holnicote Estate, just off the Minehead/Porlock road so, again, a long ride over the moor to get there. My family must have driven over with a picnic and, to end up the day of serious riding, we were all to participate in a Walk, Trot, and Gallop race. All went well until the gallop bit. Robin unfortunately in the lead, hearing the others catching up, stopped to, as usual, buck and this time he dislodged me. They said I was not wearing my hard hat, which I never believed; in those days hats were just held on by a length of elastic under the chin, it must have come off. I came to lying on the picnic rug beside the car. Nearly everyone had left, the field looked quite empty. There was a discussion about what to do. I insisted I was quite all right to ride home and I was allowed to!

There are different ways to ride from Holnicote to North Hawkwell. I think I must have chosen to go the lower route. Up to Chapel Cross then onto the lane leading to Luccombe Allers, through Ford, Wootton Courtenay and then up over East Harwood Farm to home. At least that was the plan although having been concussed I can't be sure. I must have passed out somewhere along the lane as I came to deep in the woods below Dunkery, Robin making steady uphill progress through the trees, in a direct line for home, with no track to guide him. Theory proved correct, Robin, in charge, taking me safely home.

As with most people there were two sides to Robin's character. Hunting was always a rather daunting affair. Either I stood a good chance of being bucked off or of having a fall when riding the narrow paths in Horner Woods. Robin would insist on galloping along on the outside edges of these paths; one little landslide could have resulted in a nasty accident. Father would look back and call out to me to get him off the edge, I would pull the inside rein which only resulted in Robin still being on the outside but with his head turned to the middle which was, if anything, the more dangerous of the two options. The little banks we used to canter over, landing with that lovely dropping sensation of floating in the air, have now been excavated and are actually the remains of a medieval village!

I was fourteen or fifteen when it was decided I should move onto a horse and a young, Exmoor/Thoroughbred bay mare of about 15 hands, was purchased. She was quite a handful, very green and wilful. We were having a lesson in a little field up the lane, a most unsuitable place for a riding lesson as it was on a steep slope. She kept napping (refusing to obey) at the gate leading out of the field. My riding mistress went outside the gate and, as I tried yet again to get her past the gate, leapt out cracking a hunting crop. The mare leapt forward, took off along the top hedge, turned sharp left down the slope and I came off. My riding stick, a cane one, had a knob at the top. Somehow, I must have landed on this knob as my upper front teeth were knocked out. This happened on a Friday and I had to go all weekend with the nerves exposed which was painful as, every time I opened my mouth the air hit the nerves. I was unable to eat anything solid, even drinking through a straw caused the nerves to tingle. I fully understood what people mean when they talked about sore teeth setting ones nerves on edge. What a relief to go to the dentist on Monday morning where he must have either removed the nerves or blocked them off. There was enough stump left on both teeth for them to be capped which involved putting a peg into each root and attaching a false tooth. Many years later, in Canada, I had to have the next one in line also capped; gold must have been at a high as the dentist insisted I had a gold peg to attach the tooth to and the peg alone cost $400 dollars. When I die I hope they remember to remove the gold peg before burying me as it will still be in mint condition. This accident involving the loses of those teeth happened during the summer holidays and when I came home for the Christmas holiday it was back to riding Robin and also in the following spring holiday. I assume the mare was sold on, I never asked.

Finally there was Tufter. He had been with the Staghounds, and had been the huntsman, Sidney's, tufting horse. Father bought him, quite unsound, at Exeter market where the Staghounds had sent their surplus horses for sale. I think someone must have given him some inside information about this horse because they would not have wanted another young horse after the previous year's unfortunate choice. Tufter, was a 15 hand chestnut gelding with a few faint black spots over his hind quarters. He looked thoroughbred and I found details of quite a famous chestnut TB race horse who also had the same markings so I invented a pedigree for him.

I do not know if it was obvious in the sale ring but Tufter was not sound, he was lame in both front feet. By the time I came home for the holidays though he was sound. The poor chap had corns in both front feet, once these were removed he came sound but he never liked jumping. He was another one who liked to buck. The first time I took him hunting the meet was at Dunkery Hill Gate. Moving off he was a little wound up, he most likely thought he should be up the front, also we were heading towards home. He deposited me in front of the whole field, so embarrassing. I put a standing martingale on and he never bucked again. Why a standing martingale would stop him bucking I can't imagine, it wasn't even tight. He was brilliant on the moor, always alert, always watching. Very good in mist or fog. I always knew where hounds were, his cocked ears keeping me informed.

Some years later I made a list of the names of all the horses or ponies I had ridden and, by the time I left to work in Canada in my middle twenties there were 123 names on that list! And many more to add during the Canadian years.

Chapter 9
THE NEXT CHAPTER

Arriving home in time for Christmas after my last term at Sherborne all seemed normal but, of course, things were about to change. Once New Year was over and Liz and Jonny were back at school all the attention was on me and what to do next. I had taken Tufter to Wootton Courtenay to get him traced clipped so I was more than content looking after him, going hunting and helping on the farm but this happy state of affairs was drawing to a close. Again resisting all efforts to get me to follow a traditional route into future employment I was given an ultimatum: accept that I needed further training, secretarial, nursing, hospital almoner etc. or get myself a job. I started taking *Horse and Hound* as this weekly magazine had a long 'Situations Vacant' column. After some weeks of searching I spotted an advert that sounded promising. "Girl wanted to work in busy riding stables, opportunity for some showing experience, live in, all found. References required". I approached my local Master of Hounds who wrote me a glowing reference and I sent this off with a covering letter and my "O" level results. An interview over the phone with myself regarding my riding abilities and then Father took over; wanting to re-assure himself that I would be safe going there he asked all sorts of relevant question as to my living accommodation, meals, wage (10 shillings a week) and time off each week. Having satisfied himself that I would be safe enough it was arranged he would drive me there. There being Iford Manor, Iford near Lewes, Sussex. And here, plus my bicycle, I was duly deposited late one May day.

My father and I stood in front of the rather imposing front door waiting for someone to answer the bell. My nerves were jangling, a mixture of car sickness and feeling sick to my stomach, just like the feelings I had had going back to school at the start of every term. We were ushered into the hall and my immediate reaction was 'I am back at school', for as we walked in it did feel like I was back at school. There was just this sort of smell, of furniture polish and disinfectant and boiled cabbage. My heart fell, I thought I was through with all that.

Mrs Nelson, the owner, a tall rather gaunt lady appeared and introduced herself. A widow, I was to discover, who wore her deceased husband's pin stripe suit to church on Sundays. Her assistant, Miss Williams, who I was to meet the next morning, had overall charge of the stables and us stable girls. Maybe Father knew but I had not realised I would be joining the staff of an establishment that catered for teenage girls who did not fit into the lifestyle of ordinary girl's public schools. Maybe he thought this would be a safe environment for my first foray into the big, wide world and that was why he agreed to my being so far from home. Although we all ate together I do not remember having much to do with the schoolgirls, in fact, I think that any cross over between them and us was actively discouraged.

If I thought I knew how to muck out and look after horses it was swiftly proved otherwise. I was told I must be down at the yard by 7 am the following day. On the yard everyone looked very busy. Miss Williams found me hovering in the entrance and took me in hand. The routine was explained to me and I was shown the side of the yard I would be responsible for; the mucking out tools and the grooming kit, the muck heap and the hay and straw stores. The yard was tarmacked and sloped quite steeply away from the boxes I was to look after. There were four loose boxes on my side, all occupied and all mine to look after.

The horses and ponies were fed a hard feed at 7 each morning and again around 5pm, with a hay net to pull at during the middle of the day and again during the night. Once they had finished their breakfast they were each tied up in turn whilst their boxes were mucked out and here I came unstuck. At home the horses lived in tie stalls so all the muck was at the back of the stall; here it was all over the place, hidden in the deep straw they were bedded down on. Breakfast was at 9 and I was nowhere near finished. Miss Williams, came to my rescue. She gave me a quick lesson and helped me finish; just this once. After that it was up to me. I set my alarm for 5am and it stayed there for the duration of my time there and, for the rest of my working life it was never a chore to get up really early to get the day off to a good start.

After breakfast there were the horses to groom and tack-up for the lessons or for a ride out up on the downs opposite. To begin with I did not get much riding, I think I had to prove myself before being allowed to ride. There was so much to learn, so much to do that initially I did not miss the riding. I was taught how to pull and trim a tail, how to pull a mane and plait it up on show days. All very time consuming. And, always, at the end of the afternoon, tack cleaning. There is a specialized knack to pulling a mane or tail. If done badly it hurts the horse and hurting a horse whilst pulling the tail is not recommended. With the mane you take a tuft of hair and back comb it and then, with a sharp quick tug, you pull out what is left in your fingers. If done correctly the horse does not feel the pull and remains quite relaxed so one ends up with a thin, short length of mane all along the neck, ideal for the plaiting that is necessary for showing. Doing the tail is much the same technique as the mane ending up with a smooth finish which is then bandaged at night to keep the hair lying close to the bone. Alternatively the hairs are left long and the tail also plaited for shows. I actually prefer this method as a well plaited tail really shows off the hind quarters. Mastering plaiting took some doing and involved hours of practice. No use of rubber bands back then, all the plaits were sewn in and in such a way that no cotton showed. Once home from the show the cotton had to be snipped to release the plaits as leaving them in overnight could result in some of the hair being pulled out when the horses lay down. These horses and ponies were being shown on a regular basis all summer long so it was important to keep the mane in a manageable condition as good plaiting was essential for the overall appearance and presentation of the horse. If one of the animals in our care was going to a show we went along too, to be responsible for presenting it properly tacked up and clean. We were always correctly dressed in jodhpurs, shirt and tie, hacking jacket, hair net and riding hat. To be presentable, as the groom, in the ring was considered a very important part of the overall presentation of the animal being shown.

Although we were living in a school environment we girl grooms were so concentrated on the horse side of the business we had minimal involvement with the schoolgirls. It was my first experience at leading an independent life. It was extraordinary actually; I did not have to answer to anyone, apart from, obviously, one's work in the stables. This took a bit of getting used to. On my day off, which was actually only from midday onwards, I would ride into Lewes where I joined the library. Shortly after going there I purchased my first pair of jeans. This first clothes purchase, with money I had earned, was quite a heady experience. And my first ever pair of jeans. For some reason our jeans and jodhpurs were not included in the weekly wash so we had to do these by hand in a bucket of cold water outside the back door, using a scrubbing brush for the stubborn stains. One of the other girls showed me what to do as I had no idea how to go about it.

I also learnt how to whitewash walls here which was to stand me in good stead many years later in Canada. It was extraordinary. There was a new girl coming for some work experience. I think she was a friend of one of the girls already there. She could only come if we, the grooms, were prepared to do up what was, to all intents and purpose just a large, wooden garden shed. At least the roof was sound. We evicted all the spiders, swept out the musty corners and the cobwebs that hung from the ceiling and applied whitewash to all the walls. We lugged a bed, mattress and dressing table from the attics of the big house and found an old rug for the floor. After it was done it looked quite presentable and we all stood back with mugs of tea to admire our efforts. Now-a-days it would be cans of beer. And we never questioned that this shed was considered a suitable place for someone to sleep in.

I rode for miles once, on my bicycle across country, on one of my afternoons off to stand at a cross roads and watch the Queen Mother being driven past on her way from Lewes to Brighton. Another memorable time there was a spare seat in the lorry taking ponies to Olympia for an evening show. Would I like to go? I did not need to ask anyone's permission. I could just go. It was beginning to dawn on me that I was a free agent, responsible for my own decisions and well being.

During the working day there were deadlines to meet; for instance I would get up at 5 am as, at the beginning, that was the only way to get through my work before breakfast. This habit of early rising was to stay with me for many years. Gradually I was getting some riding. There was a big blackboard in the main block of stables and the day's programme was written up in chalk whilst we were at breakfast. There was a little stampede after breakfast to see what we had been allocated to do for the day. I remember being so excited when, finally, I saw my name beside a horse to ride. Towards the end of my time there I was given some riding lessons. It came about that I was riding out on a little, spirited, show pony which got away with me on the long canter up to the top of the downs and spent the rest of the ride trying to gallop off. I was not popular as this was a prize-winning pony and I was led to believe I had ruined it. Luckily this did not prove correct but there must have been some conversations between Mrs Nelson and my Father as I was put down for daily lessons. Up to then I thought I could ride but came to realise that, although I had attended Pony Club for years, had hunted all over Exmoor and could stick like a limpet to a bucking horse, I was totally ignorant of proper riding. For the first time it was explained to me that all good riding came from the position of my bottom, my seat, in the saddle. How the horse feels every little movement through the saddle and responds accordingly, and how one never, ever, pulls on the reins. It was a revelation and set me on the course I was to follow for all the years to come.

I was also taught how to lunge a horse, a method of training which involves working a horse on a lunge rein in circles around oneself. This was not made easy as the little indoor riding arena had uprights down the centre so one had to work the horse whilst keeping one's back to the centre upright. When lunging one does stand still in the centre of the circle you are working your horse on but learning to do so whilst keeping your back to a fixed object is one hundred times more difficult. Also one had to also keep the circle small enough so the horse did not go the wrong side of the centre post on one's right and left.

I am not sure how many months I was there. Father must have come for me and my trusty bicycle. I was returning home to take part in the packing up of my beloved North Hawkwell as we were moving. I did not come to realise just how much North Hawkwell meant to me until much later in life. North Hawkwell and North Combe had been sold. We were moving to Wootton Lodge, on the back road to Wootton Courtenay from Cowbridge. Granny had been a widow for some years and Father had his health problems; his constant bronchitis during haymaking meant he could not go into the hay fields whilst the grass was drying and being baled up. Now this would be recognised as an allergy or hay fever. He would stand at the gate of the field and feel frustrated when he saw things being done differently to how he wanted. It was decided, who by I wonder, to buy Wootton Lodge as it was big enough for Granny to have her own little kitchen, sitting room and bedroom, and Father was able to stand outside the house with a pair of binoculars and look up at most of the East Harwood fields.

It was our last evening at North Hawkwell. The packing was all done. The gloomy, oppressive atmosphere in the kitchen, the only warm room in the house, was more than I could bear. "I'm going to say good night to the ponies" I announced as I slipped my feet into my wellies and grabbed a coat from the hooks on the back door. This was September with the evenings drawing in but still some light left as I crossed the yard and walked up the stony lane and through the gate into the field. The ponies, Tufter and Robin, were half way across the field and, as I approached, I realized there were other inhabitants of the field. I couldn't believe my eyes. The field was full of deer. I slipped silently away and, at the gate, tried not to make that sharp click when I dropped the latch into the staple as that would carry on the clear night air and alert the deer to my presence. I then pelted down the lane and burst into the kitchen. My parents looked up startled. "You must come, the field is full of deer" I demanded urgently. "Please come." There was a deafening silence then Father said he would come. Mother declined and we left her there. I realize now she was devastated to be leaving and maybe just wanted a quiet time to hug her grief to herself.

Back up the lane, really dark now, pray the gate does not squeak, will they still be there? The ponies, just dark shapes, were close to the gate. We each caught one and, with our fingers entwined in their manes, encouraged them to walk back across the field. The deer were grazing peacefully and, for the longest time it seemed, we walked amongst them.

Then the moon came out from behind a cloud and with it a little breeze – a hind raised her head, ears flicking back and forth, nostrils questing. She must have sensed our presence for she gave a warning bark – all the heads came up and, as one, they flowed into motion. This rippling tide of deer circled the field, the only sounds the swish and click of their feet in the long grass and then the soft thud of their landing as, one by one, they jumped though a gap in the hedge into the neighbouring wood and a soft silence surged back. We released the ponies and, too moved for words, silently made our way home. And that was my last night at North Hawkwell.

Chapter 10
THE NEXT STEP

Once again worried discussions must have been going on; the perpetual one of what to "do with Gay". I had helped with the move to Wootton Lodge and was quite happy looking after the ponies, doing a bit of hunting and farm work and generally making myself useful but, obvious to everyone but myself, I needed a boost to get me going on a career plan. I was so set on working with horses it was decided to enrol me onto a Horsemastership, three month residential, course being run at Porlock Vale Riding School; the very place I used to ride to for pony club.

There had been a horse establishment in Porlock for many years, hiring out horses for hacking and hunting to the many visitors that came to Exmoor for the outstanding scenery and relaxing way of life. The main yards were in the middle of Porlock. There were loose boxes and tie stalls, an extra large loose box, maybe a foaling box, that had been converted into a lecture theatre with tiers of seating at the back. A very large tack room which always had that evocative aroma of leather and saddle soap recognisable the world over whereever there were stables, had two tiers of saddle racks around the walls with their bridle brackets underneath and, suspended down the centre of the room a line of retractable hooks for cleaning bridles and girths and head collars. On one wall, although now never used except for demonstrations, hung a couple of sets of harness, a hark back to the times before the development of the combustion engine when horse power reigned supreme.

Further in were more boxes and a blacksmith and farrier shop, an indoor school, paddocks and a jumping lane. All in all a large establishment. Down the road close to Porlock Weir was Porlock Ford House where the owners lived. Here was the most beautiful stable yard with an enclosed stable block with four or five large loose boxes on the left as you walked down; on the right a line of tie stalls, a large foaling box and the tack room, all paved with nonslip, vitreous, brick. The hard feed area with its secure tin bins full of oats, barley and bran was beside the tack room and equipped with a boiler for making the huge amount of boiled barley and linseed for the mash that was fed, with bran, every Saturday evening to relax the horses, bowels. This was to prevent the horses tying up in spasm in the muscles of the hind quarters or developing Azortoria on Monday mornings as Sunday was a rest day and they did not leave their boxes. All the door fittings and tying up rings on the walls around the yard were well polished brass. The hay and straw were under cover in a Dutch barn with the all important chaff cutter used every day to chop up the hay to add bulk to the hard grain. And the huge muck heap was a thing of precision; four square with combed sides, a testimony to a well run stable. There is a knack to building such a muck heap.

The house and stables were surrounded by paddocks with cross country fences in all the hedges, an indoor arena, jumping lane and a further line of four loose boxes completed the establishment. The whole formed a miniature estate devoted to horses and horse mastership.

All those resident on the course lived in Porlock Ford House. After supper on the first night we were introduced to our instructor for the course, Miss Betty Howett. The aim of the course was explained, we were assigned the horse we would be looking after for the duration of the course, the do's and don'ts pointed out. There were just two of us, myself and Tina with previous work experience with horses. We were divided into two teams to keep us on our toes I was put in one and Tina, who became a life-long friend, was in the other. I think they thought we would be a steadying influence. We were called the Blues and the Reds. This was a clever idea as Tina and I were also the only ones who had lived away from home and those running the course did not want to be dragging underage girls having their first taste of freedom from the pub just a walk away across a couple of fields. There was to be a prize near the end of the course to the winning team, points being awarded or taken away depending on our diligence, competence and punctuality around the stables, and no missed curfews.

First thing the next morning we were introduced to our horses, and given each individual's grooming kit. Then we collected our horse's feed and quickly learnt which horses were polite and stood back whilst we placed their feed in their manger and which ones could be quite aggressive and come at you with ears laid back and twitching tails. With these it was best to dump the feed in the manger and get out as quickly as possible and not go back in until they were finished. Whilst they were eating their breakfast we took down and filled their hay nets and collected our mucking out tools. These were a real job lot. Those slowest at filling nets got the worst tools for mucking out. Once we had mucked out and put most of the bedding around the walls we groomed our horses for three quarters of an hour! We did just about everything for that horse bar scrubbing its teeth.

After breakfast we changed into our jodhpurs for our riding lessons. We rode six days a week for two hours, all work in the indoor arena or out in the fields where the jumping lane and show jumps were. On Saturdays we hacked out for two hours and a hairy two hours those could be with inexperienced riders, horses excited to be out of the school situation and all the open spaces of Exmoor to play in. The instructor always led these mad forays across the moors; the competition between the teams was quite fierce; anyone letting their horse run away with them and passing the instructor lost points for their team.

Each morning some of us were driven up to Porlock to ride horses back to Porlock Ford for lessons as there cannot have been enough suitable ones to mount us all. That first expedition was a shambles. No-one appeared to be in charge, no-one formed us into a manageable group; consequently everyone just got on their allocated horse and set off, regardless of who else was ready or not. It was an accident waiting to happen. Everyone on this course was meant to know how to ride but some really had little more experience than a Saturday ride once a week and were let loose to ride fit horses down the road from Porlock to Porlock Ford for our first lesson. An instructor at the Porlock yard stood in a doorway shaking his head in amazement as he watched us all ride by; the largest students were riding the smallest horses. I, myself, at a slight 5 feet 2 inches, was on top of a tall, young, bright chestnut gelding who, I learned later, had just got off the train from Ireland. We proceeded in leaps and bounds across the yard as he endeavoured to catch up to the horse he saw disappearing out onto the street in front of him. I doubt I spared a thought to thank Mrs Nelson for those lessons at Iford Manor but, if it weren't for those lessons that horse would have been in charge, not I. By sitting very quietly and just playing with the bit in his mouth through the reins we did arrive safely, even if in a bit of a lather.

Initially the horse I was allocated to look after was a pleasant dark bay mare stabled in the indoor block, second on the left at the back. But there was trouble brewing across the way. The foaling box was occupied by a large, completely white mare of uncertain temperament aptly called Pipeclay. And she had got the measure of the girl assigned to look after her and had taken to cornering her in the box. The girl was terrified and no wonder and would no longer go in the box with her. Even after just a week looking after "my mare" I was feeling quite possessive of her but the kudos of being asked to take on this difficult horse was a boost to my ego so I obliged. So it was goodbye to my nice bay mare and hallo to Pipeclay. The first instruction "Never enter her box without your riding stick in your hand"! second instruction "Always tie her up on a short line". Third instruction "Never turn your back on her". Oh dear. There was lot of speculation as to why she was like this. One theory was she was partly blind, another was that she was just unpredictable but the one that made most sense was that she had an abscess or something on her ovaries and was only like this if she was in season. The partly blind theory cannot have had much substance as we used to jump her. One thing for sure, when lined up during a lesson, whether in the indoor arena or outside Pipeclay had to stand well away from the next horse in line as she had the habit of suddenly lunging at the nearest horse with her mouth wide open, to the consternation of who ever was riding her.

Gradually we all settled into the routine. Morning stables, breakfast, riding lessons, midday stables, lunch, short break. Our lectures were after lunch. Sometimes these were straightforward lectures at Porlock Ford involving all aspects of horse care from grooming to feed to poisonous weeds in pastures, how to make hay, to the application, with diagrams, of the aids to good horsemanship. Or we might be driven to Porlock for lectures on anatomy in the lecture box. If there was a lame horse we all clustered round whilst it was trotted up and down to determine which leg it was lame on and probable causes. Afternoon stables involved tack cleaning, changing day rugs for night ones, skipping out and bedding up for the night. There was a rota for evening stables when the horses were skipped out, water buckets topped up, rugs straightened if needed, a quick check that all was well before bed. A busy day. Every other weekend was off, from midday on Saturday to Sunday evening.

Three things of note. Putting Pipeclay's bridle on one morning, just in that vunerable moment when the stick was put down so I could reach over her ears with the bridle she seized my left arm below the elbow, carried me across the box and deposited me by the door. Her teeth did not break the skin but thoroughly bruised a large bite-sized area which came out in a very colourful blood blister. It was my weekend home in a couple of days and, although the weather was hot I wore a long sleeved shirt as I did not want my parents to see the damage. Two weeks later I was again at home, had got used to the bruise, wore a short sleeved shirt and Mother's shriek of horror when she saw my arm nearly made me jump out of my skin. Sixty years later it is still possible to make out where the injury was.

Near the end of the course I was scrubbing out water buckets at the trough in the yard and Betty came up to me and asked if I would like to stay on as junior instructor. My initial reaction was no thanks. I never had time to think it through as she immediately went looking for Tina and made the same offer which Tina accepted. Looking back I think she felt she had to offer it to me as, unbeknown to me, I was actually the top of the class but she recognised that Tina would suit her better. So that was a lesson well learnt: do not make hasty decisions, give yourself time to think things through.

And the third which still peeves me today. Half way through we were joined by an undergraduate from Cambridge and, when the official results from our exams came out I was beaten into second place by this chap. I never, ever, remember being told that I was rather good at what I was doing. Although never very brave across country, as in three day events, I was, nevertheless a good instructor and good at breaking in horses but no-one ever said. Of course those were still the days of the stiff upper lip and praise might give one a swollen head!

Chapter 11
EVER ONWARDS

After Porlock I was home for a while whilst I looked for a job. Eventually I found one in Newmarket with Miss Anne Hammond whose family owned a large yard in the centre of town. This had been a busy yard for many years, supplying black horses for funeral hearses, carriage horses and horses for hire for hunting. These eventually gave way to motorized hearses and motor horse boxes in constant use ferrying racehorses around the country. It was now a showing and teaching yard with hunting in the winter. This was my first experience of teaching. Newmarket is the centre of flat racing, the whole town is given over to racing; the jockeys' children used to come for half hour lessons in their lunch hour and we also had pupils from the American army base just outside the town. One of these was a real menace. He used to run riot as soon as he was let out of the car and paid no attention to anything his mother asked him to do, or not to! Rupert Bear, a 12 2 liver chestnut gelding, was saddled and bridled and tied up with the other ponies in the yard waiting for the pupils to arrive. Miss Hammond arrived in the yard to see this little boy enthusiastically actually swinging on Rupert's tail, She swept down the yard, grabbed the boy and handed him to his mother with instructions to never, ever come back.

We went to a lot of horse shows competing in Show Hack and Show Pony classes. We were also a trading yard. Fred Broome used to come up from Wales with a selection of, mainly, ponies. These we put through their paces and those we did not like went back on his next trip to us. Because I was lightweight it was part of my job to ride and school on anything that was suitable for our market. We also took in private ponies for schooling. The current one was a bay gelding, about 14 hh. At home this local pony was looked after by an old fashioned groom whose main aim in life was to turn out his charges in tip top condition and, to achieve this he over fed them. Over feeding and lack of exercise had resulted in a pony bubbling over with good health just wanting to run. Frustrated and bursting with supressed energy he had started to rear which was frightening his young teenage rider.

In amongst the recent load from Wales was another bay, a mare Megan, almost identical to our rearing friend and this one also reared. Extraordinary really, the local one's rearing did not disturb me at all even when, one day, as we were riding them back to their field it reared up and came down straddling the much smaller pony I was leading on my right side. But Megan's rearing was a very different affair. There was something vicious about it and it frightened me. She was returned to Wales. The local one had its hard feed cut, was well exercised, the owner came for lessons and it was returned home with strict instructions to the groom to reduce its feed and exercise it more. We never heard from them again so one assumes he followed these directions.

We had grazing areas all over the outskirts of the town. These were divided or enclosed with electric fencing, my first experience with this type of control. New ponies had to be made aware that there was a considerable sting to what looked like an innocent thin wire stretched around the inside of their enclosure. The method involved backing the animal onto the fence so they received a shock and would then jump forward so one had to have a good grasp on the lead rope or it would be snatched out of one's hand and one was left with a frightened pony galloping around with the lead rope getting tangled in its legs. One was not very popular if this happened. I actually never got used to backing ponies onto electric fences but it worked; any pony so treated would thereafter view any bare wire with great suspicion.

We did quite a lot of hunting, either with the Newmarket and Thurlow or with the Cambridgeshire Harriers. (Mrs Gingell MH.) I had never done any hunting that involved jumping and both of these hunts hunted over the fens so jumping ditches was commonplace. And a nerve racking experience this could be. Remember we were hunting horses and ponies who were going to be sold on and some, like me, had never come across ditches, let alone ones like these; great yawning chasms dissecting the fields. We had, briefly, a little strawberry roan mare about 13hh and she was brilliant. She tackled the dikes with great enthusiasm, never any hesitation, took them in her stride, it was like flying. At the other end of the scale were the ones who stood, trembling, on the brink then, feeling they were being left behind, either tried to scramble down the sides and hop across (very dicey procedure) or took off from the top with a great lurch that nearly unseated one. There was a parson who hunted regularly with the Newmarket and Thurlow who carried a coil of rope over one shoulder to help pull out riders or horses stuck at the bottom of one of these horrors. Once I was sent out to accompany two girls hunting. It was a blank day and I got into trouble for not having come home sooner. Another time I rode alone to a nearby meet. We had a busy morning so I turned for home after a couple of hours. It was a warm day and I was thirsty so I stopped at a pub for a cider. Not sure what I asked for, it was delicious but, oh dear, it was very strong. I was definitely a bit the worse for wear, drunk in charge of a horse. At least the horse knew where home was.

To begin with in Newmarket I lived with Miss Hammond and her parents in their big house up the hill out of town. Mr Hammond was a very ill man and it was decided I should move into the lodgings in town in which previous employees had lived quite happily or so I was told! This was a disaster both socially and politically.

So the hunt was on for different lodgings. Racing in and around Newmarket is a huge industry employing many hundreds of people. And landladies did not like letting out rooms to girl grooms. Girls spelt trouble, at least in their opinion. But I did manage to find a pleasant land ady in a pleasant house but that is all I remember as things were beginning to unravel generally at work. Mr Hammond had died and I think I was getting on Miss Hammond's nerves So once again it was time to phone home. Looking back I realise how lucky I was to have a home and be welcomed into it after each adventure. The difference being, this time, that I was very thin and on the verge of a nervous breakdown.

In Minehead, shortly after coming home, I bumped into Captain Peck. He told me a group of people around Porlock had got together and were starting up Porlock riding school again. Would I be interested in the position of Stud Groom? I jumped at it; so started another chapter in my life. I don't think I ever knew whether this group had actually bought this little estate or were leasing it. However it was, we were starting from scratch. A bunch of horses had been bought in Ireland and shipped over; a mixture of thoroughbreds and some more cobby types, all living out. I remember the order of the day was: catch them up, brush off the saddle area, saddle them up and, if time before the lesson or hack out, brush off the remaining mud! Not how I had been trained. It was all very informal, we worked hard, we had so much fun and things gradually fell into place ready for the new Horsemastership courses we were going to be running. I was breaking in horses and we got a certain amount of hunting as every thing on the yard was for sale.

So many horses came and went that I do not really remember all of them. One stands out. We took three or four to a local meet of the Devon and Somerset Staghounds. I was on a chestnut cob, about 15hh with a hogged mane, called Clonmell. And cobs can be very strong. We found and went up over to come out on the open moorland towards Hawkcombe Head. Back then all the land to the west of the Whitstones/Exford road was open land dissected with steep moorland combes with little rivers running through, superb riding country, lovely to gallop over. This land has since been enclosed, fertilized and turned into grazing pastures. On this day our quarry was heading for Badgworthy Water and the Doone Valley. The steep Exmoor combes all have narrow zig zag paths going down into them and then up the other side. Very useful if you knew where to find the start but Clonmell was having none of this sissy nonsense of riding along the edge of the combe looking for the path. She took the bit, a Pelham, between her teeth and went straight down over and straight up the other side and did it again at the next combe. I had never experienced anything like it, she was brilliant and so safe footed, nevertheless not the recommended way to ride this country. Also, you may have gathered, she was in control, not myself, not running away exactly, just getting on with the job in hand.

All good things come to an end. A recently retired, I believed, Colonel Jamie Crawford joined the staff as chief instructor. And used to working with civilians he was not. He would come out of the office which was in a little yard up by the house, calling my name, all the way down to the stable yard; everyone with in a half mile radius would be aware that I was wanted. Nothing I did seemed to satisfy him. For example, every Monday morning I used to sit in the gallery at the end of the indoor arena and observe the horses. It was the best way to assess how each horse was looking, whether it was happy, did it need more feed or less, up the hay ration or reduce it. This quiet hour or so was a good way to start each week. An overview of all in our care. This practice of mine was considered not necessary, I should be being busy, not sitting around.

 I struggled on for a while, for I'd been there at the beginning of this new venture for Porlock and was reluctant to leave. I loved the hunting, got great satisfaction from successfully breaking in horses and the teaching of all things relating to good stable management to each new intake of students. Being constantly hollered at became very wearisome and somewhat degrading as I knew I was good at my job and seemed to be liked by those I worked with. I recognised it was his way, especially in front of visitors, to emphasize just how tight a ship he ran. This was at my expense. No one minds being reprimanded for wrong doing if it is justified but not in front of other people. With my dignity still intact I was, once again, on the look out for a new job!

Chapter 12
MENDIPS AND THE LAKE DISTRICT

Once again I was on the move. This time I had wheels as Granny bought me a little car, a Morris Minor registration GMC 1. Wanting a complete change I found a job with Major and Mrs Portal in Westbury Sub Mendip, a village on the road between Wells and Cheddar at the foot of the Mendip Hills. Here all that was required of me was to care for her horses; two hunters, a couple of brood mares and their offspring. Some showing of the youngsters in the summer and hunting with the Mendip Farmers in the winter. Oh yes, also included, combing the white cats for fleas before lunch on Sundays and clipping the toe nails of the two bull terriers as and when needed.

I never questioned their ages. I was there in 1961. I believe Major Portal was then in his early eighties and although persuaded to stop riding and hunting as his balance had become very wobbly and he was falling off too regularly for comfort, he was still managing 4 miles walking the dogs every morning. Mrs Portal must have been a few years younger, early or mid seventies so they were both born well before the turn of the century. She was a remarkable lady and very stalwart in her attitude to life. As a young girl she broke two side saddles whilst having falls out hunting. When her father bought her the second one he told her he was not buying another one for her. After she broke this one she had to go to the Master of Hounds of the hunt she rode with to ask his permission to ride astride. That must have been quite a daunting interview as ladies just did not ride astride in those days. She drove ambulances in both world wars; in France in the first one and London in the second.

We ate all three meals in the dining room. Mrs Portal did the *Telegraph* crossword each day; she started it over breakfast, continued it at lunch and hoped to finish it at supper. She never went to bed until it was completed. Once a week we had curry for lunch followed by steamed ginger pudding. One's taste buds had a bit of a beating that day. We also had tea around the fire each afternoon and often toasted crumpets on the fire.

I must have been working quite hard as I never put on any extra weight. One of my jobs was to creosote the big field shelter in the fields we had on top of the Mendips, close to the village of Priddy, called Buckingham Palace by the locals as it was quite large. Considering I am allergic to creosote I wonder how I got away with that job, I suppose because it was very airy up there and the field shelter was only three sided there was a constant supply of fresh air. And also to keep on top of the ragwort that grew strongly in the fields and is poisonous to certain livestock, especially, when dried in hay, to horses. Digging up the ragwort was just plain back breaking and boring. Stable duties included the exercising of the two hunters, one for Mrs Portal and the other, more often than not I rode hunting too. I was getting lots of hunting. Having never touched alcohol it was a bit of a revelation when the meet was at a pub or private house, to be handed a glass of straight whisky or port. Mrs Portal did not like the whisky so I, who also did not like it was handed hers too and, to be polite, had to drink it. The most revolting drink though was rum in hot milk. The days where refreshments were served were, actually, red letter days for me; the more one had to drink before moving off the less daunting the prospect of jumping the huge dry stone walls.

Mrs Portal had a strict regime for exercising and getting the horses fit after their summer holiday. She rode with me to begin with to show me the fields she had permission to gallop in and my way around all the lanes. As the horses became fitter and I knew my way around I did all the exercising; ride one lead one. It was quite exhilarating galloping two horses together on our fast exercise days.

Mrs Portal did her best to provide me with a social life. On the top of the Mendips lived a Miss Lucy Jones. She liked her racing and had a yard full of beautiful thoroughbreds for point-to-point races. She often took her girl grooms to the theatre in Bristol and I was included in these outings. Mrs Portal used to get invites to card evenings in a home near to Cheddar. As she did not go out of an evening I was sent along as a substitute, to make up the numbers. These evenings usually packed up between 10pm and half past. One night after such a session and Canada beginning to encroach on my sub conscious through my correspondence with my friend Tina I drove the long way home; up Cheddar Gorge, all the way, on the wrong side, for us, of the road. Just to feel what it was like to drive on that side.

I rode out one day with Lucy's stud groom, Mr Finch, a fine horseman of the old school He was riding a youngster he was breaking in for Lucy which looked ready to explode at any minute. Another incident of a horse being fed too much hard grain. I was always being accused by a senior member of the hunt of doing just that with the horse Mrs Portal rode hunting, which I never did, it was the way she rode it. Mr Finch explained to me what action to take if I was ever seriously run away with. There is only one thing to do; bale out! Once the rider is off a bolting horse it will usually pull itself up, maybe not immediately but eventually. If the rider has landed safely he just waits until the horse has stopped running and catches it up, remounts and continues the ride without delivering any punishment. Thankfully I never had cause to put this frightening action into practice.

The winter I was there was quite a cold snowy one. The lanes up out of the village were just sheets of ice The only way to get up to our fields on the top, where the brood mares and youngsters were, was to drive all the way around through Wells and up the main road. Up to now I had no driving experience in these conditions and this is where Mrs Portal was so brilliant. Instead of taking the wheel herself she had me drive and taught me all she knew about driving in snow and on ice.

Once the weather had improved we started hunting again and the season was to end in tragedy for Mrs Portal. I was not riding this day. Mrs Portal was riding the chestnut and the meet was the other side of Wells. Once hounds had moved off most of the field were sheltering from the wind with their backs to a thick hedge. There seemed to be no scent, everyone was chatting quietly amongst themselves when a hound jumped through the hedge behind Mrs Portal. Her horse jumped forward, dislodged Mrs Portal who came off and broke her shoulder. An ambulance was called for and I was left to take the horse home. Two things were worrying me; the horse was difficult, at the best of times, to load into the trailer and I had never driven the land rover towing the trailer, and the city of Wells was between me and home.

Loading took a little time to figure out. Luckily there was a lunge line in the trailer. I tied the horse up at the back of the trailer then went in by the little side door and walked down the inside of the trailer to the back and attached the lunge line to the head collar. I then walked back through the trailer and down the outside to the horse and untied the lead rope from the horse and tied it to the back of the trailer on the other side. Now I had the equivalent of driving reins. Praying that the horse remembered being long lined when it was broken in I set about persuading it to enter the trailer by giving encouraging tugs on the lunge line with one hand and lightly slapping the hind quarters on the other side with the lead rope. It took patience and time, not sure how long, but she eventually got the message and went in. What a relief. Now just to back the trailer onto the road and negotiate Wells. That must have been the slowest trailer journey that horse ever had and, for me, the scariest. Arriving home I unloaded the horse and got it rugged and fed then tackled getting the outfit into the property. No easy feat as the trailer and Land Rover were out in the road which was at right angles to the drive. Trial and error won the day, half an hour later all were safely parked up where they should be. And I never looked back. With just that one experience I became proficient in hauling trailers.

Mrs Portal had her shoulder operated on that evening and came home a few days later. I was keeping the horses fit and, one day, I went out hunting on the little chestnut and, rather late in the afternoon, my sense of direction letting me down, I landed off a wall onto a narrow lane. I knew hounds were off to my right but the horse knew home was to the left. We parted company – in so doing she trod on my right leg. As always I kept hold of the reins and remounted and, with a couple of sharp kicks, headed in the direction I wished to go. I became conscious of a feeling of my boot filling up with liquid! Once home again, horse seen to, rugged up, fed a warm mash and fresh hay net hanging up I went indoors and removed my boots. With slight horror I looked at my leg – under the skin it was full of blood. This over time, dispersed, with no ill effects.

Mrs Portal was told she would never have the full use of that arm again. Her dream of dying in the hunting field was not to be realised – she died in a nursing home. Poor Mrs Portal.

My next stop was the Lake District. To Tarn Hows Hotel just outside the village of Hawkshead and close to the series of little, connected lakes called Tarn Hows. The proprietors were Mr and Mrs Moffat. This was a riding holiday hotel. The instructor who was leaving stayed on for my first week to show me all the rides otherwise I would have been completely lost. The ponies, with a couple of weight-carrying horses lived out in fields dotted around the village and were bought up to the stable yard around 6 o'clock in the morning for their breakfast. I and my assistant, Valerie, would walk to get them, they were always keen to come as they knew there was a feed of grain waiting for them. We rode them bareback, and with just head collars, back to the stables. We usually had, at least, three each, trotting up the road. It was a little disconcerting, one morning, to find a police car lying in wait. This particular morning, luckily, we were well in control and proceeding quietly. I suspect a local had considered we were an unruly bunch behaving in an irresponsible way and had reported us. Thankfully nothing came of it.

The guests arrived on Saturdays. On Sundays they met their allocated pony and had a two hour ride in preparation for the day-long rides on the following five days. This being the Lake District every one was advised to bring proper wet wear riding gear and everyone was meant to have some riding experience; we only had one complete beginner turn up that summer and I had to upset another of our guests by allocating the horse I had given her, a pleasant chestnut gelding, to this complete beginner. My preferred ride was Mona, a little black Fell mare who took her duties seriously. She was the leader and considered her rightful place was at the head of the column. To keep the peace I gave my disgruntled guest Mona to ride. So now I had a disgruntled pony as well who did not take kindly to being back amongst the others. Taking matters into her own hands every day Mona worked her way to the front of the ride which suited her rider very nicely thank you; she now felt she was the leader of the outfit. All this jockeying for position actually did me a favour. With Mona leading us I could concentrate on the beginner. The horse I was left with to ride was closer in height to the one I had the beginner on so it was a better match. This way, having the beginner on the lead rein right beside me I could reach over and grab the back of her jacket and forcibly yank her up and down when trotting to force her to learn to rise to the movement. I kept her on a lead line for the first two days and told her if she did not learn how to rise to the trot by the end of the first day I couldn't take her on any other rides. Amazingly she mastered this technique, then she just had to learn to steer! That pony deserved a medal.

We covered between 15 and 20 miles on each day-long ride with lots of trotting and a good canter on each ride. I carried all our lunches in a haversack on my back. Each day's ride was different and each lunch stop presented its own challenge. In Grasmere, for instance, the ponies were tied up to the wall at one side of the car park; not tied up exactly, their lead ropes were just looped around the top stones. At any time they could have flicked their rope from the wall and made a run for home but they knew the routine and were glad of the rest. We all trooped into the village to a café with outside tables where we could buy drinks and eat our lunch. The Coniston ride was quite a challenge as we had to wade into the lake to ride around a fence that was built well out from the land. We went up on the fell where everyone had to hold their pony whilst eating their sandwiches, a tricky manoeuvre as ponies love bread. Also here we were on the open fell with little or no cover for those wanting a comfort break!

For a few months now I had been getting letters from my friend Tina in Canada. Her aim was to persuade me to emigrate to Edmonton. Tina had stayed at Porlock and a Mr Owen bought the riding school; he also owned the Silver Hound Country Club, outside London and proceeded to transfer everything, horses, instructors etc. to his country club effectively ending Porlock Vale Riding School. One day a certain Bob Stone, on leave from Canada arrived for a riding lesson and fell headlong in love with Tina. Theirs was a whirlwind courtship and three weeks later they were married. Before heading to Canada they spent a weekend at Wootton Lodge to visit my parents. Bob Stone and my father, also Bob, became the best of friends. Bob and Tina were to go to Edmonton in Aberta where Bob, who had been learning all about the forestry industry in Eastern Canada, was promoted to manage a huge quarry outside Edmonton.

Tina became involved in the English (as opposed to Western) riding community. One day she was judging at a show and there were children riding English in an appalling fashion. After her judging duties were finished she went over to talk to this family and made the acquaintance of Danny (Diana) Brown and her three eldest children. Although having lived in Canada for many years Danny was still very English in her speech and general outlook; finally some one on the same wave length as Tina (who had found it very lonely in Alberta with no like minded people to be friends with) who began teaching the children. Gradually Tina's attention drifted away from the riding world and she took up dog training and very successful she was too. Danny was bereft until Tina mentioned me and suggested Danny think about getting me over to take up where she, Tina, had left off. A correspondence began between Danny Brown and myself and I made the decision to give it a go.

Driving home from the Lake District was a bit of a nightmare. The bad winter of 1962/1963 was beginning. I got as far as Shropshire easily enough to stay with Roger and Margaret Bagot, long time friends of my parents who farmed in a big way. Then it snowed, heavily, and I was stuck there. After a couple of days Uncle Roger phoned up the haulage firm he used for transporting livestock to find out what the roads heading west were like. Very obligingly they suggested a route for me to take that had been cleared of snow so I set off for home. As I drove into Leominster a large tree fell across the road behind me and, as I drove out, another large tree fell behind me. How lucky was I? I continued driving. I clearly remember the straight old A39 through Churchill, west of Bristol and it being like an ice rink and I was doing 60 miles an hour. Did I have a charmed life?

It was snowing quite steadily as I drove up Cutcombe Hill and then left into Cutcombe. I parked up in front of Portway House and there the car stayed as the next morning it was completely hidden under a huge blanket of snow. And still it snowed, in places the snow was as high as the hedges. I remember seeing helicopters flying overhead delivering fodder and groceries to farms completely cut off from the rest of the world. And in all this I was trying to emigrate to Canada. I was meant to go to Canada House in London for an interview and medical check. This could not happen as the roads and railways were impassable. Canada House accepted my medical and references being provided by a local GP and paper work completed I was free to arrange my flights as soon as possible.

Chapter 13
CANADA HERE I COME

The day for leaving England finally arrived This was my first experience of flying. Knowing no better I dressed up in my good suit with girdle and stockings! How uncomfortable that was. Mother and I drove to Oxford to pick up Father who was attending Wycliffe College in preparation for becoming a minister in the Church of England and then on to Heathrow. This was February 1963. Landing at Winnipeg and walking across the tarmac into the terminal was a bit of a shock. I had never felt cold like it. Maybe 30 or 40 below zero. My nylons felt as if they were running down my legs. The terminal was in a large Nissen hut, the facilities were minimal but it is where I went through customs and immigration and became a 'landed' immigrant. A couple of hours later we re-boarded the plane and continued to Edmonton. Coming into land I was riveted to my window; all the land so neatly divided into squares, called sections I was to learn later, except where it bordered the frozen North Saskatchewan River where the sections were, of necessity more irregular in shape as rivers rarely run straight for any appreciable length.

It had been decided that I was to go to Danny's first before visiting Tina and Bob so it was Danny and her husband Jon who met me at the airport and drove across town to what was to be my home for the next two years: Blue Goose House, Sherwood Park, Alberta. Once there I was introduced to the three oldest children. The house was set up a short drive with the house on the left and a line of stables on the right and various paddocks plus a forty acre field known as 'the back forty' where I was to build a few jumps in the woody bit to encourage the children to open up and be more free on their ponies as they only seemed to ride in arenas. Knowing I was coming to work for them Danny and Jon hastily made an addition to the house as there were not enough bedrooms for us all. They enlarged their sitting room and above it built a large, en suite, bedroom and I was given what had been their bedroom on the ground floor. This had French doors looking out into the garden. That first night, being from England, I opened these, just a crack thank goodness, and found the water in my bedside glass frozen solid by the morning. I walked out to breakfast, held the glass over the table and turned it up side down. Much to everyone's amusement.

Sherwood Park today is one huge housing estate with two big business parks, back then it was a small housing estate served by a short strip mall with a bank, grocery store, hair dressers plus other small stores on a gravel road just off the main highway. Danny and I spent a few days getting to know each other and the children and the ponies; Jonathan thirteen, Jane ten and Adam eight. I was a bit thrown by the fact that the children called their parents by their first names. There were younger ones too, Mungo and Justin but they did not concern me as they were too young for riding. Then came Quincy (so called as the fifth boy) and, eventually, after I had left, Pollyanna (named after a well bred show pony in England that Danny tried to buy and failed). And Danny did not like failing at anything, be it riding, skiing or buying this pony.

There were seven ponies and one horse when I arrived. Criban a 12.2hh chestnut mare imported from England, Golden Goose a 13.2 or 14.2 liver chestnut gelding who competed in both riding and driving classes, Flora, a palomino mare about 14hh who specialized in Western classes, Grey Goose 13.2 grey gelding, and Blue Snow Goose a bay 16.2 that had been on the race track. This horse, whose stable name I have forgotten, did not look very well to me; gaunt and listless about describes her. We called in the vet, Dr Stan Maclean (veterinarians are called Doctor, not Mister in Canada and America) which reminded me of tooth paste so I pronounced his name as we pronounced it in England. I got a very funny look. It appeared that she had a vitamin B12 deficiency and would have to receive a series of shots (injections). I had never given an injection in my life, but in short order it was made clear to me that now was as good a time as any to learn. Stan was not coming out everyday for such a simple task. Wipe the area on the hind quarters with alcohol, take a deep breath, give three thumps with the side of your fist and plunge in the needle, then slowly push in the plunger until the syringe is empty and withdraw the needle. By giving the three thumps the horse seems unaware the needle has gone in. I always preferred the hind quarter although some people put injections into the chest muscles. There were also Rattlesnake, show name Brown Goose, a show hack type bay gelding, about 15hh who I showed and did a little dressage with and an unbroken dark grey pony who lived out. Danny also owned another horse, Glenlivet Grey Goose, the most striking looking grey gelding I ever saw with a white flowing mane and tail who was on the race track and not doing brilliantly well. It was decided to bring him home. Initially he went to another stable to be let down from the racing. He had been so stuffed full of hormones to try to get him to win a race that he was not safe for me to handle or have around a place where there were children.

My very first morning after the three oldest children had left for school and the cleaning lady had arrived to look after Mungo and Justin, Danny took me shopping. It was a typical February day, bright and sunny and the temperature hovering somewhere between 30 and 40 below zero. We started by buying a wonderful parka with fur around the edges of the hood and a draw string at the waist which kept me warm for many a year, until my future husband John borrowed it one day and lost it. Danny also bought me thick felt knee-high boots with removable over shoes, galoshes. It was possible to wear these boots without the galoshes through most of the winter as everywhere was frozen solid and they kept my feet toasty warm. The galoshes only came into use once the spring thaw had started. Gloves were the next requirement. You have to wear gloves working outside in these extreme temperatures otherwise your hands stick to anything metal and it is painful to pull them free. Also to prevent frost bite!

Then it was off to spend a few days with Tina and Bob before returning to Blue Goose House to start my job properly. The ponies had not been ridden all winter and, of course, everywhere was covered in deep snow or horrible icy patches where the snow had been swept clear by the wind, maybe thawed a bit on a sunny day then frozen again. That first morning mucking out had me puzzled. The ponies droppings were rock hard, were they constipated? Before I made a complete fool of myself by asking Danny I realised they were frozen! Next was to make a straw ring on top of the snow in the level paddock close to the main road, the only flat piece of ground I could find. This was right up Jonathan's street. He got to make many, many journeys between the muck heap and the site of the straw ring with the miniature tractor and little wagon. This had to be really deep to allow for compression and still be safe to use and large enough in circumference for lunging. This was the only way I could think of to begin to get some condition onto the ponies' muscles before riding could start.

Gradually a routine was established. The children had to get up early enough to muck out their ponies before breakfast and school. During the day I started lunging the ponies in rotation then after school the children. This was quite novel for them, they had never been lunged on their ponies before. Once the thaw had softened the ground and the snow water had drained away we started using the level paddock for some serious lessons in preparation for the showing season.

Danny became busy entering us in as many shows as she could. She started the season off with a bang. We drove all the way east to Winnipeg, Manitoba, some 700 miles, to compete in their big, indoor, spring show. That was a long day's drive along this fantastic highway seemingly on the top of the world until we descended into deep green verdant valleys which were in such contrast to the flat, brown, prairies above. I had never been to such a big event. The ponies lived at the show ground. We stayed in the Canadian Pacific Railway Hotel. These are majestic hotels built by the railway company in all major cities across the country. I found it quite awe inspiring; a little country girl from rural Somerset catapulted into such glamourous surroundings. I got used to it after a while. In the two years I was with the Browns I became used to this, for me, high living. The Besborough in Saskatoon springs to mind too. The Edmonton Golf and Country Club saw us as frequent diners. I learnt to eat lobster here having never come across such luxurious eating before.

Danny purchased a trailer for the ponies to travel in for all the shows we were to attend. This was what is called a fifth wheel trailer as the hitch was locked into a well on the flat bed of the truck towing it. It carried four horses or ponies. In the front was an 11 foot room which held all the feed and tack needed for lengthy trips to shows. Behind this were two stalls then an alleyway and two more stalls. It was long, maybe 40 feet, then add the length of the truck with seating for six and you have a sizable outfit. Many were the miles I and the three oldest children travelled although, for this first trip their dad, Jon, did the driving. The whole expedition was a steep learning curve for all of us. We had none of us attended such a big show and all under cover in this huge arena. The little boxes for the horses were where the bleaches for the winter games usually were and a sizeable arena left in the middle for all the showing classes. Removing all those and building the horse accommodation must have been a herculean task each year. Winnipeg, the windy city, lived up to its name. I longed to get the ponies out for some fresh air but it was quite impossible The arena was situated in a hollow and the open space in front of the doors was steep and slippery and the wind never stopped blowing. I was left worrying about loss of exercise, lack of fresh air and all sorts of other things I might not have been prepared for. The usual routine for showing in these big indoor arenas is, always, a very early start for exercising before the actual show gets underway around 10 am. Exercise first, then muck out and leave the ponies to eat their breakfast in peace. High tail it back to the hotel for breakfast and to change into riding gear. All this we had to learn in a hurry.

Danny was also very competitive. I first realized this on our skiing trips to the mountains behind Jasper. Twice I went along for the weekend although I was never tempted to learn to ski: I was too afraid of breaking a leg so close to the beginning of my employment. Whilst the children were on the slopes Jon took me out driving to get used to driving on the right hand side of the road before I took my driving test. Never mind some nice safe quiet roads to practice on; the only roads were the ones up the mountains, well ploughed but extremely slippery with ice. Thank you Mrs Portal for teaching me how to drive on snow and ice. Saturdays were practice days, Sundays competition days. Once the competitions were over Jon had to phone Danny to report the day's results. If one of them had done well that person could not wait to phone otherwise it was left to Jon to make the phone call to say how well or badly everyone had done.

We attended shows all over Western Canada. Myself, Jonathan, Jane and Adam with three ponies initially going up to four once I had Rattlesnake going as I wanted. I particularly loved training him. As a reward, sometimes after a schooling session I would work him loose in the paddock. I used some of the exercises my friend Tina did with her dogs and he seemed to like it. Beside me he would do slow walk, fast walk, slow jog for trot then fast jog for a speedier trot. He would stop when I did and would stand and wait to be called to come to me if I left him and did not go too far in front of him. And about turns. Through all of this he worked with his ears back, totally concentrating on what I was asking him to do. It was brilliant, we had such a rapport.

There were lots of one day shows in the Edmonton area and we also travelled further afield for bigger shows; to Calgary two hundred miles further west and Red Deer, halfway between Edmonton and Calgary. We followed the fair circuit all over Alberta. I've had the map out, the names of towns and townships are all so familiar, I just cannot remember which ones were on the fair circuit. I do remember what fun they were. They combined classes for everything to do with the horse on the prairies; from the showing classes, both English and Western, through the rodeo competitions such as saddle bronc and bare back riding on bucking horses and bull riding to steer wrestling for the boys and barrel racing for the girls. And, if lucky some cattle cutting too. Cowboys riding quarter horses cutting out specific steers from the herd, the horses working in team with their riders, usually with ears laid flat back as they concentrated on the steer required: a wonderful partnership. And going on all day the music from the fair ground set up to the side of the showing rings. The ponies lived in tented stables on the show ground and ourselves in a local motel. At one a mistake had been made and we were booked into a 'family' room with two double beds. Not my idea of fun. Jane and myself shared one bed and Jonathan and Adam the other. Sharing with Jane made for an extremely uncomfortable night, she was so restless. I made sure about the bookings for all future weekend shows we attended after that weekend. Everything at home ran on strict disciplinary lines; the longer we were away from home the more unruly the children became! Quite a responsibility.

Pony Club had arrived on the prairies the year before. This was centred at Donsdale Stables on the far side of Edmonton. I quickly had to get used to the vast distances one drove to get to the various events. I was soon wheeled in to give lectures on grooming and tack cleaning, minor ailments and other related subjects to do with the care of the horse. I took up doing some dressage here as they had the correct size arena which we did not have at home. It was decided we too needed an all weather arena. One day a large bulldozer arrived to hollow out an area for a school. Unfortunately it never really worked. There was a limit to the number of trees that Danny would allow to be felled to accommodate this. It was at least rectangular but not large enough for practicing a dressage test. This was filled with sand, too much of it, it was very heavy to ride in and enclosed with wooden panels which the ponies could not see over but the horses could. This made for some interesting schooling sessions.

Our friendly rivals at all the local shows were the MacDonald family. Where the idea sprang from I have no idea but Danny and Mrs MacDonald decided we would go east for a friendly competition; the USA versus Canada. It may have been through Pony Club. We would take four ponies, two of ours, two of theirs, four children and their large truck plus driver Joe and drive across Canada to the Hamilton Country Club somewhere outside New York. Edmonton to New York is around 4000 kms. We would go across Canada but come back through the upper states. The children used to take turns in the truck whilst myself and Mrs Mac shared driving their large Mercedes car with the other children.

Accommodation had been booked in advance so we had breakfast before starting each day's drive and there were lots of places to eat at the end of the day. It was during the second day that I started to feel unwell whilst we were having a comfort stop and a bite to eat. I was eating a slice of apple pie 'a la mode', flavoured with cinnamon when I realised something was not right with me. I have never flavoured apple pie with cinnamon since then! Either that night or the following one I lost my rag. Not feeling at all well, sick and tired, we arrived at our overnight horse accommodation. We appeared to be in the middle of a forest, there were no stables as I understood them, just some rough corrals. I threw a tantrum which did not go down well with Joe, because our show ponies were going to have to spend the night tied to trees! I was still so very 'English'; it took me a long time to work out why Joe disliked, or even hated, me. He and his wife had emigrated from somewhere in the Midlands, Birmingham maybe, and here was this posh sounding English girl throwing her weight around (most likely the very thing they had left England to get away from) the fact that it never bothered me one iota about class or background, it is how you are in the present that is important.

We survived. The next day was our last for a few days. We arrived in Ontario for a much needed few days of R and R. We all needed it. The ponies needed to unwind, get out into the paddocks and have a good roll. I was dispatched to see a doctor who diagnosed a very nasty ear infection, almost mastoid, and put on antibiotics and told to stay in bed for two days. That explained how much I had been suffering for almost the entire trip. The two days kept me well away from Joe.

Once again we loaded up, this time to drive into the states and find the country club. Wow, what a place it was, no expense spared, beautiful grounds, grandiose stabling and wonderful arenas. We were made so welcome. Various entertainments were laid on. We drove by coach into the centre of New York and went up the Empire State Building followed by an evening cruise on a very large yacht around the island of Manhattan. The drink flowed, the buffet food was good and I was bored! There was also, one evening, a barbeque at the club. On another night we ate out at a popular sea food restaurant where I had clam chowder for the first time; it was so delicious and I have never had it so good since. One afternoon I was surplus to requirements and went back to the motel. I must have been feeling homesick as all I wanted was a cup of tea and a jam sandwich! They call jam over there jelly. If I had asked for a jelly sandwich I just might have got what I wanted instead of the huge plate of ham salad that arrived.

The day came to leave. We did not time it at all well as we hit the early morning rush hour traffic. And we were to cross the George Washington Bridge. I was driving. We were on a four lane highway, all moving fast. Imagine my horror, coming in on my left was another four lane highway and we all had to merge. Frightening really does not describe the situation. Even the children sensed the tension in the front and fell silent as Mrs Mac tried to help me safely negotiate our way across. Once on the other side I just wanted to stop the car, get out and scream and there was nowhere to do just that.

Driving through Pennsylvania was delightful; the tidiest state I ever drove through with its white clapboard houses, picket fences and green, green lawns. We skirted the large towns so I suppose I did not get a true picture of the state as a whole but it looked so clean and wholesome to my uneducated eyes. Then came trauma. We made a long study of the map because we knew that ahead of us lay Chicago, a city to be avoided at all costs. We studied the road map, pinpointed a service area with good parking for the truck and arranged with Joe to meet up in the restaurant, built across the highway from the parking area accessed by an overhead walk way. We were up there having some refreshments at a table overlooking the highway and, to our complete consternation watched Joe in the truck drive right past below us heading for the centre of the city.

We could not follow him, he was long gone. If I remember correctly he had Jonathan with him. All we could do was drive on up through North Dakota and wait for him at the border. And here we waited and waited. Joe ended up right in the middle of Chicago and went the wrong way down a one way street system which caused a massive traffic jam and lots of police. Eventually he received a police escort to get him out of the city but all this took hours, he had no where to overnight and ran out of money. He had to put up for the night and wire for money We had all the paper work regarding all of us and the papers for the ponies and, obviously, most of the money. The border post was situated on a minor road just outside a very small community which turned out to be to our advantage. We were travelling as a unit so one could not just cross the border, we had to get re-united. Our lodgings for the night were on the Canadian side of the border. All this had to be explained to the Customs people which took a bit of understanding. Not only was half the party missing but they had a person with a British passport to contend with. Eventually we all became very friendly and dodged back and forth through the border with just a friendly wave of the hand as we kept checking for the ponies to arrive.

To round off that year Danny entered us in the big Vancouver fall (autumn) show. I am sure a lot of this travelling was to give me a great time and I loved every minute of it, well, most of it! We travelled down in one go. Going through the Rockies was brilliant except for one doubtful moment as there was a raging forest fire and they were stopping all vehicles and taking any suitable men from the cars to fight the fire. Luckily one look in our truck with me and Jon and three children and accompanying trailer laden with live stock and they let us continue on our way. There was a cousin of mine from New Zealand holidaying in Canada. She had been out to visit me in Sherwood Park, travelling by Greyhound bus. Unbeknown to me at the time, she was also travelling that day to Vancouver to fly home. The bus had had its usual comfort stop in the Rockies and the driver failed to do a correct head count before starting off again and left her behind. Luckily there was another Greyhound not far behind with an empty seat so she was able to make her flight home on time.

That trip out to Vancouver was just magical for me. I was loving my job and to get all these trips also was fantastic. I have some lovely photos of the journey out to Vancouver as Jon was happy to stop and look at scenery. As well as the show we did some sightseeing in Vancouver itself. I expect we did quite well as we were beginning to get noticed at all the shows we attended. The rosette board at home was filling up nicely to everyone's satisfaction, and, more importantly we were getting noticed as evinced the following year when were allocated better stabling at the big shows!

Initially I was to be in Canada for the one season. We were all having so much fun and getting on well together I was offered a second season with them. I jumped at the offer. Danny and Jon flew me home in time for Christmas absolutely laden with gifts. Jon must have been busy making his presence felt as I was swept off to one side and pre-boarded! The most amazing gift was a huge ham liberally decorated with slices of lemons and oranges, studded with cloves and beautifully wrapped in Christmas decorations.

I returned to Canada at the beginning of February to get ready for another show season. It was very much a repeat of the first year except things were not so easy this time around. I think there were undercurrents in the marriage that I was not fully aware of causing ripples in what seemed a secure family home. Danny was more critical, more expecting of our efforts. Being a recognised force now on the show circuit put more pressure on us and took some of the joy out of our trips. Maybe I did not approach it with quite so much enthusiasm, maybe Danny's hopes were just too high. Looking back I realise there was friction between Danny and Jon. Jon was too often coming home very late from work. At the bigger shows he was too often using these occasions for business purposes. Having better stabling meant we also had better tack rooms and Jon, instead of watching his children in their classes, frequently took over these to entertain clients. The liquor laws were very strict at that time so what he was doing was quite illegal. He often forgot or quite overlooked arrangements made between himself and Danny as to which of them was to be at home babysitting whilst the other was watching the older ones competing. Who knows. I do know the children and I got into the habit of tossing a coin into the air as to who was going to make the phone call to report to Danny before we started our journeys home. If we had done well the children were all too keen to make the call. If our efforts were not up to sctatch by Danny's standards I made the call. Looking back I realise what a load of responsibility I was carrying yet I slept well and looked forward to each day.

Disaster did strike one day though. Coming home very tired and late from a show a tyre blew on the truck and we jackknifed. How to describe a jackknife? Well, the truck ended up at a funny angle on the verge with the trailer half on top of it, half turned over. We were all OK, shaken but fine and the ponies, even half on their sides were, surprisingly, quite calm. A trainer travelling with us was desperate to get home. He decided that, without towing the trailer the truck would get him back to Edmonton. He persuaded me this was the only course of action to take, unhitched the trailer and drove off leaving myself, the children and the loaded trailer at a truck pull-in with minimal catering facilities on a very hot day. We were there for hours. Luckily the ponies were used to long journeys, we opened all the doors to create a draught and, bless them, they were very good. We were there for hours waiting for a relief truck to rescue us which it did eventually, driven by a quite exasperated Danny. There had been no need for this trainer to abandon us, there was not much wrong with the truck and if we had just driven quietly along we would have got home. I'm not a mechanic, I wouldn't know.

Extraordinary what happened next. Some boy scouts driving by stopped to help us and two lots of neighbours arrived with horse trailers. The ponies were so calm you would think they ended up each journey half on their sides in a tipped up trailer. With help from the scouts guiding the hind quarters and a bit of a scramble the ponies unloaded and, without any fuss, obediently walked into the new trailers. Danny never believed the blow out caused the jackknife, she always maintained I was traveling too fast and she never let me drive the rig again, which was nonsense.

Having this accident did not help the pervading general unease, that slightly uncomfortable feeling of not actually being in the right place at the right time. We all knew I would not be returning for the next season as I had been in discussion with a ranching couple who bred Arabians in a big way on the other side of town and I thought that job sounded interesting and much closer to Tina and Bob.

Chapter 14
MEETING JOHN

During the summer of 1964, at local, weekend, shows I gradually became aware of a very slim, attractive man who always seemed to be exercising when I was. We used to ride a couple of circuits together, nothing very much was ever said! Then I would catch glimpses of him at Donsdale Stables, hovering in the doorway of the tack room where I might be giving a lecture to Pony Club members. Again, nothing much was said (I find that hard to believe now). So the summer went on. John, I subsequently found out, helped out the MacDonald family when not doing his day job as curator of a theatre so we were on the same showing circuits as the MacDonalds were and competing in much the same classes.

Then a momentous decision was made or was made for us. The Government of Alberta decided to include horses in their exhibit to The Royal Winter Fair held every fall (autumn) in Toronto. All the provinces send exhibits of their best livestock. The Browns' and MacDonalds' show ponies were chosen, this year, as part of the Alberta exhibition, an honour indeed. The die in life's lottery was cast. All the exhibits went to Toronto on a special train and girls were most definitely not allowed, praise be. All that male testosterone at loose on a train for three days crossing a greater part of Canada in late October/early November does not bear contemplating.

The MacDonalds offered John the equivalent of three weeks' salary if he would take a leave of absence and go as groom on the train. I was despatched by air and met in Toronto by Danny's best friend (can't remember her name) who put me up with her mother and I used to take the tram to the arena. And I was to go shopping; on Danny's orders. I can just hear Danny saying to her friend "for goodness' sake take her shopping for some decent clothes". Me, completely oblivious of the matchmaking machinations of Danny, in somewhat of a daze, went shopping. I had never been in stores like those department stores in Toronto. Edmonton had the same department stores but not nearly such grand ones and so much choice. The friend was a very canny shopper whose tactic was always to bargain and, in nine cases out of ten, she usually won. She used to wait it out; having bargained for a reduction in price and been refused she used to just hang around the counter, sometimes for very long periods of time, or, after a wait she would go away and return the following day to begin all over again with the bartering and was, more often than not, successful in her purchase. Luckily we did not go through this routine for me; I would have found it very embarrassing.

So, whilst waiting for the ponies, I suppose, we went shopping. Not really knowing why except I was moving into the big hotel with the family when they arrived and supposing there would be dinners to dress up for I found myself with a rather super, off-white, just below the knees dress with a coil of beads around the neck that would go anywhere, matching shoes etc. I think I must have had tunnel vision for many years. My work meant everything to me, whatever my job I would be completely absorbed in it so it never entered my head that Danny was actually matchmaking between myself and John.

I don't remember unloading the ponies. Again that would not have been a seemly place for a girl, especially as they arrived at night. John must have unloaded the lot and settled them down. We shared a tack room which was in the middle of our row of stabling so there were plenty of opportunities for bottom patting, which John quickly took advantage of, as we were for ever, seemingly, meeting in the doorway! Strange that. And think what today's feminists would make of it. It was strange, it was fun, it was a giggle. I think we laughed our way through the entire show, with Danny busily pulling the strings in the background. She must have really enjoyed herself with me, being me, totally oblivious, again!

We often didn't go to bed until midnight. I believe John was meant to sleep in the stockmen's accommodation, more often than not he slept in the tack room as I remember arriving, often at 4am, to find him still asleep in there. We could only get into the arena to exercise at this ungodly hour. Everyone had a designated time slot and we got the short straw. After everything was exercised we mucked out, to constant criticism from John about my 'English ways' fed the ponies and off to the stockmen's canteen for breakfast. Because of living with Danny, I knew nothing of Canadian food so I was swiftly introduced to 'eggs easy over or sunny side up' which I did not understand at all the first time the cook asked me. Bacon, eggs, pancakes all served with a liberal helping of maple syrup. Maple syrup on bacon? What ever next. It was all so much fun. And sleep was in very short supply.

It was decided by someone, maybe even John who was used to theatre from his day job, that he and I should go to a show. *The Merry Wives of Windsor* was on so John arranged the tickets etc, asking me first one assumes. By now I had joined the family in The Duke of York Hotel. John was picking me up there. You have to imagine me at, barely, 8 and a quarter stone, very slim and fit with almost black hair, wearing my new dress. Half the Italian show jumping team were in the elevator when it stopped for me to get in. There were appreciative whistles from them all. I did not know where to look! But fun.

The show wound its way onwards with mixed blessings for the Alberta ponies. We were trying to sell Golden Goose there; the potential new owner came to try him out and stayed to watch the class. G G refused to jump, bolted out of the ring almost running over the prospective purchaser! Despite this catastrophe the sale went ahead. Flora, a palomino mare of Danny's was also sent to the show. As she was not part of the Alberta exhibit she came by truck; three long days on the road.

And we lost track of her. No-one came looking for us to tell us she had arrived and where she was. For a while we were very perplexed. I had left behind, in Alberta, an immaculate cream mare. What I found after two anxious days of both John and myself searching all the stock pens outside the arenas was a filthy, scrubby looking individual who had been tossed into a corral and forgotten. We'd walked past her twice, not recognising her. She survived, not sure how, was hosed off and dried and then I had to clip her. I did a very poor job. Cynthia Hayden, Britain's leading carriage driver walked past and offered me the loan of her clippers! Ironically she did the best of the Alberta ponies being placed in her Western class

I don't remember much of the last days at the show, not surprising, us beavers were so exhausted. I was going to stay with friends of my parents before flying home for Christmas. The rumour machine was keeping the telephone lines hot back in Edmonton. Theoretically I was working for Jon Brown and the rumours had me having a hot affair with my boss. The different spelling; Jon versus John was ignored, there was this exciting affair going on 'back east'!

Once the show was over I spent a few days with these friends of Mother and Father's in Toronto before flying home. This time it was to part of England I did not know. Father, who had finished his training and been accepted into the Church of England was now a curate in the parish of Goole, on the east Yorkshire coast in the Diocese of Sheffield. Mother and Father were not travelling light. They had two ponies, one dog and numerous cats to look after. Luckily they found a flat out of town, part of a large house conversion called Hook Hall, a tall red brick, rather austere looking building standing proud in the flat countryside, viewable for miles around, and a field for the ponies nearby.

The wind was cold as only wind on that coast could be, seemingly straight from Siberia. One wrapped up very warmly for the daily walk beside the canal with the dog to visit the ponies. John and I must have exchanged addresses because it wasn't long before letters from John began arriving in England on a regular basis, always signed 'lovingly John'.

This time I was home for a couple of months. Returning to Edmonton I was met by Tina and Bob, and spent a couple of days with them and renewing my acquaintance with John before moving to my new job at the Arabian Stud. This was a very different kettle of fish from working for Danny. They did not understand what it entailed to employ a girl and one who was living in as well. I had a good sized bedroom but it was in the basement with, typical basement, the windows at the top of the walls so there was a certain amount of light but no views and I ate all my meals upstairs with the owners. I just did not fit in, there was no comfort. What a relief it was to have John to spend some evenings with. At the farm I felt more at home in the caravan where the farmhand lived with his wife and young child.

I was not enjoying the breeding side of things at all. Again the farmhand put me wise to happenings. He advised me not to go near the barns when the stallion was being put to a mare. He found the language and goings on most abhorrent and told me to keep well away. The young foals were separated each day from their mothers for about an hour. They were tied up on a long wall opposite the brood mare boxes and they used to throw themselves around something awful at the end of their ropes and get in a right state.

I found riding and showing these Arabians quite different to the way I did things. Riding in the English style classes same as normal but for the Arabian classes one was meant to, sort of, liven up their performance; all heads up with flowing manes and tails carried high. The mares were fine but the stallion was a different matter altogether. For some reason I was sent into the arena with the stallion wearing a hackamore (bitless) bridle and instructions to keep out of the ruck. Impossible. Too many competitors. I got hemmed in on the rail, nearly lost control and was signalled out. Truth be told I should never have been put in this sort of situation.

John and I were getting to know each other during our evenings out. Not every evening at all but enough to relieve the stresses of the job somewhat. Neither of us had much money, we existed on pizza mostly with black coffee, cheap and satisfying. I had bought a little car so was able to visit Tina quite regularly too. Our next show was the Calgary Spring Show. Luckily I drove my own car down. Nothing seemed to go right and it all culminated over cleaning the tack one evening. I am a very good tack cleaner and everything I used was cleaned daily. I cleaned my tack with my usual speed and also some spare western gear that I was not even using and considered I was done for the day. The proprietress decided otherwise and I thought, literally, to hell with this. I packed up my car and drove back to the ranch, packed up my possessions and left. I arrived at Tina and Bob's quite late; being spring on the prairies it was light till late. Happily they were at home and were so kind and there was no question but that I should move in with them until I sorted myself out.

I started doing some freelance teaching even going back to Danny's where our differences seemed to have disappeared and she helped spread the word that I was doing this. Travelling the long distances necessary between clients on the prairies ate up much of what I earned; but fuel was cheap and I had enough to pay housekeeping to Tina and it was summer time, what more could one ask?

John and I were seeing more and more of each other. One evening we were out driving and we stopped the car and got out and walked across a property, a typical piece of prairie land, owner unknown, until we were out of sight of the road. We sat on a grassy knoll with slews and swamps around and ducks flying in pairs (that's important) in and out, lots of quacking and splashing going on all around us. We were idly chatting about spring and everything pairing up; maybe he felt I was hinting, I don't know, I was most likely just feeling romantic. Anyway, he opened up. He told me his early history. Up to this point I had really no knowledge about his early life at all, he always shied away if I tried to probe.

There were two brothers; Dick and Jack often called John who lived in Lewes, Sussex. Their father had owned all the land between Lewes and Brighton and owned race horses who were trained up on the downs. All in all they were bought up in a very privileged way until the day they were summoned for an interview in the library. Their father told them he had little money left and the best thing they could do was to emigrate. He handed each boy a cheque, said there would be no more!

That must have been such a shock, talk about being thrown in at the deep end. They selected Alberta, Canada for their big undertaking. They applied for and were granted a licence to homestead and they each settled in the area of Ranfurly to the east of the city of Edmonton. After they were established Dick sent to England for his fiancée, Sylvia, to join him and Jack (John's father) fell in love with Iola, the stunningly beautiful daughter of neighbouring ranchers. Both brothers married their girlfriends and John my future husband was born on the 18th of December 1935. This was during the depression, and things were not good for the brothers. They were too newly into the ranching life to have built up any reserves. Dick got work driving road graders but I am not sure what extra work Jack managed to find. In 1938 Jack made the decision to take his family and return to England. They settled in Lewes.

Jack went to work in the agricultural industry and, once the war started was away a lot of the time. Their second son Mayla was born in England. Iola then had a third son, Paul. Jack was not the father of Paul and after the war was over Iola, with the three boys, returned to Alberta. John went on to say how awful his mother really was and how because of all this awful history he shouldn't be asking me to marry him. It was great theatre; to this day I can picture it so clearly, especially the ducks. Of course all this touched my deeply hidden romantic heart strings and the rest is history. I wonder how he would remember it.

Danny's plans had reached fruition, John and I are engaged to be married! We lost no time settling on a date: August 7th 1965. We found St Mark's a small, beautiful church in the west side of Edmonton and a hall for the reception. Danny knew of a dressmaker so she and I went shopping for material for my dress. My mother's favourite flowers were Lily of the Valley and we found material covered with a pattern of embossed lilies which I thought was a good omen. Bob Stone gave me away and Jane Brown, despite having her jaw wired together (she had got impatient with a horse whose tail she was plaiting and stuck her sewing needle into his hind quarters whereupon he upped with his back legs and kicked her in the mouth) was my bridesmaid. John's sister Karen was meant to be the other one but she backed out. Dick Brenton was John's best man. It was a lovely wedding and everyone seemed to enjoy the reception. We were driving out to Vancouver Island to stay with Uncle Dick and Aunt Sylvia for our honeymoon, staying at Dick's cabin in the Rockies behind Golden on the way.

Above: A very young me with Mother at Brockton.

Left: Taking our very gentle and patient 'Smithy' for a walk. Dungarees, obviously to grow into!

Below left: Father tending to his sheep at East Harwood. Dunkery in the background.

Below right: Aged three with 'Betsy', our Old English Sheepdog.

Above: Father and Mother, with Liz, myself and Jonathan sitting on the doorstep at North Hawkwell.

Left: The three of us on a very young 'Robin.'

Below: Gay with Robin, Mother, Liz with Pixie and Choti the Golden Retriever. Jonathan with Tommy and Granny behind.

Top: A lesson in progress at the Porlock Vale Riding School's Arena. Me on grey behind the instructor.

Above: Riding 'Pipeclay' in one of the paddocks at Porlock.

Left: John in our courting days. Unloading competion horses at Toronto Railway Station following three days crossing Canada, to compete at the Toronto Royal Winter Fair.

Above left: August 1965, Leaving St Mark's church, Edmonton, Alberta, following John and my marriage service.

Above right: Preparing to cut the cake at our wedding reception.

Left: Pamela on Goldie in front of the barn at Puckle Road.

Above left: John holding a very young Bridget, with Pamela and Kaiser, in front of the cottage at Puckle Road.

Above right: John, minus beard, when he was District Commissioner of the Victoria and Saanich Pony Club.

Left: My girls and me in the garden of Puckle Road.

Above left: Vancouver Island, spring 1984 the last time I backed a horse.

Above right: Preparing to compete in a 'Quarter Horse' class at a local show riding Western style.

Left: Kaiser at ease on the hay with Alex.

Above: Norman and me celebrating his 80th birthday with a party in the garden.

Left: Gunns Farm as it was when Mother, Bridget and I first viewed it.

Below: Gunns Farm after the extensive renovations.

Above: Jason collecting in the harvest!

Left: Martha blissfully happy, in her favourite position on Norman's chest.

Below: Festa patrolling the lawn.

Chapter 15
BEGINNING MARRIED LIFE

I remember, on our honeymoon, wanting to throw away my wedding ring. It came about this way. We were going to spent our first few nights in Dick Brenton's cabin before going on to Vancouver Island to visit John's Uncle Dick and Aunt Sylvia. We set off rather late in the afternoon to drive to Dick's cabin situated in the mountains behind Golden. A long drive so we arrived in the dark. It was a lovely little cabin; one large room downstairs and a large bedroom upstairs and an outhouse where all outhouses are, well some of them, in the middle of a piece of rough ground so no-one could mistake where you were going. I do not believe we even had a flashlight so were groping around in the dark. The next morning I realised just how remote we were. I had never lived amongst the mountains and found them very awe inspiring and felt almost threatened by their majesty. At least the bed was a comfortable one with clean sheets and proper pillows and quilts!

Early the next morning it was off to the nearest store to get in some necessary food supplies and a flashlight. After that John wanted to go exploring so we started following the logging roads further and further into the mountains. These single track narrow roads are cut into the mountains facilitating the logging operations. The dirt roads were either very dry producing clouds of dust in their wake or slippery with mud if there had been lots of rain. Precipitous drops, hare-pin bends and water hazards characterised these roads winding their way up the mountains, crossing creeks and valleys, water tumbling down the slopes; every possible danger you can think off appeared to be on those roads and I strongly felt we should not be on them. I can only think that the trucks were on a oneway system as passing places were few and far between; up the mountain to load up the huge logs in the mornings and down in the afternoons. And these trucks stop for no-one, they have right of way and take no prisoners so meeting one was a scary business. Finally after one hazardous crossing of a large creek with water pouring down the mountainside an actual passing place presenting itself I persuaded John to turn around. Where is your adventurous spirit you might well ask. Well, I don't have one

On our third night there Dick turned up at about nine o'clock. This was when the first shock of my married life occurred. Dick walked in the door and the atmosphere changed, it was very odd. Although I did not recognise it at the time it was the forerunner of things to come. It was the beginning of being relegated to "the little woman" status. John and Dick proceeded to catch up on all sorts of topics I knew nothing about. Bedtime came and went and still they talked.

Eventually I went to bed by myself and still they talked and every word, especially every laugh came upstairs. Sleep was impossible and I couldn't even read as there was no electricity. Taking all this into account it was not an auspicious beginning to married life.

On our way out to Golden to begin the long day's drive west to Vancouver Island the car began to make an unusual noise. We found a garage in Golden who were prepared to help us but not for some time. It was blistering hot in Golden and we spent some very uncomfortable hours waiting and wondering if the car could be fixed. (Also, we were doing the honeymoon on my money and you know how odd I am with money, poor John.)

Eventually the car was fixed and we were on our way and, at some point, arrived with Dick and Sylvia on the island. And here things between John and me that were lurking just below the surface, began, very subtly, to change. Here it hit me; in the space of a very few days I had become a possession, John's possession, and it was particularly noticeable when we were with David. It was the most dreadful shock. I was twenty-eight, I was an independent person who had loved being courted, I was treating John as a loving wife (or how I perceived my Mother treating my Father) and here I was, suddenly not being considered, treated as if I was of no account because it was important for John to give the "I am the man here and my wife knows her place" impression. One step behind. I was no longer a person in my own right able to make my own decisions. I was being regulated into that male attitude to 'their' women, so prevalent back then but never experienced in my own family. It was a very uncomfortable feeling. It had started whilst Dick was with us in his cabin. Then on the island it escalated. This attitude became particularly obvious when we were out with John's cousin David and his family. David's wife was definitely 'one step behind' and I don't think she even knew it. I was the visitor there yet I was never once offered the front seat of the car. If I had been I would most likely have said no, I would sit in the back with Bev but it was just assumed I would sit in the back because that is where wives sat. There was never any question but that the women sat in the back seat of the car, the men up front. It was the way it was done that bothered me, an acceptance that this is how it is done and no exceptions. Men up the front, little women in the back. Yuck. God, I was mad. But also sick to my heart because I knew I had made the most dreadful mistake in marrying John. Of course one did not live together then but I often wonder if we had I might have retained some independence. So I sat in the back seat and took off my wedding ring and, thought about dropping it out of the window. I wasn't quite brave enough and I loved him, didn't I? And you don't do those sort of things on your honeymoon. I had made my bed and I must lie on it.

Many years later with my second husband Norman we used to visit friends who farmed near Bude in Cornwall and we always went out for a drive after lunch. Owen always asked me if I would like to sit in the front and, because I had been given the choice, I always sat in the back with Joice where we would quietly chat whilst Owen and Norman enjoyed a good farming natter up front. I know I wasn't the easiest person to get to know. I expect David and Bev found me cold and unfriendly and, of course, being me, I would have withdrawn into myself as I do in unfamiliar circumstances. Let's face it, we didn't have a lot in common and John had only met them earlier in the year when he went out there for a visit and to reconnect with his father's side of his family. There is a lot to be said for spending one's honeymoon away from other people, especially relatives. Looking back it cannot have been easy for John either even though they were his friends and relatives. If he felt as I did it is a wonder we stayed together as long as we did.

Back in Edmonton we organised our next stage. Before we became married John had a change of jobs and was returning to what he most enjoyed; being outside working on the land. John got a job with a Mr Scott Durling who lived in Westlock a small town some 50 miles north of Edmonton. Scott had barns and corrals on the edge of town, a men's clothing store in town and many quarter sections of land out on the prairies east of Westlock. John was to be general ranch hand and in the store one day a week for Scott's day off. John's decree, I was not to work!

We had no furniture and hardly any money. John's mother Iola suggested we go to the Sally Ann, the local Salvation Army charity shop or thrift store as they are called in Canada. John was ashamed, I was enchanted. For extraordinarily little money we bought a table and chairs, kitchen cupboards – lovely little pine ones with screen doors to keep out the flies, a couple of easy chairs and, one presumes, a bed. We had received a lot of necessary household goods as wedding presents. We were all set.

Scott owned a small apartment block in town and we were given, as part of John's wage, the use of an apartment in it. Steps went up the outside to a small balcony at one end of the building leading to the second storey. The door of the flat opened into a large, bright sitting room with picture windows looking south with a fireplace at one end. Kitchen off this room and bedroom and bathroom beyond. The lane outside this building led directly across the main street down to the barns where John was to spend many of his working hours. Standing on the balcony outside the entrance door to this level I could actually see the roofs of the barns across town. Not a large town but pleasant enough.

So began a rather strange existence. One whole day was spent cleaning the flat and unpacking. I swept and polished, bought some groceries, did some cooking. Not only do I not possess a spirit of adventure, my sense of humour is somewhat lacking too. John coming home to our first home with his first supper ready to be served walked to the end of the sitting room and ran his finger along the mantlepiece checking for dust. This action was meant to be a joke; it fell flat!

Then what. I was not welcome in the barns. I was certainly not welcome anywhere near the clothing store. It was dire. If I did wander down to the barns there really was nothing for me to do. Nothing to ride and no-where to ride to. John so busy being the breadwinner he was working all hours. How often I stood on that balcony, looking down the lane that crossed town and led directly to the barns, waiting for him to come home at the end of the day, to eat a dinner drying up in the oven. And, of course, It would be too humiliating, too losing face for John if Scott were there and I turned up looking for him and give the impression, Heaven Forbid, that it was I who ruled the roost.

It was an extraordinary existence. I was so frustrated; no job, John virtually ignoring me in preference for his boss and his job. I wasn't even granted an existence during working hours. It was as if I, or any wife, maybe, was an embarrassment. John definitely thought the little woman's place was in the home. Did he never look at how I lived my life before him, how active I was, how good I was at what I did? He had been around so much latterly as I led my busy, satisfying life, had that not registered with him? Did he really think I could be satisfied just being a housewife? He often worked long days out on the quarter sections, repairing corrals ready for winter and mending wire fences. I don't actually know why I am still alive. In boredom, because I wasn't allowed to get a job, I'd drive out to see him but he couldn't stop to chat even if it was just stringing wire fencing (this , above all shows just how very single minded John could be). Feeling pushed out I would leave and drive back to town as fast as the car would go down those gravel roads, I mean really dangerously, until I frightened myself and would stop and sit in the car beside the road shaking like a leaf. Why did I stay. I was bought up with a strict sense of duty; once you put your hand to the plough you kept it there.

Once or twice I drove down to see Tina. On one of these trips I stayed for a few days. John could not understand how a new bride could go away so soon after our honeymoon. Quite easily actually. I think this was the time Tina asked me If I would look after Jeffery, her old collie dog, whilst she and Bob went on holiday. He was on a special diet and I had to be so careful but what joy to have a companion. He was with us for several weeks and I handed him back in as good a condition as he came. When he died Tina asked for a postmortem and they discovered he only had one kidney. Brownie points to me for keeping him healthy whilst they were away. Using the pretext that Jeffery needed a good run out of town I persuaded John to allow us to go onto the quarter sections for that purpose. We would usually park close to where the actual homesteads had stood. There might only be a hollow in the ground where the root cellar had been, or some rhubarb or a thicket of blackcurrant bushes gone wild to indicate the past presence of human habitation. I loved finding such places. The sense of past endeavours, of dreams that came to fruition or crumbled into dust. No-one left to tell the tale, but I could dream as I wandered around. And John gradually came to accept my presence out there and even initiated me into the art of stringing wire fences.

Somehow it came about, we were to break in a horse, a palomino gelding. I suspect John was meant to actually do this, but I started lunging it then tacking it up and lunging it with all its gear on. Everything seemed to be going really well. We did all the introduction to having a rider, me, leaning across it then putting a leg over, then sitting upright and John led us around the corral. All seemed OK, he felt quite relaxed, so John let us off the lead line and all hell broke loose. He started bucking on the side of the corral furthest from John, real rodeo bucking. John thinks I lasted close to the rodeo time of ten seconds then I was gone and that horse kept bucking until he had bucked himself clean out of all his gear. It was a spectacular display of power. I believe he got sold on to a bucking string where, I suspect, he might have originated. He certainly knew how to buck. And I lent weakly against the corral fence hugging to myself my recent reckoning that I was most likely pregnant!

I started attending the local Anglican church just a block from the apartment. I was enjoying the familiar ritual, yet no-one made any friendly gesture towards me. I had thought I might find a social outlet through the church. Not to be. I had been going for a few weeks when, one weekday morning, there was a knock on my door. Outside were two members of the congregation and they were collecting for some cause or other. They could come collecting but not extend the hand of friendship to me following each Sunday service. I never went back. I wonder if they noticed.

In the ground floor apartment directly beside the stairs, in fact their doorway was under the bottom of the stairs, lived a middle-aged German couple. I never saw much of the husband but I used to drop in for a cup of tea sometimes with the wife. Really the only person I got to know in the whole of Westlock. She hardly spoke any English, but we used to get on OK unless her Hutterite friends were in town for market day. Then communication was all smiles and head shakes as they only spoke German. I bought a goose from them.

Having discovered I was pregnant I just wanted to talk to my Mother. This was no easy matter. We had no phone and phoning England back then was almost unheard of. I arranged a call using the public phone box three blocks over and behind where we lived. I had to book the call to co-ordinate our time. It was very tricky and the first time we did not connect which was upsetting to put it mildly. Somehow I managed to get the arrangements sorted and, on our second try, we managed to connect. I am standing out in the cold, on a street corner, light snow gusting around my ankles, in a one-horse sort of town on the Canadian prairies bawling my eyes out. Poor parents, what must they have thought although very pleased to hear they were to become grandparents. Tactfully I omitted to tell them about the bucking horse.

I think we had Christmas in Westlock, was the goose for Thanksgiving or Christmas? So much of that time is lost from my memory. Things were again happening in a mysterious way. Danny again, believe it or not. She must have been aware that things were not too happy in Westlock so when she bumped into the Dean of Commerce, Dr Hugh Harries, from Edmonton University they got chatting. Hugh had learnt there had been an extremely good hay harvest the previous summer. Because there was so much of it, it was selling at rock bottom prices and, being Dean of Commerce he thought he had spotted an opportunity to make some money. He employed an agent to buy up whole stacks of this hay; a stack being anything from one thousand bales to five thousand. He then, again through an agent, started buying beef cattle from the auction marts to eat this hay. Having gone about things sort of backwards he found himself without any one at the ranch to oversee his newest operation. He was looking for a manager for his feed lot operation, a job including horses, and a cottage to live in. Danny immediately got busy on our behalf. I can't say the wires began to hum as we had no telephone, nevertheless communication was established and it was agreed we would go there. John handed in his notice in Westlock and we prepared to move.

Chapter 16
OUR NEXT MOVE

Leaving Westlock was, for me, no hardship. John had been out to the bungalow we were to live in on the ranch. It was bitterly cold, both inside and out so I went to stay with Tina and Bob for a few days whilst John thawed out all the pipes and generally warmed up the place. He found a tractor that would start, all the other vehicles were frozen and would not start. He was rather torn between getting the bungalow liveable in and working on the trucks that were needed to haul all the hay. He decided the more pressing need was to get the bungalow warmed up so I could join him out there. Not only to housekeep this time, I was needed as a driver too! One good thing to come out of the Westlock experience was a frank discussion on how we would manage our day-to-day living. It was agreed that whatever we did there would be a role for me, that I would be part of the package, so to speak. (There would always be areas where it was not practical for me to be, such as de-horning mature beef steers or getting involved with loading cattle at the auction marts – both extremely unpleasant events that I wanted no part of.)

Once the bungalow was warmed up and all the pipes unfrozen, so there was running water and the toilet flushed, John drove out and picked me up. The first morning there, after breakfast, John was outside seeing to things and I was exploring the sitting room. It was darkish in there and I stepped forward to look at a picture hanging on the wall and stepped, literally, into space. I landed , although still upright with a spine jarring shock, on the floor of the cellar, the trap door of which John had left open to try to let some warmth into as the water was piped into the house that way. There were no steps and it was no good calling for help. Somehow I managed to lever myself out of there and slammed the trap door behind me. Rather a nerve shattering beginning to the new year

Outside it was certainly bitterly cold. It took me a good five minutes each morning to get dressed up for any outside work. I quickly learnt how to layer all my clothes to provide the best insulation, especially at my waist. Last on, when I could barely bend over my many layers, were my trusty felt boots. One felt a bit like Michelin woman. I was certainly determined not to get cold.

The first job, on my very first day out there, was to persuade the three quarter ton truck to start. This we did by towing it up and down the gravel road outside the ranch entrance. John completely exposed to the biting cold on the tractor (45 below and a windchill factor on top of that), myself inside the cab of the truck equally cold although without the chilling effect of the wind. Up and down that piece of road we went, again and again until at last when I wasn't sure how much more cold I could take, the engine broke into a throaty roar and we were off. John unhooked at the speed of lightning, whizzed around on the tractor and headed home leaving me to execute yet another three point turn, at which I was becoming most proficient, so I was able, also, to return home. In the yard the tractor was quietly rumbling away to itself, John nowhere to be seen. Leaving the throttle slightly open to keep the engine of the truck running I went to investigate and found John indoors, already divested of his outer garments, almost hugging the boiler in an effort to warm up.

The telephone was on a party line, a novel experience for me as anyone who shared the line could listen in; a practice much frowned on yet irresistible to lonely housewives. One had to be so careful of what one was saying, it was best to stick to the strictly necessary in any communication. It could be frustrating as it always seemed to be busy exactly when one most urgently needed to use it. Mainly the phone calls were about the next delivery of cattle or where to go for the next load of hay. Quite often we would arrive home long after dark to find a corral that had been empty that morning now full of bawling cattle demanding water and feed. Whilst I saw to getting a meal John would be grappling with frozen drinking troughs because although meant to be heated they, too often, were not. And can't thirsty cattle bawl? Once the noise had eased off I knew the problems were solved, at least for that night, and John would be in to eat. The following morning, first thing after breakfast, the new cattle had to be inoculated, against shipping fever or some such thing to do with all the trauma of being through the auction marts. I followed John as he worked his way amongst all these new arrivals, me carrying a huge bottle of inoculation fluid and John jabbing the cattle in their rumps as we went with a syringe that would do about ten cattle before needing refilling. Why we never got kicked or stamped on I am not sure, maybe the sheer crush of cattle kept us safe.

Our quest for hay took us all over Edmonton and the surrounding area. I drove the three quarter ton truck and John drove an enormous rig whose engine had 16 forward gears and four reverse ones. On one journey, luckily when I was with John, the gear shift became loose and came out in John's hand. We headed for a garage that specialized in these sorts of trucks, me crouched on the floor holding the gear shift in place. One farm sold us a lot of hay that necessitated us going back more than once. I used to go indoors and visit with the wife. Again a lady with little spoken English, we used to sit in her sun room where she grew masses of pelargoniums and enjoy each other's company over cups of tea. One day she shared with me some recipes from a woman's magazine for Scotch griddle cakes or American pancakes and I still use these recipes today.

Another time, at another farm when we had both the trucks, the hay was difficult to get at, the snow having drifted in and filled the alleyways between the long stacks of hay. The farmer did not seem to have any means for dealing with this snow and John battled backwards and forwards with the small truck trying to pack down the snow and make headway for the large rig to get between the stacks for loading. I was keeping warm in the house with the wife and her two youngsters and, as the afternoon dragged on I became increasingly aware of a certain amount of tension in the house. It was getting close to the family evening meal time and we showed no sign of being able to leave. Eventually, with a sigh, she got out a big mixing bowl and mixed up a batch of pancakes and fed us all these with steaming hot coffee for which John and I were extremely thankful. We got home about midnight this day. My most scary drive home though, was the day my load shifted. In the wing mirror I could see it developing a distinct lean, luckily to the verge side of the road. I slowed right down, every curve or bend in the road was treated with extreme caution. I crawled around right or left angled turns and we arrived home intact. What a relief.

Then came the day when I had to drive to the stock yards myself for cattle. We had been out early to collect yet more hay for the increasing number of cattle Hugh kept buying and were looking forward, for once, to a cosy night in when the phone went. It was the cattle mart office to tell us there was a small bunch of cattle waiting to be picked up and no arrangements had been made for their transportation. Although still daylight when I left it was dark by the time I arrived but no matter as the stock yards were well lit; the stockmen were sort of surprised that a woman was driving (women did not go to stock yards back then, not nice places to be) they did not actually know what to make of it. I think they expected the drivers of the trucks to help with loading and I, obviously pregnant, was going to be no use for that. I sat in the cab watching them debating. Eventually, whilst I grew more and more uncomfortable, they went off and with much yelling and prodding the cattle were loaded and I could set out for home. Going up a slight incline the engine started spluttering and then conked out; I had enough momentum to drive the truck onto the verge and there I was, in the middle of nowhere with a load of restless cattle and no way of contacting John. Eventually a guy in a blue car stopped and asked if I was alright. I explained the situation and he said he would drive to the ranch and tell John what had happened. The inordinate time I was away from home had began to worry John so he was somewhat relieved when this good Samaritan turned up. Our car was out of fuel so John filled it up with red petrol which was illegal to use in a private vehicle. At least that meant he could come looking for me and it was sheer bad luck that, the following day, I ran into a police fuel checkpoint and ended up being summoned to appear in court to explain myself. I made John go and plead in my place and we got off with a reprimand.

It was by now completely dark. I was sitting in the truck wondering what to do when a car came screeching towards me, did a perfect U turn and pulled up in front of me. John to the rescue, was I glad to see him. Open the hood and peer under; Conclusion, the fuel pump had broken. Back to the ranch to fetch replacement pump, back to the truck, replacement pump just would not go in, back to ranch to wait for daylight, first light back to truck, truck and cattle all still together, replace pump, so easy in daylight, drive cattle home. Just another one of 'those days'.

Little things happened, some to lift our spirits, some to dash them to the ground. Soon after settling in I was sitting in the fly-screened porch one afternoon enjoying a few minutes of quiet when I felt myself being watched. Turning slowly around I spotted a grey long haired cat staring warily at me from under another chair. I made encouraging noises but it wasn't having any of that so I got slowly up and went into the kitchen to find something for it to eat. Obviously hungry it nevertheless took its time before leaving the security of the chair to sample what it was being offered. So began many years of association with Alex, the most faithful, brave cat you could hope to meet. He once walked across the middle of a pen full of pigs keeping himself between me and a pregnant sow.

Tina and Bob came to dinner one night, a long drive of about 60 miles one way. We had not seen them since the New Year when John picked me up from their place. This was the first entertaining we had done since we got married! It felt great laying up a dinner table with our wedding presents, the canteen of cutlery, the fancy tablecloth with matching napkins and cut-glass glasses. I made a fabulous steak and kidney pie which went down a treat. It was a most enjoyable evening and uninterrupted by any sort of crisis

Then there was the load of Aberdeen Angus steers who took fright at something (we were later told that American Aberdeen Angus are renowned for being flighty) and stampeded during the night they arrived and completely demolished their corral. Once the snow began to clear from the land we turned bunches of steers out into the nearest pasture where we fed them directly from the back of the large rig. I used to drive this whilst John stood on the back throwing out the hay. The frozen ruts of mud from the previous wet autumn made driving quite tricky. However carefully I was driving the truck had a perverse tendency to lurch from rut to rut. Not only was my baby bump getting the bouncing of its life there was John's safety to consider too. An unexpected sideways lurch and I could have seen, in the wing mirror, John losing his footing on the slippery deck and flying through the air.

There was a pregnant cow out here amongst the beef cattle (how did she get there?) and once she gave birth she turned so protective of her calf her eyes turned red and she was both mad and dangerous. Somehow John managed to get her and the calf into a secure pen in a barn. I went up to look at her. I had never seen a mad cow before and, believe me, it was a frightening sight. She was too dangerous to keep around so was sent off to the auction mart for someone else to cope with. I was always worried about some unsuspecting new owner getting hurt.

Sunday afternoons were our only time off in the week or were meant to be. Until Hugh started to make a habit of driving out to chat to John. We could even be standing beside the car, obviously ready to go somewhere. "Could I have a minute of your time?" more often than not would turn into an hour or more before we could leave. My getting the lunch earlier and earlier to get John away before Hugh arrived seldom worked. It was so frustrating.

At some point I thought that maybe I should tell a member of the medical profession that I was pregnant. I asked Danny for advice and she said I should sign on with her gynaecologist in Edmonton which I duly did. He liked his pregnant ladies to keep exercising, encouraging them to play tennis and go to the gym. So, on top of our daily busy lives I did a bit of riding, just tooling around the yard or out onto the pastures close to the buildings where the snow was not too deep. These were Western horses that I rode in my English saddle as the horn on the western saddle was beginning to dig into my bump. Came the day when we needed to ride out and find a small bunch of assorted ponies that were on a section of land away from the main ranch that nobody had thought about all winter. Hugh hired a helicopter to fly out to find them so we knew roughly where to go and look.

We rode out east across the pastures, bucking our way through the snow drifts that had built up along all the fence lines making opening the gates difficult. I would hold John's horse and, when he had the wire gates open sufficiently for us the two horses would do huge lunges to get us through the build-up of snow. Great fun. We came out on a road which we crossed and knew the ponies were somewhere in the next pasture. We passed an old wooden barn and I had an urgent need to pee so popped inside out of the wind. I will never forget how incredibly warm my wee felt and how it gently steamed on the barn floor.

We had only ridden for another five minutes or so and our search was at an end. The bunch came to find us and needed no urging; instead of us herding them along they followed us eagerly to the gate. We opened the gate and I went through first to turn them right to head for home around by the roads. I was galloping along behind them when John, who had to shut the gate galloped up behind me and shouted 'can't you go any faster'. I thought I was galloping fast but he passed me like a streak of lightning, his horse flat to the ground, to get ahead of them to make sure they made the next turn left for home which they were going to do anyway as they knew the way. It is no wonder that my daughter Pamela, like me, is a bit of a limpet on a horse.

Hugh's family always spent the four summer months at the ranch, living where we were living and commuting back and forth to Edmonton. I asked where would we live and it was suggested the bunk house. I had a look, it was basic in the extreme, the baby was due the beginning of June and my parents were coming out later in June. I am not sure how the next move came about. I don't think it was anything to do with Danny this time although one could never be certain what contacts and deals were made at The Golf and Country Club!

Mr Arnold, who years previously, had been Mayor of Edmonton, had bought a dairy farm and a herd of yearling Ayrshire heifers for his son who then decided he did not want to be a farmer and was refusing to have anything to do with the venture. Enter John and Gay, John with no experience of dairy farming but who could hand milk a cow and Gay who had left her only experience at the age of four! John had known Mr Arnold for years and the prospect of tackling something completely different appealing to both of us we agreed to give it a go. We were, once again, on the move, the third move in under a year and not even married a year either.

Chapter 17
NORTH NORTH-WEST TO ONOWAY

At the end of April John, Alex and I travelled out to Mr Arnold's farm This was situated 4 miles from the hamlet of Gunn (a garage, filling station, general store and phone box located just off Highway 43 W of Edmonton situated on the shores of Lac St Ann). The farm was 3 miles of gravel road and one mile of gumbo from the highway. Gumbo; the most dreadful type of mud to drive after heavy rain, or when the frost was coming out of the ground; it was like driving through very thick soup. One learnt to go with the mud, let it take you almost into the ditch before correcting the slide and then be suctioned into a new direction; and pray no other vehicle was coming towards you.

The bungalow was of fairly conservative design built over an undeveloped basement; up wooden steps into a lobby with a wood-burning cooker in it, and a twin tub washing machine, then into a fair sized, properly outfitted, kitchen with room for a large table and chairs at one end then into the sitting room with two bedrooms and the bathroom off. Large picture windows let in plenty of light and it had a pleasant atmosphere.

Besides the heifers there were young pigs and breeding sows, thankfully no bull. We immediately had our hands full, not only with taking on the care of the livestock, but no-one had started to prepare the arable ground for sowing the spring wheat. Many a night I would go to bed only to wake up a couple of hours later and realise John was still not in. Unable to go back to sleep, partly as the baby was becoming more uncomfortable day by day, partly wishing John would come in. I spent hours, either standing up nursing my back or in the rocking chair, at the big window watching the lights of the tractor slicing into the night across the field opposite as John just kept going, right to left then left to right.

We were both working very hard, I as much as my swollen tummy would allow and John flat out to get the seed grain sown. We had to make time to drive to Edmonton to see my gynaecologist as my actual due date was uncertain. We were no further forward as he thought I was still some way off. He was pleased, though, with my weight. I had gained only nine pounds throughout the pregnancy! He was very fierce with any patients who gained a lot of weight, he certainly did not believe in the 'eating for two' practice. And lots of exercise which I was certainly getting.

Late the following afternoon the young heifers broke out of their pasture and ran through the buildings and onto the newly sown field. There were no fences and they were heading towards the road with their tails over their backs, bucking and kicking and in the mood to run. Of course I responded to John's call for help. Running down the side of the ploughed field was not easy; can't you run any faster came the encouraging calls from way on my right where John was running down the middle of the field. At which point, completely out of breath I felt a lurch in my belly as the baby turned and dropped. And that was me done with running after that unruly bunch. John stopped following the cattle and cut diagonally across the field and, with a super human effort, managed to reach the opening onto the road before the heifers and turn them back.

Following that initial lurch nothing else seemed to happen for quite a few hours then I began to get uncomfortable twinges and we decided that my labour was starting. Of course the birth canal was not ready, no-one had opened the sluice gates yet the baby tried to start its journey into the outside world. If I had any waters to break there cannot have been much of it as I never felt it come away. We headed into Edmonton, 50 miles away, to the Royal Alexandra Hospital and thirty-nine hours of torture. It transpired that I was so physically fit through all my hard work and the riding that my muscles were unable to relax, they kept tightening up and trying to force things along. As it was a first baby, they did not want to do a caesarean. They said my waters had broken, if so there was very little as I was not even aware of it happening. They said it was a dry birth, but surely every birth could be described as 'dry' after the waters have come away, and not a drop of sympathy or kindness to be had anywhere on that labour ward. Eventually I was wheeled into theatre and put out and the baby was delivered by forceps and, immediately whisked upstairs to the high dependency unit and placed in a heated cot on Oxygen. There she stayed for three or four days. As she weighed well under 5 pounds she would not be released until her weight went up to 5 pounds. All I could do was walk up to another floor and look at her through a plate glass window. I ask you. How inhuman was that. To have gone through all that pain, to have suffered all the indignity of being prodded and probed for hours on end and all I could do was look at it through a plate glass window. I have no recollection of the baby's arrival, no immediate holding and bonding (most likely the importance of this not recognised even then or would not have even been acknowledged as the labour wards were quite without sympathy or comfort in their attitude to childbirth).

I was on a six-bed ward. I was the only patient without a baby present. The baby was still 'the baby'. I was meant to express milk for her, a nurse just threw the apparatus onto the bed, a quick explanation and I was left to get on with it. There was no way. For starters there was no milk and no proper help forthcoming. I was very thin, my breasts were as flat as pancakes, well, not quite as I was wearing a bra, and super sensitive. Hence the baby had to go onto formula. I was feeling pretty useless at this point.

Then came the third day. No-one told me that the third day after giving birth can be very emotional. John came into see me that evening. He sat very stiffly on a chair beside the bed in almost complete silence. It was awful. After he left I went into complete breakdown. I was in a right state and they would not call a doctor. I pleaded for one. Eventually, as I was upsetting the others on the ward, they took me into a small room behind the nurses' station and got me some tea. And there I stayed for most of the night.

The following day the baby was bought down to me. John and I had already decided to avoid all family names and Pamela had been decided on, followed by Gay. So, Pamela Gay was bought down to me and I was shown how to give her the bottle of formula and a few rudimentary lessons on how to care for her and how to put on the diaper. The feeding did not go well and putting a diaper onto such a small infant very tricky. I was finding the whole experience quite frightening. This fragile being was now in my care and I did not have the experience or knowledge for this stupendous task.

I was instructed in the mysteries of making the formula and the necessary hygiene for keeping everything sterile. Basic good housekeeping really. The diapers were viewed, somewhat with dismay, as I had made them myself and I am no seamstress.

Danny always had a diaper service. The dirty ones went into a special sack and were collected once a week when a package of newly clean sweet ones were delivered. No way would I find such a service where we were going to be living. There must have been ready-made ones available, most likely quite expensive, and only obtainable in a big department store down town or, maybe, through a catalogue (we had no catalogue). And who had either the money or the time for a 60 mile round trip for a packet of diapers. Certainly not us.

One day later and we were being discharged. The only laugh I had during this whole experience was getting under the shower on the morning we were to leave with my bra on. I was almost hysterical with laughter. A nurse suggested I hang it by the window in the hope it would dry there which it partially did before we left. John came with a carry-cot and, loaded down with diapers, formula and bottles we left. We went first to a flat owned by the Arnolds. Why I do not remember. I remember, vividly, though being left there with Pamela as John had something important to do. The carrycot with Pamela in it was placed on the kitchen counter and she started to cry. The feeling of absolute aloneness weighed me down, the silent flat and this baby crying on the counter. I was incapable of moving, frozen to the spot in the middle of the kitchen floor and terrified.

I pulled myself together, I had to hadn't I? I lowered the carry-cot onto a coffee table and was able to pick up Pamela and walked up and down trying to soothe her. All the time I was asking myself where was John, was I meant to be feeding Pamela, did she need changing? The questions going around and around in my head whilst Pamela continued to grizzle. Anyway, you will be glad to hear, we sorted ourselves out, John returned and we headed for the farm.

That night when john undressed he turned his back to me and I gave a shriek of horror. His back was lacerated from side to side. That fateful third day he visited me in hospital he had been grinding grain at the farm and his shirt tail had got caught in the power mill he was using. He had been dragged onto the blade and was unable to reach the switch to turn off the machine. Using all his strength he managed to pull free and extricate himself from the auger and live to tell the tale. Except he did not tell me the tale that night in hospital and I was left with the impression that he was not interested in either the baby or me. No wonder I broke down. He said afterwards that he did not want to worry me by telling me what had happened!

So there we were, our little family back home on the farm. My carefree life was now at an end. No more just hopping into the truck with John for a trip out to buy groceries or acquire a much needed piece of farm equipment. My place was at home with Pamela as, in those days, that was where mothers and babies were meant to be. An unexpected problem arose when Pamela developed an umbilical hernia. The doctor was not too concerned, for a while she wore a wide bandage around her stomach and she was not to be allowed to cry! Can you imagine. One bit of knowledge I had picked up along the way was it was good for babies to cry, it developed their lungs and exercised them. Well, goodbye to that theory. Life then became rather complicated. Pamela turned night into day. I wonder if it was because she had been born close to midnight. She slept blissfully all day long and was awake and crying all night. John was out all day on the farm except for meals and would stagger in around 10pm for a good, if short sleep and Pamela would wake up. Not an ideal situation. I believe we became a little fraught through pressure of work and lack of sleep. John needed his few hours of sleep, Pamela demanded attention all night, or so it seemed. I was incredibly lonely although trying to carry on; we were tired and stressed, not a good combination for a new baby.

Then my parents arrived. We were to meet them at Edmonton Airport. We studied the maps and decided to go across country to get there. A big mistake which made us late, poor Mother and Father, their first plane journey, a long one at that, and no-one to meet them and no way of either party being able to contact the other. Not a good beginning. The whole situation was far from ideal. Father had had a major heart attack a few months previously and had, obviously, been given the all clear for the holiday BUT the farm was a little remote. There was no phone and there was this baby awake all night. I think Father looked on it as a big adventure, he made contact with the local Anglican minister in Onoway and was signed up to be involved with the church as guest preacher which was great. Mother, who was a bit concerned because I was rather thin did some cooking and took her turn at nursing Pamela and also devised plans to have her more awake, especially in the late afternoon.

Pamela was to be christened and Father was to perform the office. It was arranged to hold the ceremony in the little wooden chapel on the shores of Lac St Ann. And afterwards back at the farm for tea and cake. John's mother Iola, brothers

Paul and Keith and sister Karen drove out, it was a lovely day and a pleasant time was had by all.

Shortly after the christening Father hired a car for our trip out to Vancouver Island to spend a few days with Dick and Sylvia. John could not leave the farm. We drove through the Rockies. We stayed one night at Three Valley Gap, in a motel. It was very odd; soon after we arrived all I wanted to do was go to bed. Mother asked what on earth was wrong with me, I did not have the answer but, ever since, down all these years, arriving at a motel or a cabin for an overnight stop I seem to go into a dark place; uncooperative, cold and just plain difficult with a strong desire for a deep, hot bath. After we were settled in and had a cup of tea Father drove back up the road aways and painted a picture of the mountains with the road running through them.

I forget just how many weeks my parents were with us. Father kept busy with painting and services with the local Anglican community. They were going home overland by train from Edmonton to Quebec City which is were my Mother's Mother had been born and stayed until her parents died when she and her sisters came to live in England. How I wish I had asked some questions – I am just not a curious person. From Quebec they sailed home on a merchant navy ship that took a small number of passengers.

Chapter 18
MARRIED LIFE AND FARM LIFE

Returning home from leaving Mother and Father at the train station in Edmonton the house seemed rather empty and quiet. Pamela was becoming quite active, wriggling around more on the changing table and in her bath and showing an interest in things around her. It was time to introduce more solid food so our weekly grocery shop now included tins of baby food; tiny jars of pureed meat and vegetables and tins of puddings and fruit. Following the traditional way it was meat first then pudding and, almost immediately, I hit a snag. Pamela would not eat the meat mixtures, she only wanted the puddings. A battle of wills ensued. In desperation I drove out to Gunn to use the public phone box to talk to the paediatrician as we were not signed up with any local medical practice and he was very kind and patient with me. "Feed her the pudding first then, if still hungry, she will eat her meat and veg"! How simple. I did feel a little foolish; I had become a much more flexible person since living in Canada, yet the old rules of my growing up years obviously still had a strong bearing on my thinking.

The grain was ready to harvest. Mr Arnold agreed that John needed help and two men were employed. John had to drive to Onoway each day to collect them and I provided a midday meal, at twelve noon. John decreed that I was not to eat with them, something about being an embarrassment to them? I hovered in the kitchen end ready to exchange main course for pudding and coffee. John came in with them and left with them, never a word for me. One day I tried to retain him with me for a couple of minutes chat and he would not stay. John being John I can only think he did not want to appear to be in thrall to his wife. Once again we were back to the 'little woman who must know her place' One day I cracked, as they walked out of the door and, yet again, John would not pause. I threw all the crockery right across the room, some of it even hit the window. I can't remember if I was screaming or in a silent rage, most likely the latter; my upbringing again, do not raise your voice in anger. Being melamine nothing broke, it was just a horrible mess, smears of gravy and puddings on the table, on the chairs, on the floor. Weeping with frustration I cleared up the mess, loaded Pamela and all her stuff into the truck and left. I drove to town. I could not see any point in going to Danny so, rather feebly, I just went to Iola (mother-in-law). And poured it all out. By the time John arrived some hours later (how he got there I have no idea) I had Iola firmly on my side so it was a good thing I did go to her rather than Danny. I think it would have been a very different outcome if I had gone there.

We stayed the night, there were frank discussions which cleared the air and it was suggested we needed some time off; we had had none since moving there,

John had not even had the advantage of the trip to Vancouver Island in the summer. We were well into October by now, winter beginning to get a grip on the land, the slews or lakes beginning to ice over. A herd of some 30 Aberdeen Angus cows and their bull had arrived to winter with us. A weekend away was arranged and Mr Arnold's son, the one who refused to farm, was persuaded to come out and look after things. It was almost dark when we arrived home. John went out to check on all the stock and found a most dreadful situation. The first I knew of it was John rushing in to tell that Mr Arnold's son had opened a gate he should not have done and the Aberdeen Angus had gone through and walked out onto the newly formed ice on the nearby lake. Some cows had drowned and he was taking the tractor and ropes down to see if he could save the bull. And I was to get ready to help once he was back. I would be needed to resuscitate the bull if he managed to drag him out of the lake!

Rushing back in John told me the bull was standing in the barn and to do what I could to dry him and warm him. I went to look. This huge animal was just standing there with frequent deep tremors shaking his whole body; if you are not used to Aberdeen Angus bulls, and I wasn't, the task was daunting. Dashing back into the house I placed Pamela in the play pen and admonished her to be good! Grabbed all the towels I could lay my hands on and dashed out again. I covered the bull all over with the largest towels, having to stand on a bale of straw to reach his back, that's how huge he was, and went to work on his extremities. Who would ever have thought that a lecture I attended all those years ago at Porlock would stand me in good stead now. The important routine of looking after a wet, exhausted horse by getting the ears and legs warm and dry first which would facilitate the whole body recovering. First the ears. He was just standing there with his head drooping so it was easy for me to reach up to his ears which I gently worked around with the smaller towels, around the ears, down over the eyes and cheeks then up again until the tips of the ears began to feel warm. Then down each leg, beginning in the well behind the elbows and down to the hoof and up again until the hoof showed signs of drying. Then the back legs, starting up between them then down each leg in turn until these hoofs too showed signs of drying. Once again onto the bale and rubbing vigorously I worked my way along his spine from the back of his ears to the top of his tail. How long was I there? Anybody's guess. I know I didn't leave him until I was reasonably sure he was warmed up and showing interest in a leaf of hay. Back in the house Pamela did not seem to have missed me at all! John eventually came in, cold and exhausted from saving cows but, unfortunately, some had already drowned before he found them. Why had we gone away at all?

A few days later, unbeknown to us, the owner of the cattle had come by to look at his herd and, of course, found the numbers did not tally. Around supper time later that day the Royal Canadian Mounted Police arrived, asked to speak to John and the next thing I knew he was being put into the back seat of their cruiser and driven away. I watched from the window. Never a word to me, they just drove away. Many hours later they delivered him home. We had no phone and John, being John, never thought that he should drive out to Gunn and phone Mr Arnold to tell him what his son had done. Only after the RCMP had been involved did John explain what had happened; he was facing a charge of cattle rustling for God's sake. Incredible where misplaced loyalty can land you. The Aberdeen Angus were duly removed from our care.

Thanksgiving was upon us. I just cannot remember how we communicated with the outside world, most likely by public phone on our trips to town for groceries. We were invited to spend it with Iola. We got all the chores done then loaded up Pamela's needs and drove into town in the late afternoon. I think Paul and Karen were there also for the meal. Iola was at the stove making a rum sauce; she was stirring this light brown glossy sauce in its pan and, at times, a slurp of rum would go into the sauce then a sip or two into the cook. It was the most delicious sauce I have ever tasted and I have never managed to replicate it, how ever many times I have tried!

By now we had piglets arriving and, also, dying and we did not know the reason why. John decided we should take a couple to the vets in Spruce Grove and I grabbed at the opportunity to take some dirty laundry to the laundromat. Leaving Pamela in John's care I set off. The cab was full of laundry and dead pigs so I was unable to have the heat turned up as that made the smell worse. I was barrelling down the highway minding my own business and revelling in being out alone when I saw, coming towards me down a very steep hill, a large truck that had jackknifed. It was filling the road and totally out of control. Instinct made me revert to the British side of the road to get out of its way and it hit my truck on the passenger side door and sent me into the ditch. If I had stayed on the correct side it would have stove in the driver's side door with much more damage to myself. As it was I was knocked out and there was blood on my neck from a cut on my head. I came to being talked to by a telephone engineer who happened to be on the road and witnessed the whole thing. The truck driver was unhurt and I understood later he had applied his brakes at the top of this steep hill and they had frozen on causing him the loss of control. My friendly telephone engineer said he was taking me into the hospital in Spruce Grove and helped me into his vehicle and off we went. I remember being confused and just doing what I was told. In the hospital they sewed up my head then the RCMP arrived and took me off to the police station which is where John found me. He was so angry 'what business did the RCMP have in taking me from the hospital and interrogating me when I had been knocked out and was in no fit state to be answering questions.'?

I suppose John must have got to hear of the accident through 'bush telegraph'! He must have been loaned a vehicle, maybe from the farmers down the road as this is where he left Pamela; in the care of the grandmother who did not speak a word of English and was cuddling and cooing to Pamela in her native tongue when we arrived to pick her up. Pamela seemed totally unfazed by the experience.

These same kind people were our closest neighbours, just a half mile up the road before we got to our place, who had not noticed they were occashionally missing chickens thanks to Vicky, our chocolate Labrador. Vicky was given to us by my friend Tina, she was a lovely dog who was never tied up even if we left the farm for any reason. We began finding the odd white chicken in our yard which was a bit perplexing as we did not have any of our own and were not allowed poultry as we were breeding pigs for slaughter. Coming home one day who should be trotting down the road in front of us but Vicky tenderly carrying a white chicken. Mystery solved; we rounded up the chickens once they had gone to roost and returned them to sender! Once she had been found out I don't remember her doing it again.

To return to the saga: I have no idea what happened to the dead pigs or the laundry. It must have all got sorted and, eventually we got our mended truck back and I was given $100 dollars compensation which I immediately spent on a horse! A young liver chestnut gelding which I think had been backed otherwise why would I have saddled it up one day for a ride without any preliminary lunging etc. What joy to ride again although I admit I was a tad shaky when I first got on him; I had had a baby and not been on a horse since the one in Westleigh that bucked me off. Willy Bum! He used to enjoy wandering onto the patch of ground where the clothes line was and pulling the frozen diapers of the line, scattering clothes pegs everywhere.

The next exciting event was the arrival of the phone. There was no phone when we moved in. We knew the phone was coming, we even knew the date and the time. I was watching from the big picture window and saw the phone company trucks pulling up at the entrance to the farm at the far side of the wheat field. Until the ground froze we drove around the edge of this field on a rutted track but since the freeze up we had been cutting, in a diagonal line, straight from the house to the road and the cable laying machine followed our tracks from the road to the house, diagonally across the field. The machine sliced into the soil and laid the cable all in one go. Such a slick operation. It seemed no time at all and it was beside the house and there was a knock at the door. It was one of the engineers who asked where I wanted the phone. I indicated a spot on the wall beside the window. He drew a X on the wall, went outside, drilled a hole from the outside and came back in carrying a phone which he then connected to the cable which he had pushed through the wall, made a connecting call, said "there you are, all connected," and left. Incredible. And I couldn't think who to call! Sad really.

On Christmas Day we drove to Iola's then settled down to endure the coldest part of a prairie winter with the thermometer often dropping to 40 below. Basically we fed the livestock and tried to keep the water flowing, as always, it seemed to me, we were never ready for winter. Pamela continued to grow and become much more active. At some point, as she did more during the day, she ceased to try to turn night into day so we were, after many months it seemed, actually all sleeping through the night. Pamela never crawled, she rolled everywhere and at great speed too. We were to learn, many years later when Pamela had just started in her senior school, that crawling is a very important part of a baby's mental development.

February slipped into March and we were beginning to wonder how this venture was going to pan out. The Ayrshire heifers were still running almost wild, no attempt had been made to introduce them into the milking parlour and were, I presume, due to start calving at some point. I think things were looking a little dicey for us and here entered Danny again. She must have been a bit concerned else why, completely out of the blue, would we get a phone call from a Mr Carpenter on Vancouver Island asking if john would like a job managing their competition yard and there would be work for me too if I wanted? Danny by now was well into the horsey world of Western Canada and had taken up jump course designing which she was very good at, hence the connection. March is the most dreadful month on the prairies. You get spring-like days, temperatures, maybe, just into double figures on a sunny day in a sheltered spot then, wham, another blizzard hits and one is back to square one. We did not take much persuading!

Chapter 19
HEADING WEST!

Having made the decision to accept the job on Vancouver Island we just had to hand in our notice and make the necessary arrangements. The break with Mr Arnold did not go smoothly, he was reluctant to re-imburse John for things we had purchased or additional expenses we had met out of our own pockets. It did get sorted in the end. Never one to rock the boat I did not question too closely the final sum, I was just glad we got something back. There were arrangements to be made, not least what to do with the horse. Some neighbours kindly agreed to keep him for us until such time that we could send for him. We did not have many worldly possessions! What we had fitted into a small trailer and so we set off. One baby, one dog that we already knew was not going to be allowed to come with us to the stables, one cat and ourselves all tucked into our beat up old Plymouth car.

We travelled down through the Kootenays where we had an invitation to break our journey with Dick and Valerie Brenton. We spent a couple of days there then continued our journey. Arriving at the ferry terminal for Vancouver Island we had a bit of a shock when we looked at the hoarding displaying the prices for the ferries. Even pooling our resources we did not have enough money to get on one! Desperate searching ensued. I remember feeling rather sick in the pit of my stomach. Then tucked in the very back of John's wallet he discovered a $20 dollar bill that he had no recollection of possessing. It was unbelievable. Our only conclusion, Dick, knowing John rather well, had slipped it into John's wallet when no one was looking, thus enabling us to pay the fare and board the ferry that was to carry us to our new life far from the prairies. Once on the island we were to stay with Uncle Dick and Aunt Sylvia at Cobble Hill for a few days. John had to have an interview with the Carpenters and, if successful, we had to find a home for Vicky. Here Aunt Sylvia came up trumps with news that neighbours of theirs would love to have Vicky so that solved that worry: they loved her to bits but recognising her need to be free they did not stop the gap in their back fence and, one day, some people on their way to church ran her over. They were very upset.

Dick and Sylvia's home had a good sized balcony overlooking the valley below and here, Pamela, just short of her first birthday, choose to get up and walk. Quite literally, she got to her feet and was off. Aunt Sylvia was cock-a-hoop that Pamela had chosen their balcony to take her first steps. Me, I was really miffed, I still am actually. But why? To this day I cannot work out why this should be so.

Interview successfully accomplished we were all set. If John and Mr Carpenter had taken an instant dislike to each other, we would have been up the creek without a paddle as the saying goes. But here we were, employed and a house to live in! This was a two-bedroom Pan abode dwelling with good sized sitting room laid with a parquet floor overlooking the yard with kitchen behind and steps leading down to a grassed area where Alex spent many hours pretending to hunt but, in reality, curled up sleeping. Very pleasant all round. The property was set back off Prospect Lake road and the lake itself was just a little ways further on, and comprised the main house, two enclosed stable blocks with good sized loose boxes, an outdoor arena and various paddocks. Plus the house we were in.

This was, in effect, a boarding stables but of a high standard. Mrs Carpenter had a good quality show hack and everyone boarding their horses there were into showing, either show jumping or hunter classes; it was a highly competitive yard. For some reason they seemed a bit wary of me. I had thought I would get a bit of riding but that only happened twice. I got a ride on one of their jumpers to take part in a jumping clinic and got one ride at a show. It was a ridden hunter class, no jumps, and I rode a dappled grey gelding and won the class! And that was it for the duration of our time there. To keep busy I whitewashed the whole of the second block of stabling and, in a hidden corner, left my signature!

The word spread far and wide amongst John's family, that we were on Vancouver Island, even down to the States were some remote cousins of John's lived. Lo and behold, they had always wanted to see Vancouver Island and, without much warning, they arrived on our doorstep. They had a daughter, around two years of age, with no table manners and not being taught any either. The husband, deprived of male company during the day, would, each night, at bedtime, suggest that he and John went for a walk. John's usual time for getting up was six each morning and this wretched man was keeping John walking until one or two in the morning. Of course I was not allowed to say anything, about this or the sticky floor or anything; they were our guests and I must put up with it.

Looking back I find it rather interesting that, for the time we were at the Carpenters, John and I never shared a bed. Our bedroom window looked over to the yard and I felt very exposed sleeping there and was totally unable to relax enough for any high jinks. John and I never discussed this aspect, either then or at any time afterwards.

For the life of me I cannot remember how we met the Pinks: Alf and Yvonne and their many children. They lived on an acreage at the end of the road and we became very friendly with them which was great. I started giving riding lessons, so good to be back in the horsey world I understood. One night the idea of Pony Club was broached. I imagine Alf and Yvonne did most of the ground work. It seemed no time at all until The Victoria and Saanich Pony Club was formed with pink and brown as our colours. The first few meetings were chaotic to put it mildly. No-one knew what to expect. The children and parents and ponies or horses arrived in all sorts of costumes with all sorts of bridles and saddles, a real jumble of English and Western gear. Teaching was a challenge as too many who came were not receptive to new ideas. Gradually over the following weeks some sort of order was established. One of the most difficult things to tackle were the bits. Everyone figured some sort of curb bit was essential for keeping control of one's animal, but they could not understand how a plain snaffle bit was sufficient. With, maybe, a martingale. And how ponies were actually better than horses for the younger rider and, of course, an English style saddle. The whole point of joining the Pony Club was to educate. We tried to go along with those who did not want to change saddles but very soon those who wanted to continue in the club changed to an English saddle and snaffle bridle (the tack shops must have enjoyed a bonanza) and we were off. Stable management and general care and feeding of the horse played a huge part in our early education of our members as well as regular riding sessions.

There is a big Fall (autumn) horse show in Vancouver every year. Knowing there were competitors coming down from Alberta we arranged for horse to be bought down and he was collected from the show grounds and came over to us where he lived with the Pinks. It was great to have him with us once again

My private teaching was building up, having a sturdy playpen was such a bonus as I would set it up in a shady corner of the field where Pamela seemed content to play or snooze away the time as I taught. We were beginning to feel at home on Vancouver Island. Came the day when Alf told John that the company he worked for (Steels), a tug boat company pulling barges of oil up and down the coast and amongst the islands was looking for a cook for their main tug boat. John took the job even though he really knew nothing about cooking! I wrote him out some basic recipies which I doubt he used and the hunt was on for somewhere to live. John McIvor and his wife very kindly offered us their basement rooms under the main house. Two large rooms, one we used as the living room as it had basic cooking arrangements at the back and the inner one for sleeping. These rooms were not underground, they opened out onto the forecourt of their property. The floors were concrete so the first thing I did, with John's increased wages, was to go into town and buy the largest oval braided rug I could find so Pamela had somewhere soft to play on.

We knew this was temporary, it was so kind of the McIvors to let us camp there whilst we looked. Friends were keeping an eye out for somewhere for us to live and one of them spotted an advertisement in the paper: "Cottage to rent on large acreage. Some care taking duties." With a phone number to ring in Vancouver. I lost no time in making that phone call! I remember I had to be there for 10am on a Thursday and I also had the directions: off Puckle Rd which was off Island View Rd which was off the Sidney to Victoria highway up a long drive; a quarter of a mile. John being at sea this was all up to me!

The first thing one saw as one negotiated the rutty track (drive!) running up the left hand side of the fields was a two storey red wooden barn up on the ridge ahead. The large fields on the right were divided by substantial hedges but they were no longer separate fields as the centres had been cut out to make a runway with a wind sock on one side near the end of the runway. Driving up I was hailed by a woman wandering around near the wind sock. I stopped and lowered my window. She asked if I was there to meet Mr Bernard and when I said yes she told me there was no point in my waiting as the cottage had already been rented out. For some reason I did not quite believe her and drove on. The drive climbed steeply on a curve around the barn to straighten up and pass the barn. Across a small, flat piece of ground on the left was a long open shed which housed a Silver Ghost Rolls Royce! Behind the barn, sitting on a small patch of rough grass (the potential lawn) was the cottage I had come to see. Further on, on the edge of a wood was the main house, rather imposing looking with a veranda surrounded by trees and a paddock.

The property was owned by Mr Frank Bernard a businessman from Vancouver who flew his own plane, hence the landing strip. All the buildings were on this ridge which fell away behind to more level fields ending at Island View beach on the Straights of Juan De Fuca. The whole property was some 60 acres. I parked up and looked around. My stomach was in knots, I was so nervous and the woman waiting had unsettled me badly. There was a lot riding on this interview and just standing there I knew I wanted to live there and I had not even seen inside.

I watched the plane come in and land and taxi up the slight incline to come to a stop. I did not see what happened next but it seemed a long time before Mr Bernard appeared. I guess there are certain procedures one has to do with a plane after a flight, then he had to talk to The Woman. Eventually he appeared and went straight away to show me the cottage. Essentially this was a plywood shack being glorified with the term 'cottage' with four rooms and a bathroom tacked onto the back accessed through the kitchen which had a oil burning cooker, on the same principle as an Aga and, as we found out the first winter, this cottage had almost no insulation. If you are practically homeless one does not quibble over the niceties. After a brief look around and a ten minute interview the cottage was mine, the rent was low as we were to caretake the big house and generally look after the place in the owner's absence. I explained about John going to sea on two week shifts; two weeks on two weeks off and that seemed acceptable to Mr Bernard; he must have decided that I was more than capable of looking after the place. We had the use of the barn, the paddock and the fields at the back and we could make hay on the front fields. There was not much to do. The Bernards flew in and out for the odd weekend but did not think that would inconvenience us at all as long as we never had livestock loose on the front fields. As we only had a dog, a cat and one horse at that time this was easy to agree to. All decided with a hand shake. However primitive the cottage, the relief at having found somewhere to live was enormous. Moreover it was more than I could ever have dreamed about. Sixty acres to, almost, call our own. I could not stop smiling, I just wanted to jump for joy.

Chapter 20
PUCKLE ROAD, HURRAY!

The relief of having somewhere to live in such a super location had me floating on cloud nine. And for it to be decided so quickly was amazing. From being, virtually, homeless to having a roof over our heads in just ten minutes, incredible! I just could not keep this news to myself but had no means of letting John know what was afoot until, thankfully, he rang 'ship to shore' and I could tell him. Ship to shore is not the easiest way of communicating especially if one of the parties is excited and keeps forgetting to say 'over' at the end of a sentence! There was no waiting around, I did not have to give notice to the McIvors as we were there on a friendly basis and the cottage being empty there was no reason not to get on with it. Pamela and I could move in right away.

Friends rallied around and loaded our meagre possessions onto various pick up trucks and we were away. Unbeknown to me Pamela had found the ex.lax, a chocolate laxative, and helped herself. Luckily the floors were just plywood as she was running all over with excitement leaving trails of dribble from her back end from room to room. This did stop, thank goodness, as I had not realised just how much danger she might have been in, ignorance is bliss.

I had been made aware of the one real snag to this caretaking business and that was the water situation. Mr Bernard showed me where the well was, well two actually, close together in the woods below his house. Across the paddock, through a small gate and follow the track. If one well ran dry you had to prime the pump in the other one, a skill I had never come across before. I thought I will tackle this once John is home and hope we do not run dry in the meantime. So one of the first jobs once John was home was to get to grips with learning how to prime a pump and how to move the mechanism from one well to the other, or at least parts of it that needed connecting each time.

There is a law isn't there? I believe it is called sods' law which refers to things going wrong, always at the most inconvenient time. Well, these wells stuck strictly to sod's law. When they ran dry it was always at the worst time of day, getting supper, putting the children to bed, visitors arriving, you name it that is when it would happen, quite often after dark and when the Bernards' had guests; town folks used to turning on a tap with no recognition of any water restrictions. It was impossible to actually see well enough down the well to ascertain how much water was left and however one tried to manage the situation it inevitably ran dry at the most awkward of times. Many is the time I would be down there, usually in the dark, often with rain dripping down my neck, lying on the ground attempting the change over without actually dropping the flashlight down one of the wells.

My greatest achievement was during a spell of very cold weather and the whole system froze up. By now we had animals to look after and cows especially can make their feelings known if they are thirsty. To this day I do not know how I did it but I managed to reverse the whole system and, instead of the water flowing to us then up the rise to the big house I got it flowing in the opposite direction through a system of hoses and managed to water the stock and have some in the cottage too. I gave myself a pat on the back for that one.

During that first afternoon I became aware of there being a donkey somewhere around. It is difficult ignoring a donkey demanding attention, but as the noise did not go on for too long I didn't go looking. It wasn't until a couple of days later that I spotted a tall woman going past clutching an armful of hay wearing what looked like a very expensive jumper. She never looked our way or knocked on the door. Not friendly at all but once I had accosted her and we became friends I realised she was just being rather 'English' and doing things according to her outlook on social behaviour. I find it difficult to describe, something to do with not having been introduced in a social or acceptable setting? This was Diana Evans whose husband Jim managed the local sewage works and they had a daughter Susan hence the donkey Cello. They had started off married life in Africa, Kenya maybe, where I think they lived rather a special life with servants as Diana knew nothing about housework or cooking or so it seemed to me. She was on a sharp learning curve and they lived in a cottage a short walk away through the woods from us which was why it was so ideal for her having Cello so close. We struck up quite a friendship. One Christmas it actually snowed overnight and we woke up to a white world and, after breakfast, we walked through the snowy woods singing carols to visit the Evans, a magical moment long cherished.

Alex, the cat, accepted this move as he had all along, very stoically, and, I think, revelling in being back on a farm with the big barn and acres to go hunting in. I am not sure how long we had been there before friends starting asking me wasn't I nervous living up the long drive with no property within sight let alone calling distance. Well, there was Diana in the woods to the south of us and Jady Wright's farm just to the north, through a wire fence, now that was within calling distance if one stood at the wire fence and hollered loudly. I really was not bothered but these friends got me thinking a bit. Really kind of them to be concerned but a bit detrimental as their concerns were making me a little nervous. One friend took the issue even further. She phoned me one day and said she knew of a dog who desperately needed a new home. I suppose this arose because I had got a sort of Labrador from a rescue centre and it was completely unsuitable and had to go back. This dog she phoned about lived in town, was never exercised and the owner had been told to find it a proper home. What was it I asked. A German shepherd! Was I a German shepherd owner I asked myself and I really did not think so. I had watched my friend Tina with one of hers and was aware they needed a lot of control and keeping on top of and I just thought I was much too lazy to be bothering with a whole lot training. Horses yes, I could certainly keep on top of stroppy horses but a GS? I don't think so.

Nevertheless, as always doing what I was told to do, I drove into Victoria and found my way to a street of terraced houses just back from the town centre. I remember feeling quite apprehensive and even more so when the doorbell was answered by a middle aged man and no-one else at home. In we went, down the hall to the kitchen which was at the back of the property. He said the dog was outside in the yard but he, the dog, was very friendly. He opened the back door and in bounded the dog, all excitement and action; the kitchen immediately shrunk or seemed to. He was called Prince and very handsome. It turned out he was never walked, he spent his days in the back yard, his only excitement and exercise was rushing up and down the length of the small enclosure and making vain leaps trying to reach the neighbourhood cats parading along the top of the walls, just out of reach. And occasionally, of an evening, he would share a bottle of beer with his owner!

What a dilemma? I did not want a GS yet how could I leave him there. Not giving my brain a chance to override my heart I said I would take him, loaded him into the van and drove home. Now what to do with him. There was a wire enclosure where once there had been a hen house. I had him in the house at night and put him into this enclosure during the day. I must say he behaved beautifully. Two days later John came home and I introduced them. John immediately announced that no dog of his was ever confined so I countered with 'fine, on your head be it'. And off they went down onto the airfield to become acquainted where Prince ran wild. Apparently he just ran and ran and would not come back. To John's frustration he could not remember the dog's name; instead of Prince he yelled Kaiser (the name of friends' GS) and the dog immediately stopped and returned to John and he was Kaiser ever after. And he was never shut up again. Even if we were away for the day or even a weekend, he remained loose and never left the property. He was the most wonderful dog.

Things were good. John was in a steady job with decent pay, I loved where we were living, normal marital relations resumed, we had the horse and acquired a house cow and a couple of beef calves to rear on. Then, in the New Year, winter hit. Vancouver Island generally enjoys a mild winter climate with the odd exception and our first winter on Puckle Road was one of those exceptions. It was so cold in the cabin, the cooker quite inadequate as a form of heating. For the first time we actually looked around the outside and realised the walls of the cabin only rested on the ground at the front. The ground had a gradual slope to the rear and the wind was whistling underneath with nothing to stop it. Then it warmed up a little and snowed. Once that had stopped we shovelled snow up against the walls and that stopped the wind blowing underneath excepting for the bathroom which was too high off the ground to do anything about. The icicles hung some 2 feet long from the edge of the roof and one could scratch pictures in the ice on the windows inside. Some kind friends lent us an oil filled radiator to plug into the socket in the sitting room which did help to warm us up. The cats took to lying as close as they could to it!

On one of his home periods John lost no time in building a 4 by 8 foot glassed-in porch which made a huge difference to the warmth of the place. Spring came, we acquired some white picket fencing which we erected across the edge of the bit of grass in front of the cottage and encouraged that grass to turn into a lawn with some shrubs to differentiate our bit from the drive. Coming home one summer's morning I found a hummingbird in the porch. Seeing me in the doorway it started dashing itself against the end window in a bid to escape. I stood very still and it came to rest on the shelf under the window. Slowly I stretched my left arm towards it, and keeping my back towards it I edged closer. Out of the corner of my eye I watched it as it cautiously hopped onto my extended index finger. If I had not seen it do this I would not have known it was there as I felt no weight from it. Ever so slowly I carried it to the open doorway and it flew away. I felt so privileged to have been so close to this amazing, beautiful bird.

Having resumed marital relations it was not long before I became pregnant again. J refused to wear a condom apparently "it was like washing your feet with your socks on"! I could not bear the thought of having a device fitted so took other precautions which, obviously, proved ineffective. I had already tried being on the Pill; in those early days the pills were far too strong and virtually knocked me out, I was like a zombie when I was taking them. I know exactly the night Bridget was conceived; I remember fluffing around for a while before actually joining John in bed which must have been a mistake as I woke up the next morning knowing I was pregnant, and I was right.

The summer before Bridget arrived Pamela and I went to England. Father had the living of Eldersfield in Gloucestershire which was very much a farming community and suited him down to the ground. Whilst there they asked if I would like to have a holiday (as if being there was not holiday enough for me) and I chose the Lake District much to their delight. We were driving out of the village of Elterwater when Father stomped on the brakes and did a rapid reverse. We wondered what was happening. He had spotted a battered "For Sale" sign lying on the top of a garden wall. I am going in he said where upon he got out of the car and disappeared through the gates. He was back very shortly, it was definitely for sale and we were invited in! Father on a mission. We spent a very pleasant couple of hours there, enjoyed tea in the sitting room where Pamela had her first taste of Chocolate Fingers and kept asking for more. She was a big hit with the owners. Father just fell in love with the place and resolved to buy it for his retirement, which he duly did. After two glorious months I returned home to Canada.

Whilst at the vicarage my sister Liz and family came to stay and for Liz's daughter Nicola to be baptised although I might be wrong about that as she was no longer a baby. There is a photo of the grandchildren sitting on Robin, a repeat of the three of us sitting on him at North Hawkwell when we were children. The journey home was a nightmare. By then I was heavily pregnant and I don't believe they allow a woman these days so far into pregnancy on airplanes. I wished I wasn't on one for sure. Vancouver Airport was grillingly hot and the walk to the plane for Vancouver Island very long and Pamela very tired, I was so exhausted.

The order in which we acquired animals after Kaiser is lost in the mists of time. We acquired a Jersey cow called Daisy who was in calf. This is really where I learnt to swear. Milking her was a nightmare, she was adept at kicking and extremely accurate with her aim once she felt she had given us enough. More often than not she would kick the bucket over just when I thought I had got enough for us; she was determined her calf got the bulk of her milk. John got on with her better than I did, maybe he could kick better than she could as we had a lot more drinkable milk when he was home.

I am trying to remember when we acquired Bimbo. Pamela was two and a quarter when we moved to Puckle Road so I think it must have been the following spring when Diana mentioned she knew of this old pony who might suit Pamela. Or was it Mary Moss? We had made the acquaintance of Mary and Paul Moss who had three children, Nick, the oldest then Katie and then Jeremy. Mary became my dearest friend; if she had a problem health wise with one of her children's ponies she would phone me for advice and if I had a problem health wise with one of my children I would phone her; a mutual support system that worked extremely well. To get back to this pony. Bimbo was old, no-one knew quite how old he was, a bay gelding, about 14hh with lots of white hairs scattered through his coat, certainly his teeth were very long. He was such a sweetie and seemed to keep his winter coat all year round so became rather hot in the summer which is when we used to give him a trace clip. One felt absolutely safe when Pamela was riding him, he was so gentle and obliging. She had lots of fun with him, her first horse show, her first Pony Club camp which we held at Puckle Road, her first ride all by herself down the drive and up the parallel road to visit friends.

Life settled into a routine with John working two weeks on and two weeks off. He was enjoying the job, especially once he left the galley and became a deck hand. Eventually he became responsible for arranging the oil sales. The company services all the remote First Nation communities and lumber camps up remote inlets on the coast north of Vancouver. He made some good friends; one Christmas he came home with some dried venison, absolutely wonderful flavour from one of those friends. Another time was not so happy for me. It was his first company Christmas party held on a small island off the ferry terminal where the owner actually lived. I waved him off at about half past one, he was picked up by Alf Pink. And he never returned. Afternoon turned into night; eventually, quite late I could stand it no longer and phoned the Pink household where I learnt that they, Alf and John, had gone on to a party. When I phoned where they were I could hear the sounds of a rip-roaring party in the background. To get to this party they drove right past the turning to Island View Road which led to Puckle Road and and never thought to just turn in and, at least, tell me where they were going to be. Afterwards I learnt that other people had their children there who were just put to bed somewhere for the duration. I was so angry, and hurt yet another example of the little wife knowing her place.

I remember the summer of 1969 as being a busy yet happy time. Of course some of it was spent in England which might have contributed to the general aura of well being. John came and went at regular intervals, Pamela was enjoying riding Bimbo, we acquired some laying hens, Pony Club and teaching keeping me feeling fulfilled and needed.

Chapter 21
FURTHER TALES FROM PUCKLE ROAD

We acquired some hens and a cockerel. I think we were trying to be as independent as possible. We had the cow and beef calves growing on, but growing vegetables proved an exhausting enterprise. Quite often on Vancouver Island it may not rain from May to September. Saanichton Fair was always held during the first weekend in September. If this weekend happened in the first days of the month one was guaranteed a dry show. If the fair was held, say on the 6th or 7th of the month it was always wet. Year on year you could depend on this weather pattern back then before global warming.

We had a beautiful cockerel with the chickens, very handsome. They had a run to one side of the barn but were usually let out once they had laid their eggs during the morning. I think Pamela was about three. She used to love to carry around the lunge whip and play games at rounding up things and trying to make it crack. This day she must have decided it would be more fun to actually round up something alive rather than imaginary and went into the hens' run. The first I knew of it was when I heard her screaming. I rushed to where the sound was coming from and found Pamela pinned up against the wall of the barn by the cockerel who was beating at her bare legs with his wings. John immediately gave him away to some close neighbours where he settled in happily and never did that again to anybody. Back in the day when one wormed your horses by sprinkling powder onto their feed and hoped they would eat it proved disastrous. One year I wormed the horses, and none ate their feed that night. Stupidly I threw all this waste food onto the muck heap where the hens used to scratch for goodies, and they all promptly died. I did feel a fool because, of course, the medicine was poisonous to the chickens too and I never thought it through.

Helping to start the Victoria and Saanich Pony Club opened a couple of avenues for me. There was a small sandy area at the top of the airstrip which, with a bit of work around the edges we turned into a small arena for riding lessons and parents started asking for private riding lessons for their children. The barn had loose boxes on either side of the main alleyway which is how we became friends with Marilyn Miller. She was looking for somewhere to board her horse, so I invited her to join us and a happy, supportive relationship developed over the years; often involving a bottle of sherry after a harrowing experience. One afternoon a gale unexpectedly swept in, high winds and torrential rain. The fir trees behind the house were swaying frantically and there were two horses turned out amongst them, one of them Marilyn's. Marilyn was worried for her horse's safety, so we headed out to get them in. Sheer madness as it turned out. I was opening the electric wire gate, Marilyn behind me when, with a loud crack, a huge limb came off one of the trees and fell right between us! We caught the horses, encouraged them to scramble over the branch and were then towed to the barn, so eager were they to get into the shelter of their stalls. That was definitely a 'sherry' moment even though the middle of the afternoon.

Another time we were going somewhere with Marilyn's horse in the trailer and found a pile of gravel in the gateway at the bottom of the drive. We decided we could get through, the truck struggled but we made it onto the road. All seemed well. We crossed the main road and were driving up the short but steep road in front of us when we realised things were not quite right with the trailer. It did not seem to be following as it should, it seemed to be yawing from side to side. We got out to look and the trailer was only attached to the truck by the safety chain, obviously dragging through the gravel had pushed the hitch off its ball. We did not know what to do. As we stood there contemplating this disaster our friend Ed Bohnet came up behind us in his big truck. He thought if he supported our trailer from behind with his truck we could back up sufficiently to re-attach the trailer properly to the truck which we did. How thankful we were to be so kindly helped.

Pony Club grew and grew and as we progressed, we began to travel to the mainland to partake of inter club competitions. One day it was decided to host a Pony Club Three Day Event. I was the only one, really, who had any experience of the sequence of such events. We had the Saanichton Fair grounds for setting up the dressage arenas and the ring for the show jumping and I was living on these 60 acres of interesting terrain which, with the additional use of some of Jady Wright's farm next door meant we had sufficient mileage for the cross-country course. For the first and only time I designed a cross country course which was built by the fathers in their spare time and was a great success. These fathers went on to build other courses in BC, but I would have been unable to design further afield with John working away even if I had been asked. This was a missed opportunity which, deep down, I always regretted.

Bridget now had Zippy to ride, a Shetland-sized little bay gelding who looked like a miniature thoroughbred and was terrified of hosepipes, so we were never able to wash him down before shows. Before Canada I was quite unfamiliar with this method of cleaning a horse but took to it readily enough as it was so much quicker than the three quarters of an hour grooming that I had been taught at Porlock! Zippy was another who kept his winter coat but, rather amazingly, he allowed us to trace clip so, in the summer he did not sweat up so much. Of course, we never knew why he was so afraid of hosepipes.

Pamela was outgrowing what she could do with Bimbo or what Bimbo could do for her. He couldn't jump for instance, one would not have liked to ask him, and she was beginning to be envious of those of her riding group who were popping over little jumps whenever they liked to. I heard about this pony called Goldie. Now Goldie had been bought out of an auction by friends of mine who had felt sorry for her, very small and very thin. They thought she was a yearling. Once home they had the vet out and he thought she was three years old, and very malnourished. They broke her in once she had put on some weight and generally improved in health and their daughter Karen rode her until she grew out of her. Some people from up island behind Cobble Hill bought her and did nothing with her and eventually put her up for sale. I was telling parents of my riding students about her, and a couple went to look but were not impressed. Thankfully I woke up and went up myself. The first thing I saw as I drove up was this palomino pony trotting amongst some trees with a large dog hanging on her tail. The owners caught her up for me to have a closer look, she looked generally unkempt and was fine weight wise but with virtually no tail left. I thought to myself if this pony can cope with a large dog swinging off her tail, she must be pretty much bomb proof. So I bought her there and then, and went back the next day with my trailer and a cheque and bought her home.

A couple of days later Pamela decided she would like to ride her around to the neighbours to show them her new pony and Goldie was having none of this. She refused to go down the slope of the drive outside the barn, she dug in her toes and would not budge. I told Pamela she just had to win this one. I fetched the lunge whip and standing well behind the pair of them I added a couple of cracks with the whip as Pamela was kicking away and, thankfully, Goldie gave in and they left at a smart trot, down the drive and up the parallel road. I stood listening until I knew they had arrived and, from that moment on, we had no more trouble except she could be slightly nappy at the first jump in a jumping class at a show. Having found this out, from then on whenever I designed a jump course at a local show the first jump was always facing back towards the collecting ring thereby ensuring that most competitors got over at least one fence. The first time as a mother watching my child jump a course had me pacing nervously up and down behind the bleachers not watching at all!

Chapter 22
BRIDGET'S ARRIVAL

Bridget arrived on 21 October, 1969 at approximately 2pm. Her arrival was much looked forward to; she had a much more placid time in the womb than Pamela did. John was in settled employment and we were living amongst friends and, although primitive by today's standards, we loved where we were living with the horses and beef cattle John was acquiring plus Daisy the dairy cow who taught me how to really swear.

The due date for the baby's arrival was fast approaching and John was at sea! We had a ship to shore conversation, the airwaves of which are open to anyone listening in, "over and out", that sort of call. I am asking John to come home and John is asking for details of why he should come home just then. I was so conscious of who might be listening in to what was a rather intimate conversation that I think I said 'on your head be it' and hung up. John, of course being up an inlet somewhere along the coast north of Vancouver had to wait until they docked back in Vancouver which must have happened that night as he was home the following day.

The morning after I had a hair appointment which John was to drive me to. I did not feel quite right so we dropped into the doctors on the way. He was slightly horrified at how far advanced I was (I was a mite surprised too as I had felt no contractions) especially when he said I had to get to the hospital right away! So we headed to Victoria, bypassing the hair appointment. I guess bouncing along in the truck was bringing things on as twice we had to stop so I could get out and walk up and down the pavement as my contractions were suddenly coming hard and fast (most likely not the best course of action to take). On arrival I was whisked upstairs, no time to shave me (lucky me) and the baby arrived. John missed it all as he went outside for a smoke! By the time he returned I was lying on a trolley in the corridor with the baby on my tummy. So concentrated was he on getting back into the maternity unit and not expecting to see me out on the corridor he walked right past us, to emerge a couple of minutes later looking rather embarrassed.

Once again no milk so onto formula, the first of which did not suit. The doctor changed the formula and gave me medicine that I had to give five minutes before the feed as he said Bridget was a colicky baby and this would help sooth the stomach. And could she cry. If I tried to hold her she went rigid in my arms, almost impossible to hold. The five minutes between the medicine and the food were the worst. I put her into the baby carrying cradle on the table and stood by helplessly as she rocked the cradle from side to side. Then the feed then peace until the next feed. The extraordinary thing was she slept through the night, unheard of with colicky babies apparently. Four months later it was all over, just like that. No more pain, peace reigned.

When Bridget was two and a half going on for three my father died. I managed to get on the last flight from Vancouver before the airports shut down due to strikes although my luggage did not catch me up for a couple of days. I was in England for three weeks and when I returned there was a Jack Russell puppy awaiting me and a daughter whose speech I could not understand. We were so used to how Bridget talked we never realised she could not pronounce certain letters of the alphabet (L's and R's particularly). Pamela had been translating for her for quite some time. Lots of speech therapy followed.

By the time my Father died things were breaking down in the marriage. John was becoming increasingly frustrated and he kept up a constant criticism of me. He fell in love with a reasonably outgoing person who was up for a challenge but, once he had got her and got her pregnant she was to stay home and be a 'MOTHER' all the time. The more he tried to change me the less he liked me and the longer the talk sessions lasted. We were in the middle of one of these when we got the phone call to say my Father had died so things were on hold. Right from the beginning, once I had Pamela, John considered I should stay home "surely being a wife and mother was satisfying enough for me?" Unfortunately not.

Anything to do with Pony Club or teaching riding was acceptable because this kept me close to home. But try to go to church, well, forget it. He was a master at engaging me in one of his long discourses even if I was standing there dressed for church. Once started he could talk at me for hours at a time.

I have to ask did John feel threatened by anything I did that did not involve himself? It was so extraordinary, I was living this double life. I became District Commissioner for Victoria and Saanich Pony Club and then went on to be Regional Chairman for British Columbia and John took over as District Commissioner. Being Regional Chairman meant I had to be away more for meetings even to Toronto for the AGM. But things at home were a different matter altogether and continuing to deteriorate. No one in our circle realised what was going on, as John seemed such an outgoing person, full of fun and laughter and jokes (how I hate practical jokes). This continued desire of John's to dominate and control my life was all consuming. When and why had John turned into this different person? Or was it all me.

Things became even worse after Bridget was born, even to the point that I almost lost the use of my legs. Physical symptoms of deep emotional strain I guess. Twice, doing the supper dishes, I felt his hands around my neck. I was beginning to feel frightened. Each time he went back to sea I was taking longer to recover. The one day stretched into two or even three when I would do the absolute necessary and nothing else; horses, cattle, children, then read curled up in a comfy chair. It was becoming unsustainable. I decided to seek lawyer's advice. At the end of the first session with the lawyer he said to me "every sentence you utter has John in it, do you realise this?" Of course I hadn't, I was so busy trying to be what John wanted I could not see the wood for the trees.

Having got this far the prospect of divorce was now looming on the horizon. Mediation was suggested. John flatly refused to consider this "we were alright, we could fix this ourselves"! We were not alright. John became friendly with a member of our local Anglican church, ironically the one I had given up trying to attend! Would I attend a meeting with John and this chap? I knew him, I thought it would be OK, a friendly chat and a way forward. I agreed. It was an afternoon meeting before the children came home from school. It lasted fifteen minutes at the most; two against one, awful. I pulled out shaking like a leaf; one male deaf to anything one said bad enough, two of the same mind quite impossible. The divorce proceeded. End of that chapter of my life.

Chapter 23
ANCHORS AWAY

One summer the parents came to stay from England. They actually shipped over a small sleeping van which was the envy of many of the friends they made. One couple who lived in Washington State would have liked to buy it, but the States had bought in new laws about emissions from vehicles and this van, unfortunately, did not meet these requirements so they shipped it home again and it was eventually sold to someone in Ireland. We all loved going out for little trips in this van, parking up, making a brew and a sandwich and a couple of times we took it to horse shows where it certainly proved its worth and felt quite a luxury!

Needless to say, we had to put on some sort of a drama. We had a very large beach ball and Bridget and Pamela were taking it in turns to throw themselves onto it in the middle of the sitting room floor. Somehow Pamela managed to slide off it face first and caught her bottom front teeth on the braided rug and pulled one out. Trauma all round, panic from John "her looks are ruined" etc. Off to the hospital where it was re-inserted and held in place with some sort of splint until we could get to the dentist on Monday morning. We liquidized all her food which she drank through a straw. The dentist made a bridge to hold it in place and it did seem to re-attach itself but, many years later, it came away. Over the years the gap has closed which I had been saying all along would happen.

Luckily my parents were no longer with us for the next excitement. This was the evening when I came in from doing the last chores in the stable to find Bridget with a needle through a finger. Pamela had decided to teach her how to give an injection to a horse practicing with an orange. Somehow, instead of the orange Bridget's finger received the needle. The staff at the hospital looked rather askance at what they were being presented with. Luckily the needle had missed the membrane so the risk of infection was minimal! Also, luckily, I always sterilised needles after use so this would have been a clean needle.

Then there was the burning cruise ship which we had all heard about, on fire off Vancouver Island. Mr and Mrs Bernard were over, and he came down from his house to ask me if I would go with him to see this ship. I just abandoned my daughters! I guess I thought, if I thought at all, or maybe Mr Bernard put my mind at rest that Mrs Bernard would keep an eye on them although, truth to tell they never set eyes on her all afternoon, and off we went. I found it slightly alarming, even though I had watched it countless times, as Mr B gave a thrust to the engine to gain height to clear the telephone lines at the bottom of the field. This thrust made the plane give a sort of lurch and then we were up. We flew up the straight between Vancouver Island and the mainland west and, arriving at the ship, we circled around it watching. There were five fire boats spraying sea water over it, the passengers having been taken off. Mr B then suggested we needed a cup of tea so we flew on to Bella Coola on the mainland, landed at the airport and took a taxi into town for refreshments! Then back to the airport and flew home where all was as we had left it, the girls were fine. I doubt if Mrs Bernard even checked them, she certainly did not have them up to the house. Such is life, seize the moment.

Came the day when Mr Bernard came over and told me he was putting the property on the market and I should look for somewhere else to live. So started a series of country rentals as I was determined we were not moving to live in a town, even the small one, Sidney, close by. Eventually after three short-term rentals we ended up under the wing of the Matherson family who lived on a good sized acreage with one big house, an apartment over the stable block and a small cottage. Bridget was very friendly with the younger daughter, Siobhan. The cottage was very small; kitchen, sitting room with log burner and two bedrooms and small bathroom, and neither bedroom could accommodate two beds it was that small. On the plus side it had good stabling for the horses, corrals for turnout and excellent riding out.

Mr Matherson built a twostorey bunk bed for one of the bedrooms with a ladder for Bridget to get to the top bunk, the lower bunk was used for storage and I had a single bed in there also, so Bridget and I shared this room. We were very happy here, and keeping busy. Pamela was at Parklands, the senior school in Sidney. Here it was discovered that her reading age had not progressed much beyond Grade Three. I still cannot work out how this came about. Maybe because she was so bright, the first always to see a joke, always organised and efficient. From a very early age I relied on her to pack the trailer in readiness for going to whatever horse shows we had entered in. We embarked on a series of exercises which quickly bought her up to the level she should have been at.

I was persuaded to allow Bridget to do the same as Siobhan, that is be home schooled and enrolled her on the same courses, not realising that there was no comeback with this particular system. No work had to be submitted so no guidelines to help keep check on any progress, if any. Basically, the two girls ran wild all year, getting away with the minimum effort to appear to be actually doing some work. I thought I was supervising, how gullible can one be but, in my defence, to be able to keep the horses I had to work and the stables I taught at were a good half an hour's travel from home.

Then I became super homesick. Pamela was nearing the end of her formal schooling and deciding what follow-up training she should do. I felt as if I was in a rut, could not see my way forward at all. My sister and brother-in-law came out for a visit and I got to talking about my situation. Not sure who suggested it, but maybe return to England? Many years before my brother had made it quite plain that any care Mother needed as she got older would be up to myself and my sister; maybe the fact that mother and sister did not get on very well played a part in my thinking. I took Liz and Peter out to Pacific Rim National Park on the south side of Vancouver Island for a long weekend; a holiday within a holiday so to speak. On our last morning Liz got really stuck in. "Was I going to do anything about returning to England, if I was I had to get on with it now, we had to be there by the end of August so Bridget could start at West Somerset College at the beginning of term". She went on and on. We packed up the car to drive home; it is a lovely road, I was in such a rage I just put my foot down, 80mph at least (far exceeding the speed limit of 60 mph) to spot, far ahead, coming towards me, a police car! He must have had a camera on me as he swung around behind us and put on his siren. I had no option but to pull over. My first and last speeding ticket was issued. Luckily I got away with a fine as he accepted my rather weak explanation of why I was travelling so fast; I blamed the road! Liz and Peter went back to England a few days later, promising me we could stay with them whilst I got sorted. Lots of discussions took place and, eventually, I made the decision to return to England.

Chapter 24
RETURNING TO ENGLAND

On 4th August 1984 Bridget and I left Canada. John and I had been divorced for some years now and I was becoming increasingly homesick for all things English and I could not see any forward direction to my life in Canada. Since emigrating to Canada in 1963 there had been many up and downs. During John's and my marriage, over seven years together, there were times of great joy, times of real hardship, times fraught with anxiety and uncertainty. Working hard, raising a family we made it through the difficult times and came out the other side only to end up in the divorce court. Such is life.

Having made the decision to move back to the UK there was much to accomplish and sort out. Pamela did not want to come so she enrolled on a secretarial course in Victoria and her father was living close by but Bridget (fourteen) was very excited at the prospect.

I did not want to leave my good furniture in Canada. Mr Buxton to the rescue. He made us an 4 foot by 8 foot crate (it is surprising just how much can be got into a crate of that size) which would be shipped back to the UK. I sorted out the future for the horses; Pamela was to keep Amber, Mary who bred Choti the dog, took her back and two friends took the cats. Pamela was to continue to live in the cottage although that went pear shaped soon after I left. Bridget and I packed our bags, found bucket seats on a flight to Heathrow and prepared to take this enormous step into what should have felt familiar yet was completely unknown territory.

Before we left we were asked out to a barbecue which turned out to be a farewell party for Bridget and me and I was presented with a round silver tray and written in the centre 'To Gay from all her Friends'. John, who I thought had become resigned to our move, asked me out for dinner on the harbour front in Sidney. We had the most stupendous row, I left and got into my car and John followed in his and the insults continued through the open windows all the way up Sidney High Street. Quite memorable.

The following day Bridget and I left on the ferry for Vancouver Airport. John came to see us off and, at the last minute, thrust a package into my hand. I walked the decks of the ferry, looking back at a vanishing Vancouver Island and debating what to do with this package.

My brother Jonathan met us at Heathrow. We had been in discussion as to what I might do and had come up with a plan that involved himself and myself with Mother living with Bridget and myself that sounded feasible if very hard work. We were just on the motorway when he announced that that was not going to happen.

Talk about a whammy but in hindsight thank goodness he pulled out before we came too involved. Jonathan drove us to my sister's in West Somerset where we were to stay whilst we figured out our next move and to enrol Bridget in West Somerset College. Mother put her house in the Lake District on the market as she liked the idea of returning to West Somerset and we decided she, I and Bridget could share a house together. I was very lucky work-wise as a friend of my sister's was looking for someone for the winter to help with her horses and there was a cottage to live in. Bridget and I moved in and Mother joined us there once her house sold. We had a very happy winter there until the spring when Jenny needed the cottage for her summer letting business. She no longer needed help with the horses as they would be turned out.

Obviously I needed a job so I took up house cleaning which was not nearly so lucrative as in Canada, then became Information Officer for Exmoor National Park based in their headquarters in the old workhouse in Dulverton. This job was really interesting, meeting visitors to the area and being able to share my knowledge to help them get the most out of their holiday. One of the most frequently asked questions were how to see the red deer and Exmoor ponies.

From Well Farm we moved to a cottage at Triscombe Farm just below Wheddon Cross. One Sunday we had just finished a rather late lunch when Mother stood up rather abruptly and announced she was off to the Methodist chapel in Wheddon Cross for their afternoon service. She returned quite excited as she had been told of an old farm house, Gunns Farm, on 5 acres in Luckwell Bridge that would be coming on the market but we did not need to wait to view for she had also been told where the key was for us to take a look. Up to now our house hunting efforts had met a brick wall as we were trying to stay in Cutcombe parish and I wanted stables and a bit of land and there seemed to be nothing to suit our requirements.

The following day after Bridget was back from school we drove to Luckwell Bridge. It was spring time when the natural growth if left unchecked runs riot and covers the land in lush new greenery. Whilst not actually having to hack our way in the growth on the banks of the driveway reached out and brushed the sides of the car. We struggled with the gate and decided to leave the car where it was.

Our first impression was of entering a green jungle, a peaceful, secluded haven from another age waiting, like Sleeping Beauty, for the kiss of life. Very much in need of some tender, loving care it cried out to us. We walked up into the yard. On our left was a two-storey stone barn, large loose box on the ground floor and then a doorway leading into a darkened interior. Here were small wooden pens where calves might once have been kept, dark, dismal and damp and, high up, on the back wall a window covered in cobwebs cutting out any hope of light getting through. Next a stable with two small loose boxes with vitreous (non-slip) brick flooring, once the home of a favourite horse? Again, these boxes were divided into small pens but more light here, a more pleasant place to be. Further along a long feeding trough against the back wall indicated where once there might have been a single storey barn with stalls for dairy cows. This trough, now a flower bed, was filled with earth and the remains of long dead plants. On the right of this a high wall with a doorway leading into the field below, once belonging to Gunns, where there was meant to be a septic tank.

The key was hidden above the lintel of the back porch and, having reached it down and inserted it into the lock, we paused. It was an eerie moment; the empty windows of the lonely house before us, the gloomy buildings behind. Had we or had we not seen a cat melting into the shadows? The rickety guttering was hosting clumps of Hart's Tongue fern and soft green tendrils of creeper were peeping from under the roof tiles. All combined into a quiet watchfulness, a suspension of time.

We turned the key and tentatively pushed open the door. Even though we had permission to be there, such were our feelings of being intruders we found ourselves whispering as we crept from room to room amongst the shoddy remains of the previous inhabitants. Everywhere was dark green paint and peeling wallpaper. The kitchen floor appeared to be awash with water although actually dry. The fire box of the Rayburn cooker was full, still, of wood ash from the last fire lit there, the old arm chair drawn up close. No wonder we were whispering.

We were both fascinated and appalled. Fascinated, for we had understood an old gentleman had been living here until three months previously, loath to leave what was his home of many years and appalled at the sheer volume of work which would be ours if we followed our hearts and purchased it. Outside, the front of the house was covered in creeper which, true to its name, had crept right into the little front porch and through the electrical junction box which, combined with the water running down the wall, was a most dangerous situation for the unwary. Also it had crept under the roof, along the rafters to come out above the back door. The garden had gooseberry bushes, rhubarb, peonies, plum and apple trees, white lilac, old fashioned roses and unexpected flights of steps. In one corner was a dog's grave: "Linda. Died 11th September 1978. Aged 16 years". The rest of the in-ground was covered with a myriad of ugly corrugated sheds and the three and a half acre field was rather steep. Driven by motives we never stopped to analyse we decided this was the place for us,

The immediate family, my sister and brother and Mother's brother were appalled but rallied round. My brother had a friend who was a surveyor and we were given the name of a builder, Mr Andrew Devlin. We had the survey, Mr Devlin came and gave us an estimate, we did our sums and prepared our offer. All offers were by sealed bid, there were three. I was so jittery and imagining all sorts of skulduggery that Jonathan offered to come with me to the estate agent Stag's office in Barnstable to be present for the actual opening of the offers. And this he did whilst I sat shivering in the car in the pannier market car park. He seemed to be gone a long time. Imagine my relief when I spotted him coming back and when he saw me looking out he raised his thumb. Got it.

Then of course the hard part began. We made no major alterations, just made good what was there. I did a bit of research and traced this property back to 1714. The front rooms are, obviously, old with deep set windows in thick walls and flagged floors but, at some time, a back section was added with low doorways and a sloping roof. This was not 'cute and low' it was low and ugly and, as we discovered when we dismantled it, very poorly built. For instance, the bath was suspended between two, not overly strong timbers. Why that tub never crashed into the kitchen below remains a mystery. For many years the tenants living here used to take in guests. I have visions of Mrs Stokes calling up the stairs to say breakfast was ready and returning to her kitchen to find one of her guests already down, bath tub and all.

Somehow it all got done and we were in. We were even able to offer Christmas hospitality to my dear friends from Canada who were in the process of relocating to Wales, Anne and Ian Wood.

Chapter 25
MEETING NORMAN, SPRING 1986

I had gone with my sister and brother-in-law to one of the point-to-point race meetings held at Bratton Down, a venue we always enjoy with its bracing fresh air and far reaching views. I was standing on the bank watching the runners for one of the races cantering past on their way to the start when a voice in my right ear asked me which one I fancied. I said I rather liked the look of the chestnut that was actually going past in front of us at that moment. Then I turned to see who had spoken. There was this rather well dressed elderly gentleman with a brown trilby hat standing next to me. We fell into conversation; he told me his wife had died three months previously and how, as she was being carried out on the stretcher, she instructed him to 'look after the cats.' The paramedics suggested he stayed home for a while as the hospital would be doing lots of tests and it would be wiser for him to follow on in a couple of hours when more would be known. He was getting ready to do just that when the phone rang. It was the hospital to say his wife, Doris, had died.

My heart ached for him but I did learn he was there with his son and daughter-in-law so not completely alone although, obviously, very lonely. After the race was run we turned to leave the bank and he raised his hat to me. Being recently returned from living in Canada where such courtesies did not happen I was very impressed.

Fast forward a few weeks. Bridget, who loved anything to do with speed and horses (she had been a going concern on her 14hh pony on the Three and One Day Event circuit in Canada) had never been to a point-to-point so I suggested we went to the last point-to-point of the season being held at Umberleigh, just over the border into Devon, about an hour's drive away.

We had an enjoyable afternoon. Bridget met some friends from school which enlivened the day for her which was more than I did; no matter as I always just love watching horses, whether it be in the parade ring or racing. I had wondered if I might spot or even recognise the gentleman from Bratton Down, maybe he was not there. Having watched the runners for the last race leaving the parade ring and thinking I should look for Bridget so we could make a quick get away I did spot him; standing all alone by the empty ring. I wandered over and asked him if he remembered me. His face just lit up and, again, he tipped his hat to me. Well, well. We chatted and exchanged names and where we actually lived. Somehow he had got the impression I lived close to where he lived, can't work that one out. He seemed disappointed that I lived up on Exmoor, rather a way from where he lived in a village close to Torrington, called Monkleigh. He rather tentatively asked if I would like to visit him sometime to see his horses and we agreed I would phone him when I had a day off free to do that. I collected Bridget and we set off for home. My thoughts quite busy with this terribly lonely person I had been chatting too, who I felt so sorry for.

At no time did the thought enter my head that this was a chap I could marry. Marrying again, after the first go round, was an absolute no no as far as I was concerned, not ever to be contemplated. Nevertheless I did phone him and we arranged an afternoon for me to drive over. I found the place quite easily and, feeling slightly nervous, knocked on the door and was welcomed in. A comfortable bungalow built across the road from the farm house and all the usual outbuildings where his son and daughter-in-law lived, with wide reaching views across Devon farmland.

It soon transpired that we were not actually going to see any horses. I got the impression that Norman did not get on with his daughter-in-law and was not welcome up in the yard. Nevertheless he showed me all the trophies he had won down the years, both showing and racing as he held a licence to race under rules as well as point-to-pointing. And we had some tea. And it was time to leave. Standing by the Aga he asked if he could kiss me! Whoops. Following this surprise he suggested he come up to Exmoor, maybe for a picnic, at a future date. When I explained exactly where I lived he said, with a bit of surprise in his voice, that he and Doris had once taken a drive to Exmoor and had eaten their picnic by the phone box in Luckwell Bridge just below where I lived.

The summer rolled on, we took it in turns to meet up in Devon or on Exmoor. I was working at the National Park Centre in Dulverton which I loved as I was helping people to get the most out of their stay on Exmoor and Norman was still busy on the farm, sometimes long days on the tractor, I never questioned how old he was, he was such an active individual. We were heading into autumn, the evenings were drawing in, Norman was getting fed up with the drive if he happened to be heading home in the dusk. One afternoon we were walking up on Ley Hill and had stopped to sit on a bench looking across a combe where we thought we might see some deer when he turned to me and said he thought we should get married. Marriage was still far from my mind but, increasingly, I was enjoying his company and his courtesy and I felt safe with him. The second time I had been proposed to on the top of a hill!

Everything swung into high gear. Wedding plans were made, Bridget's schooling had to be sorted, she enrolled at 6th form college in Barnstaple and we found digs for her within walking distance. Mother would stay at Gunns until it was sold then look for a smaller place for herself. Because of my divorce the wedding had to be in the registry office in Williton and Mother paid for the wedding breakfast in a hotel in Minehead. The major hiccup was getting Norman to produce his birth certificate; he did not want me to know how old he was. I think by this point it was immaterial, we were getting married. Eventually, with some embarrassment he produced it. Surprise, surprise, Norman was twenty-six years older than I was! He was so fit and always so busy I never guessed he was that much older.

I moved down to Monkleigh, we bought a horse for me to hunt and our days were busy and fulfilling. Between hunting and returning to Gunns to keep that place looking neat and tidy for a possible sale we seemed to be forever on the road. Norman then disclosed that he had always had a longing to live in Somerset. He had been the underbidder on a farm close to Taunton many years ago, so we added looking at properties in West Somerset, always ending up having a cup of tea with Mother at Gunns. For some reason I had got the impression that Norman did not like Gunns. I thought he did not like the steepness of the in-ground and the field, much preferring to walking on flat ground. After another fruitless viewing of yet another unsuitable property, over the cup of tea in the cosy sitting room, he looked around and said to Mother 'I will buy you out'. And much to the annoyance of Cathy Wilcox our estate agent we took Gunns off the market.

Chapter 26
THE RECLAMATION OF GUNNS FARM

Norman having decided, much to my delight, to buy Mother out of Gunns there was much to be done. He followed up his offer to Mother by announcing that he could not live with either the present staircase or the back of the house, the kitchen etc as it was. Enter Andrew Devlin again who, although delighted to be offered the job of partially rebuilding the house was aghast at the thought of knocking down so much of what he had quite recently renovated. Plans were drawn up to get rid of the kitchen and lobby and build on larger, wider, foundations running the length of the back of the older part. In effect Gunns was to be turned around, a proper front door into a hall from which a new staircase would rise, a larger kitchen and utility room with back door which would open into an attached garage. This turned a rather ordinary dwelling, of which I was quite fond, into a proper, comfortable house with the added benefit of a master bedroom with en suite. The main bathroom backed onto the en suite so all the plumbing was on one side of the house. The single bedroom at the front between the other two double bedrooms was done away with to create a large bright landing. I love landings.

By leaving the back walls of the derelict cow byres standing there is protection from the midwinter, north-easterly winds and a sheltered courtyard with support for honeysuckle, clematis and climbing roses. The garage, being built onto the utility end of the house with a fire-proof door connecting it to the utility room is much appreciated when you live at 800 feet and it is bucketing down with rain and the car boot is full of groceries from a monthly trip to town. Besides the car it housed a large freezer, a small fridge for animal food, the lawn mower, my potting bench and a large accumulation of things which were rarely used but might be needed some day. I was constantly in and out. There was a door at the back leading into the front garden with a small greenhouse tacked onto the back of the garage. All very handy. The bungalow in Monkleigh was put on the market and, luckily, a cottage in Wheddon Cross came on the market for Mother to buy.

Of course all this needed supervision and many were the journeys we made between Monkleigh and Luckwell Bridge. The ugly, corrugated, outbuildings were taken down and what could not be sold were put in a natural depression near the bottom of the field and buried deep enough for the depression to be filled and turned into a small riding ring for me for schooling horses and giving lessons. We also bought a hen house and created a fruit cage as well as a well-drained patch for growing vegetables. We had quite a busy summer. There were ten sheep in the field keeping the grass sweet for Tanglewood Bey (Tangle) my little riding mare, and a few hens providing us with large brown eggs. These were Norman's concern. The sheep were pampered all winter with grain, hay and a shelter against the elements, and the hens must have been the best fed in the all of West Somerset. Tangle we shared – I rode her and Norman did all the "donkey" work – the mucking out and carrying of water buckets, hay and straw. He also grew all our own vegetables which, with the soft fruits from the fruit cage, guaranteed a freezer full of home-grown produce for the winter.

We were many months without a dog after losing our beloved terrier. We talked about getting another dog, but could not agree on size, shape or colour. My eldest daughter became impatient and exasperated listening to us twittering away, and took matters into her own hands. One evening, as I was taking it easy in my recliner, she staggered in and unloaded an armful of four-month-old Labrador into my lap! I don't know who was the more flabbergasted – Norman or me – or indeed the puppy who had never been in a car before, never into a house and so never onto anyone's lap! For the first and only time in his life, he was somewhat subdued. Having only ever lived in a stable he was quite relieved when we all trooped outside to make him up a bed in one of the loose boxes. Being yellow, I immediately named him Jason, after a long-lived dog of the same breed belonging to friends of mine in Canada.

Having acquired what was obviously going to become rather a large dog, I decided to start as I meant to go on. Before letting him out the next morning, I introduced him to a collar and lead. I spent two days bonding with him. Everywhere I went, except upstairs, that dog came too. He became my shadow; he learnt the boundaries of the property, his corner in the kitchen and his night-time stable. When I was away he stuck to Norman.

After us, he loved his food, the cats, going for walks or rides out in the car. He was a very bouncy, active dog, and although he adored cats he would not tolerate the stray Toms we got around during the spring and summer. We would never harm one, but Jason chased them away pretty smartish!

With all the media-hype building into an almost daily tale of dog horror stories, I decided to take proper precautions and enrolled Jason and myself in the local dog training classes. For the first three lessons, Jason was brilliant, only wanting to please, then he became bored and set his agile little brain to work trying to second-guess everything that was required so that he could do the exercises his way. Unfortunately, in the "Lie Down and Stay" lesson he discovered that if he rolled over and waved his legs in the air, everyone laughed. We might have overcome this if I hadn't thought it was rather amusing as well! Future sessions of this exercise were only accomplished reasonably correctly if I stared, stonily, into the distance, all the while aware, out of the corner of my eye, that Jason was waiting for any excuse to do his clown act. Undoubtedly his best, and favourite, exercise was the Long Sit and Recall. He never once broke the Sit and in the Recall would launch himself, like a projectile, down the slippery wooden floor. He never quite timed his sit in front of me correctly, and it was only by taking a swift step sideways that I avoided being knocked into by a seventy pound dog sliding past me on his bottom. The whole exercise was carried out with my staring sternly into the distance and Jason sporting a large grin.

I think that cats, like the tramps of old, must have a sign language. With arrangements of sticks and stones at the entrance to properties travellers of yesteryear could give out vital information to other Gentlemen of the Road. The signs would tell of such things as the presence, or otherwise, of a guard dog, the possibility of hot water to brew a can of tea or even, hopefully, the offer of food and drink. I can't imagine how cats communicate such information, but the signs on our gate must have indicated "friendly abode, suckers for appealing eyes and empty tummies" for three of our four cats were strays.

First came Suzy, our long-haired grey, spayed, female, and the only one of our cats who was actually invited to be part of the household. Her ears became quite bald and shiny and she spent a lot of her time sleeping indoors, and less time out hunting, for which I was truly grateful. She used to be very quick at catching birds, which she liked to eat in the dark, behind the door of the wellie-boot room. Unsuspecting visitors had been known to come out rather fast when confronted by a large fluffy grey ball emitting crunching noises and spewing out the flight feathers of some luckless swallow.

Next was Big Black Tom. I put him at a year or so younger than Suzy. He weighted 14lbs at his last check, and was totally black, with a medium-length coat. In his younger days he used to, literally, bowl over any stray cats trying to home in on his territory. However, finding the weight of his years and his increased girth more suited to a sedentary life style, he spent hours beside the Aga. He would lie at the base but, ever wary of my feet, he preferred the narrow counter built over the electrical works, where he soaked up the warmth and was in constant danger of falling though, to give him his due, he never actually hit the floor the act of slipping usually being enough to waken him.

Tom loved to get upstairs, and when he was in the mood for some loving he lay in wait, listening for Norman to arrive downstairs to make the early morning tea. As Norman opened the kitchen door, Tom shot between his legs to get to the stairs before Norman realised what had happened. Spurred on by the resulting bellow of "Tom, you fool", he galloped up the stairs and along the landing. I would hear him coming, to land, with a thud, on our bed, much pleased with his strategy.

Smarty, our long-haired ginger, arranged things to his own advantage and well-being in a very decided fashion. He and a black kitten were dumped beside a busy minor road leading out of a quiet Devon village. The black one was soon run over, and the ginger one, left on its own, made its way up to our farm where we were living at Monkleigh where it attracted Norman's attention by peering down at him from the top of a haystack and wailing. Here, for a day or two, Norman fed him until he realised that he was feeding half the village cats. The latter, having their own homes to go to, soon stopped coming around when Norman stopped putting out food, but not so the little ginger kitten who, all along, must have observed Norman's comings and goings between the bungalow and across the busy road and the farm. A couple of days later at bedtime on a wild, wet night we heard a cat crying outside the side door, and there was the ginger kitten, blustered with rain, trying to shelter in the limited space by the door. He hovered there, weighing up his choices – the cold, wet, hungry freedom of the outside against the tantalising aroma of warmth and food, but possibly also captivity, beckoning from the open door. Being the sensible fellow he was, he chose the open door, and as he hesitantly slipped inside we both exclaimed 'what a clever little cat you are' and named him Smarty.

Luckily, we enjoyed being busy and looking after stock, and were not for ever wanting to go away on holidays. We derived great satisfaction from our friendly four-footed family, and the crowing rooster with his harem of motley hens. Once we envisaged that our retirement would be one long procession of country pursuits, but, getting so much pleasure from our home and animals, we only went to those Horse Shows and Race Meetings that we knew would be most enjoyable.

Chapter 27
JASON AND MARTHA

Jason was one of life's observers. Not for him the hurly burly of the chase, the headlong pursuit of prey. Coming across a rabbit lying doggo in the long grass in our field he stood and watched as it raced towards the hedge. Once the rabbit had reached the safety of its burrow, Jason put his nose to the ground and fathomed out the line of scent. With his questioning ears and feathering tail he gave a good impression of a true hunting dog. Arriving, eventually, outside the burrow he looked round with a happy grin on his face. Obviously I was meant to applaud this feat of tracking. It was just as well the acquisition of our daily dinner did not depend on his hunting abilities!

At home Jason spent many hours outside the grooming box. Sitting bolt upright or lying watchfully with his head resting on his crossed front legs, he was strategically placed for monitoring the infrequent activity on the lane at the bottom of our short drive, or for supervising tacking up if there was the possibility of a ride out with Tangle. On our walks he would stand and watch things that attracted his attention with an enquiring look on his face and his tail gently waving. This could be another walker, a buzzard on the ground, a squirrel running up a tree or a blackbird scuffling among last year's dead leaves. Any one of a number of things would hold his attention. Seeing him standing on a knoll looking alertly into the dip beyond gave a moment of pleasurable anticipation. He would turn his head impatiently towards me as if to say 'hurry up'. Usually by the time I got there the object of his rapt attention has gone about its business and I was none the wiser. It was a joy to go walking with such a dog.

I well remember the beginning of December 1988; 6.30pm of the first Monday to be precise. My daughter and her partner had been for the weekend and they had left, at the crack of dawn, absolutely laden with extra bedding and warm clothes to help ease life in the miserable caravan in which they were living. I had been busy all day, tidying and setting things to rights again. Having made a conscious effort to have our meal ready early, I was looking forward to a long sit down by a good log fire, as the weather was turning decidedly chilly.

This night I went out of the back door and nearly trod on a little scrap of white, black and tan cat. It shot off under the car and then, as I stood still, it came out, looked up at me, and spoke. A small head, one bald ear and a much distended stomach. Obviously female. My heart went out to her. I put some food onto a saucer and gave it to her. She took two huge gulps of the food and paused for a moment to go 'Brrup, Brrup' (Thank You, Thank You), before returning to finish off what I had given her, in double quick time. She then retreated to the back of the garage and settled down on the grass bag of the lawn mower and began to wash.

I spent the next hour phoning all around the neighbourhood to see if anyone had lost a cat. This was rather a pleasant exercise, as once we are into winter we seem to lose contact with our neighbourhood acquaintances. Searching for the owner of this cat was a good excuse for some friendly conversation. Sadly, no-one I spoke to had lost a cat so, deciding to search further afield, I wrote out a notice to go into the village Post Office window the next day.

At bedtime that evening I took a small feed to the back of the garage and placed it just under the bumper of the car. Very warily, she jumped off the mower and went to the feed. Again, partly through gulping the food, she paused to go "Brrup, Brrup", whilst shooting a quick glance at me. The garage was bitterly cold and while busy covering up the sacks of potatoes and carrots I thought to fix up a bed for the new acquisition. Hoping that she would accept my offer, I placed a cardboard box with some warm bedding on top of the mower box and stood back to watch her reaction. She walked around me at a distance and eventually jumped up and into the box. I closed the garage door, figuring that she would most likely leave through the cat flap during the night, and went to bed.

Lo and behold! She was still in the box the next morning! She quickly jumped out, under the protection of the car, went up near the back door and demanded food! After eating a light breakfast, light because I didn't want to overload her tummy, she sang to me the most incredible noise I have ever heard from such a small creature! She stayed in the garage all day, except for one mad dash to the flowerbed to do her business, when she thought that no-one was looking!

I had a good heart-to-heart with Jason about 'this poor, starving stray, and how pretty she was and so appreciative of my feeding her and giving her a warm box, and she was a nice kitty and not to be chased', all the while keeping him firmly in hand on the lead as we went in and out of the garage. A stranger coming upon me unawares would have thought me quite ga-ga talking to Jason in this fashion, and the resident felines seemed not to know that she was around. I found myself muttering at intervals 'I already have three splendid cats, I need another one like a hole in the head'.

But, here she was and here, she had decided, she was going to stay. Even though she would not let me touch her, she always thanked me when I fed her and at other times she sang to me, walking up and down under the back bumper of the car, just out of reach. In blissful ignorance, little knowing what was in store for us both, I continued to try to make friends with her.

By day three this cat was getting a little bolder, actually venturing to sit just inside the back door. Jason was treating her with caution, giving her a wide berth, but at the same time wagging his tail furiously, and the "gang" had noticed she was there. Well I never, they scattered in all directions, hissing, spitting, backs up and threatening to leave home. Fortunately we have three doors into the house because, for 24 hours no-one would come near the back door. Suzy would only use the front, sunroom, door, or the sitting-room window. Smarty would arrive, complaining bitterly, on the kitchen window sill and, in fits and starts, allow himself to be persuaded in through the front door. Tom was the first to give in and walk past her into "my own house, dammit!". Suzy took a little longer, but I was getting thoroughly fed up with the circus performance produced by Smarty. He seemed bent on embarking on a new career as a trapeze artist, as he took to making flying leaps off counters, over her head to the door, even once whizzing past my head as I came in the door, emitting a howling, screeching noise as he went.

The following day she was showing signs of having been a house cat, being determined to establish herself within the confines of the house despite what the other cats had to say, and they said plenty. Had it been summertime, with a plentiful supply of rabbits just up the lane, I believe they would all have eaten out, but as it was winter, and a cold one, they continued to return home for meals. Protesting bitterly at having to go anywhere near the new arrival, they nevertheless ate two good meals a day. As I had seen no sign of disease in her, I permitted her to stay in the utility area and decided that it was time to give her a name. As it was Christmas time and I was by now certain that she was pregnant, I named her Mary, but decided that this was bordering on the sacrilegious and changed it to Martha. The unexpected cold snap was really becoming established and the garage was freezing cold with draughts sweeping in under two doors. That night, Martha put herself to bed in a corner of the utility and I let her stay.

To keep her safe from bullying by the others, I had to shut her in, which meant that they couldn't get to their litter tray. I moved this into the kitchen and made another one for Martha. By giving Suzy, Tom and Smarty the run of the dining room as well as the kitchen, I made sure that Suzy could hide herself away in the old bread oven to one side of the open fireplace in the dining room – the 'boys' would occasionally beat up Suzy if shut up in too confined a space for long. They thought it great to be allowed to sleep in the dining room – lots of comfortable seats, so necessary for a good night's rest after a busy day spent, in the main, eating and cat-napping.

From the utility it was a short step right into the kitchen, and the next day Martha took up residence on the mat by the Aga, and began her training as an opera star. One of us had only to stand by her and say a kind word, and she would look up at us and sing, and sing, and sing. The strength and durability of her purring quite at odds with her strange, thin little body. Gradually, even Smarty accepted this invasion of his domain and we continued, in an atmosphere of increasing calm, to Sunday.

Chapter 28
THE CHANGING SEASONS

On Sunday morning I heard Martha sneezing. I was filled with dread and my over-sensitive stomach muscles clamped up, as if in a vice. All the while busy with Sunday lunch, I kept looking at her and wondering, was she sickening? Or not? What was the matter? Would she infect my other cats? These questions, and more, played round-abouts in my head whilst I coped with roast beef, potatoes and parsnips, two veg. and a pud. My mother and her dog joined us for lunch, and afterwards I walked the two dogs.

We were blessed with some good Rights of Way and, invariably, I followed the same route. For years I appreciated the changing seasons, watching over the same piece of countryside, week by week. There was a choice to be made – the short, sharp, climb or the longer more gradual, uphill gradient. Even feeling stuffed from over indulging at lunch, I preferred the short, sharp pull. Once that agony was over, I strode on across the fields with comparative ease. Before striding on, however, I had a breather, to look down the slope and reflect on the changes each season brings.

Each spring the blackbird, from the hawthorn opposite my bedroom window, serenaded his mate nesting snugly in the honeysuckle close by. Robins darted in and out of the lilac tree on the front lawn, their beaks stuffed full of moss and twigs. Overnight, it seemed, the rooks wove their untidy bundles of sticks into nests, high in the bare branches of the many stands of beech dotted around the countryside. Everywhere the trees and hedgerows thought forth their summer finery. First as tight, glossy buds, followed by the unfurling of those buds into a haze of soft green leaves, all fresh and smiling in the welcoming sunshine. The grass thickened into a dark green mantle over the fields and, all around, there was evidence of the exploding rabbit population, badgers spring cleaning their holts and the mole's frenzied subterranean activities.

Buzzards drew attention to themselves with their high, plaintive mewing as they lazily wheeled and climbed on the thermals rising from the valley below. The fields filled up with ewes and their young lambs and for April and the beginning of May, we walked elsewhere. Strange dogs, even well under control, pose a threat to newly-lambed ewes and, hating to see them running and 'baaaaing', often leaving their lambs behind, I gave this route a miss.

More time was given, in summer, to propping up the gates, seeking to cool down in the breezy gateways. With arms resting on the top bar I enjoyed the ever-moving patterns of sunlight and shadow on the hills and valleys as the clouds chased across the sky playing "peek-a-boo" with the sun.

The fields changed colour overnight as farmers threw all their energies into haymaking. Tractors, with cutters or balers, went steadily on from mid-morning, when the dew had evaporated, through to late at night. They were often to be heard long after dark, hauling bales, their headlights slicing into the balmy, summer nights. The air was full of the soft drone of bees busy collecting nectar from the profusion of wild flowers that, following each other in pre-ordained succession, kept our banks and verges in a constant kaleidoscope of colour. My flower garden, being semi-wild, needed much attention throughout spring and summer. Each year the wild part threatened to take over the cultivated section, and I asked myself, "When is a wild flower not a wild flower?" – "When it's a weed growing in my flower borders".

Of all the seasons and the many moods of this hilly region, winter most caught my imagination. Even if the weather was mild, the well-worn tracks, where the outlying sheep and cattle followed the trail of fodder across the barren fields, proclaimed "It is Winter". There was a feeling in the air, everything is dead-ish, sleeping – if cold and frosty, one could even say enduring the waiting period, before the first stirrings of spring would bring the promise of renewal. The dogs ranged hither and thither, picking up the scents of badger, fox, rabbit or buzzard.

In times of hard frost with, perhaps, snow on the tops, snipe would come in. If Jason put them up from the wet, marshy areas where the little springs rise which feed our River Quarme, they would break away in wild zig-zag flight, uttering loud, hoarse, cries. Occasionally we surprised a fox working a hedgerow or curled up tight in a sheltered hollow in the middle of a field, seeking warmth from the weak winter sun. Oftentimes, a buzzard would lift off as we come over the brow of a hill, to skim away just above ground level, leaving me with a feeling of wonder and delight at the ease with which such a large bird took to the air.

But, this December day, I walked fast, hoping to obliterate the small knot of gnawing worry sitting, like indigestion, somewhere below my midriff.

Chapter 29
THE BEGINNING OF THE STRUGGLE FOR MARTHA'S HEALTH

Coming in from the walk all seemed very peaceful, Martha was sleeping beside the Aga and Mother and Norman were well away, in front of a dying fire, in the sitting room. I rattled around, mending the fire and moving the kettle onto the hotplate for tea, effectively waking everyone up, and the dogs flopped down, well exercised and content, for the rest of the day, to doze until supper time.

At supper time, although Martha ate, she was obviously going off her feed as she didn't quite finish, unheard of for her. On Monday morning I noticed she had had diarrhoea in the night, luckily in the litter tray, but plain to be seen that things were not right in her bowel department. She didn't want her breakfast. She looked bright enough, was still practising her scales, but her breathing was becoming shallow and rapid. I rushed us through an early lunch to make it to town, 10 miles away, for afternoon veterinary surgery.

Martha showed no objections at being put into our cat carrying crate, adding weight to my theory that she had either escaped from a moving car or had been dumped, well out in the countryside, to fend for herself. There were a couple of protesting "me-ows" during the drive, really because she wanted to hear my voice as she was making no effort to escape.

Our friendly, cat-loving vet Mr Denham gave her a most thorough examination. Although her lungs were wheezy she did not have pneumonia, and he decided that a long-lasting injection of antibiotics would put her right. At this point it was established that she was not pregnant and Mr Denham suggested that I make an appointment for the following week for her to be spayed. I thought "Fine. Not much wrong here", and returned home, criticizing myself all the way for having taken pity on a stray.

By midday of the following day, Tuesday, I was getting worried as Martha would neither eat nor drink. In the evening I found her vomiting white, bubbly stuff and discovered that her bowel movements were showing signs of blood and becoming increasingly loose. I began to feel desperate. I do like to be in control of all aspects of my life, and here was a situation developing that was promising to run out of control. Children and animals are fine until things start to go wrong with them. In these situations I become excitable and run around in a panic, feeling totally unprepared and unable to cope. At nine I telephoned the vet's, a pleasant-sounding lady vet whom I did not know was on duty. Although willing to see Martha, we decided that she was still well under the influence of the previous day's antibiotic injection, but I had to get fluids into her. Glucose in water, preferably, but failing that sugar in water.

Of course, I didn't have any glucose. With the best intentions in the world, first aid wise, I never seem to have the exact thing required. When in doubt, I always telephoned my good neighbour and friend Mary, who lived below our vegetable garden. She didn't think she had any glucose either, but phoned back very quickly to say that she had found some. It was definitely oldish, as the price tag read 50p, but as it hadn't been opened we figured that it would be alright to use. By the wavering light from an almost exhausted torch I dashed out into the cold, dark night to get the precious packet. Coming back in, I saw Martha drinking from the water bowl, and five minutes later she was vomiting, the same white, bubbly stuff as before. I rushed to phone the vet, terrified that she might no longer be at the surgery. When her calm voice answered, I made myself sit down on the telephone chair whilst I talked to her. Fresh instructions. Martha was to be kept away from the water bowl. I was to get glucose down her every hour, keep her warm and take her to the morning surgery. With great difficulty, by using a horse syringe, I got some liquid down her and then turned my thoughts to making her warm and comfortable.

Until Martha became really ill, I never realised how the draughts whistled across the floor of our kitchen. When we designed the kitchen, it was intended that the Aga be on the east wall with its electrical works on the left and a small counter built over as a work surface. The glass door to the utility was to be next on the left, so standing cooking I would receive lots of light from this door and the north-facing kitchen window. This arrangement had worked very well in our previous home in Devon.

Unfortunately, when the site engineer for Aga came, I was not in. Upon returning, I found that the Aga was to be on the south wall with the electrical works on the right and, as you have guessed, my back to the light. I put up some resistance to this plan, but to no avail. The builder and Norman blinded me with theories as to why the Aga had to go on the south wall. Eventually I shrugged my shoulders and conceded. With hindsight, I realise that it was just simpler and more convenient for the chimney to be installed straight up instead of putting in an elbow! Most likely they had already bought shares in the soon-to-be-privatised electricity companies because, even in the middle of a brilliant summer's day, I had to put on the 8ft strip light to make a sauce! To go back to the draughts and their exclusion. I rigged Martha up in the cage as close to the Aga as it would go. She had a warm hot water bottle and various layers of newspaper and blanket, so that when she was either sick or incontinent I could remove a layer with the least possible fuss and disturbance. I wrapped the cage with blankets and on the outside placed a large seat from an old armchair, standing up against the side. This would have worked very well if the Aga had been on the east wall, she would even have been out of the draughts, but as the space was very limited between the Aga and the door, the cushion stuck out a little. I tripped over it a couple of times until I automatically swung a little wider on my journeys back and forth. Norman found it more difficult. Each time the cushion ended up under the kitchen table from the toe of his boot. I patiently replaced it until he too became adept at avoiding it.

Each time I ministered to Martha I found this cushion very comfortable to kneel on. Martha was not amused at my efforts to induce her to take some liquid. There is a knack to inserting a syringe into the side of a cat's mouth so that the liquid goes down its throat on the inside, and not down the chest on the outside. It is useless to insert the syringe and then give a good push on the plunger. Using a 20cc syringe to administer 5cc was making things difficult enough without contending with the struggles of the cat, and our first efforts, whilst not actually drowning her, did little to make her feel better.

I stayed up until midnight so Martha had three lots of glucose, and then I got up at 2.00 am, 4.30 am and 6.30 am. Each time involved a clean up and change of bedding and a row over accepting any liquid, my kneeling on the cushion and Martha backing into a corner of the cage.

Chapter 30
GETTING TO GRIPS WITH A NEW ROUTINE

At 7 o'clock I took Norman up a cup of tea, got dressed and informed the poor man, quite sharply, that if he wanted to eat breakfast with me he'd better get out of bed pronto as I was heading for the 9.00 am surgery. Again, Martha made no objection to being carried in the cage or to the journey. Mr Denham confirmed my feelings that she was seriously dehydrated and, except for her bowel movements not being the colour of mustard, showing all the symptoms of Infections Feline Enteritus. My next immediate worry was for the three cats back home, but Mr Denham assured me that, being older, they were likely to remain immune. As I had to return to Minehead in the afternoon, I left Martha there so that she could be given fluids intravenously.

There were two ways we used for travelling to and from Minehead. We went via Wheddon Cross, Timberscombe and Dunster or up over Dunkery and down through Luccombe to join the Porlock to Minehead road. I decided to go home over Dunkery.

The pleasurable feeling, once we had left the main road, of driving "up into the hills" drew like a magnet. The narrow, twisting lane to Luccombe, then the slightly wider road up Chapel Steep to Webbers Post. Here the car had a five minute breather, if we were in no particular hurry, for Norman to search, with binoculars, for a sighting of deer, whilst I wandered amongst the whispering pines hoping to catch a glimpse of the shy, elusive tree creepers. Then up again, through the hairpin bend, there were resident kestrels, tirelessly hovering on the currents of air or gliding over the contours of the hill, searching for prey, and so to the top.

In winter we kept our eyes peeled as the deer, appreciating the absence of summer ramblers, were often seen, on a wind-free day, browsing or lying up, out in the open. The climb, which seems endless from the back of a horse, was soon accomplished in our modern conveyance.

On this day I was scooting along when, halfway down the incline towards Dunkery Hill Gate, a quiver of movement caught my attention. Giving a quick look in the rear-view mirror, I slammed on the brakes and pulled into the side of the road. A large hind was trotting through the heather towards the road. Behind her came a mixed herd of hinds and half-grown calves, with a young stag and pricket bringing up the rear. They looked quite disturbed. The lead hind, with head well up and ears flicking nervously back and forth, searched for the danger. There was a hesitation at the road, but, once determined, they flowed across just in front of me, swinging around away from the road and looking back from whence they had come. I wondered what had startled them until I heard a voice yelling at a dog to "come to heel"! The danger past, the herd wandered deep into the combe and I continued home much cheered by the sighting, serving to remind me there were other things still in my life besides the desperately-ill cat.

We returned to Minehead in the afternoon. Hoping to see deer again we went over Dunkery. The road was very quiet, and we surprised a pair of red grouse drinking from a roadside pool; the last sighting of these birds on the Dunkery moors, but saw no deer. After a busy couple of hours spent getting hair cuts, buying groceries and picking up a supply of books from the library, we went for Martha.

Deep down I had been hoping that the vet would keep her in overnight, but no such luck! She had been given an injection of Dusolyte under her skin and looked much filled out. This injection was to replace lost body fluids and, being full of essential vitamins, give her system a boost. We came home armed with liquid oral antibiotics and instructions to get liquids inside her.

Every hour for the rest of the day and every two hours during that Wednesday night I got small quantities of glucose and water down her. I thought that she was thin when she arrived, but she was positively plump then compared to how she was now. I was almost afraid to handle her, she was all skin and bone, with a lifeless coat – and she felt very fragile indeed. There was no escape – she lay in the cage, dribbling stuff from her rear end and resenting the resulting change of bedding every hour before I gave her some liquid from the syringe.

Occasionally, she leapt out of the cage to lie beside the Aga, looking all stiff and obviously in pain. If she then wandered off, I would put her back into the cage and swab the floor where she had touched it with disinfectant. I was forever washing my hands so they were becoming very sore, red and chapped. The eczema patches that, in times of stress, break out below my thumbs were having a field day and looking very ugly. My mother suggested that immersing my hands in a bowl of Dettol might prove beneficial, rather than constant washing, and how right she was.

Although my hands started to heal, I did not want to prepare any food with my hands – not to mention finding the time to do so! Giving a sick cat liquid each hour might not sound too bad until you come to do it. The hourly attention took up at least a quarter of an hour each time, so three quarters of an hour from the last hand washing it was time to start all over again.

Bread making went by the board. It had taken me four years on and off to come up with a brown bread recipe which worked in the Aga. The whole exercise could have been achieved in half the time if I had just thought to buy an oven thermometer, and at least have known the temperature with which I was attempting to cook. Persistence finally paid off, and I had stopped buying bread. Now, however, I filled up the limited space left in the freezer after stuffing it full of home-produced garden fruit and vegetables with some shop bread.

I found it most satisfying to donate loaves of bread to fundraising coffee mornings. How eagerly they were snapped up. Equally satisfying was to have a cupboard full of Bramley apples for winter use and shelves of home-made jams and chutneys. My squirreling instincts were uppermost during the summer months anything that couldn't be eaten at the time of harvest was preserved in some way. For healthy living it is essential to keep as close as possible to Nature's larder and to avoid the colourings and preservatives with which so many foods are treated these days.

Jason was taking the sudden lack of attention in good part. He knew that something awful was going on, and would sit as close as he was allowed to the Aga and watch all the fuss. If my temper became a little ragged, he retired to his corner, from whence he could keep an eye on proceedings without the risk of being yelled at. Norman took over giving him his daily exercise. Tom, Suzy and Smarty kept well away, appearing at meal times and bedtimes, otherwise leaving the kitchen to Martha and me.

Norman was beginning to feel lonely and neglected. Increasingly occupied as I was with the cat, Norman sat by himself in the evenings. Endeavouring to keep things as normal as possible, this evening after our meal, I repaired to the sitting room. Determined to stay awake, I dropped into a deep sleep, forgetting to warn Norman about the alarm clock. It cannot have been funny, snoozing away in front of your warm log fire, TV burbling in the corner, when suddenly an alarm clock of which you had not been aware jangles into life, causing your sleeping wife to leap to her feet and stumble from the room for yet another stint of nursing. Jason leapt into the air barking wildly. Suzy, until then peacefully sleeping on Norman's lap, painfully dug her claws into his knees as he jerked awake. His resultant yell of anguish brought Jason running after me to the kitchen, with his tail between his legs. We decided, for the preservation of our marriage, to discontinue this particular experiment.

Chapter 31
A RACK OF RUINED BREAD

The orderly procession of our days was totally disrupted. Our early morning tea roles were reversed. Norman was now the one left lying snugly in bed waiting for tea to arrive, and no cuddle and cosy chat about our plans for the day either. It was 'Drink up and get up, please' as I dumped a mug of tea on his bedside table. Then a mad dash outside to feed Tangle and let Jason out, administer to Martha and feed the others before attempting breakfast.

The further into the crisis we went, the closer came Norman's toast to resembling a burnt offering, thereby lending weight to his contention that toast is nothing but 'a rack of ruined bread'! The threat of an electric toaster to add to the already over-cluttered counter tops drew ever nearer. Jason, quick to take advantage of the relaxing of mealtime rules, took to sitting as closely as possible to Norman. With his tail gently fanning the floor and his big brown eyes watching every mouthful, he pleaded to be allowed to help with the burnt crusts. His pleading was not in vain. Some mornings, such was his consumption of toast, I might as well have laid a place at table for him!

Norman was so lucky because he could keep busy outside with the daily chores. Once he had struggled through breakfast there was Tangle to dress up in her New Zealand rug and turn out in the field (she was most likely wondering why she wasn't being ridden each day); the sheep and chickens to feed; the box to muck out and Jason to walk. I envied him his busy morning in the fresh air away from the hourly nursing, the smell of disinfectant and the overall worry.

By Thursday afternoon Martha was again serious dehydrated. I felt I wasn't giving her enough nourishment but I was doing the best I could with the instructions which 1 had been given. Hindsight tells me it was maybe for the best that she wouldn't eat, but I couldn't help feeling that my nursing was lacking some essential ingredient. I am sadly deficient in experience when it comes to caring for small animals. I have never felt inclined to take on the impossible task of trying to save fledgling birds by feeding with a pair of tweezers or baby hedgehogs with an eye dropper. Now, even to my untutored mind, it was apparent that Martha needed some more veterinary attention.

Norman elected to come with me to Minehead for the evening surgery. We left Gunns in brilliant moonlight, clear, cold and sparkling, a hint of frost to come.

Martha had a hot water bottle well wrapped in blankets to lie on and more blankets were draped around her cage to keep out draughts, really quite a performance to get ready for these expeditions.

On the lower ground, between Timberscombe and Dunster, we encountered patches of whispy fog, and Minehead was beneath a thick, white, woolly blanket. This was very confusing and a reversal of the normal situation. So often, for weeks it seems, we, who live on the hills, have our heads in the clouds whilst Minehead and Porlock enjoy clear skies and sunshine, and here I was, on my mercy mission, reduced to a crawl in familiar streets suddenly made strangely outlandish by the fog. With both side windows down and the cold clammy air swirling into the car we crept forward, searching for the turnings we needed to arrive facing the correct way on the one way system outside the surgery.

Maybe because of the fog Martha was the only patient. The poor little thing was removed to the back room for a repeat injection of Dusolyte. From my seat in the waiting room I heard her cry out as it was administered. At this point I really began to question what I was doing. It was becoming such a battle for us all. I sat there going over in my mind the words to use to Mr Denham to explain why we should call it quits on this cat. Of course, when confronted by Mr Denham and a plumper-looking cat my words dried up. As he pointed out, she was still showing so much interest in what was going on around her, she even sang to him five minutes after the injection, how could we put her down? Reassured, we drove home with some additional instructions. We were to 'get some food into her' but how was not explained!

Twice that evening we force fed her, some steamed cod with a little melted butter to help it down. A messy business. Norman trying to hold a struggling Martha on the kitchen table so I could insert tiny slivers of fish into her mouth and stroke her throat to encourage her to swallow was most stressful. Martha was surprisingly strong, greasy fish was from one end of the table to the other with Jason continually trying to catch any bits which fell onto the floor. The resulting loss of tempers evolved into a scene from some ghastly nightmare. The only difference being that this was for real, I wasn't going to wake up and find it was a dream dissolving before I had grasped the gist of it. It was time to review the situation.

Norman retired to the sitting room where, arriving with a placating cup of tea, I found him immersed in the battles and troubles of other people's lives as seen through the medium of the 10 0'clock news. Hadn't he had enough storms and strife for one day? Jason was curled up tight in his basket. He had not enjoyed the shouted threats and counter threats that had reverberated around the kitchen table with the velocity of a ping pong match. Martha was lying innocently back in her cage. I wondered what to do next?

Obviously devising a better way of producing some nourishing food had top priority. A soup, perhaps? A thick soup that would go through a syringe seemed like a good idea. I boiled up some rice, added a joint of chicken and placed the pan in the bottom oven of the Aga to cook overnight, planning to rub the chicken and rice through a sieve once they were thoroughly cooked.

Norman went of to bed and I settled down to catnap in the sitting room with the comforting ticks of the alarm clock for company. At 2.30 am, having decided I needed long enough in bed to achieve a deep sleep, I went out to the kitchen to give Martha one more drink and clean up. Things were looking bad. She was no longer lying as cats do, curled up tight in a ball or stretched out relaxed, in front of a heat source. She was lying braced with her feet hard against the bars of the cage and her head thrown back. A horrible sight. If I hadn't thought I was close to cracking up I would not have contemplated leaving her alone. I was so tired, so strung up and probably sending forth very negative vibes. The thought of sitting there, helpless, watching her die was too much for me. Making her as comfortable as possible with her hot water bottle and blankets, I crept away to bed.

Once upstairs and in bed, although not expecting to, I did achieve a couple of hours of that deep sleep for which I longed. Waking up well before the alarm clock went off was a disappointment, but I did feel refreshed and was able to tiptoe downstairs without waking Norman. More than half expecting a dead cat, I was much heartened to find her looking a little brighter and holding up her head to watch me approach.

The morning went on much as usual. Burnt offerings for Jason, more clean ups for Martha and persuading her to take, via the syringe, some of the soup. This was not to my liking and I started searching through my cookery books for beef tea recipes. Rapidly running out of blankets for her I threw all of the soiled ones, with a large measure of disinfectant, into the washing machine and set it to its hottest programme. Afterwards, I wondered just how wise I had been, I should have burned the lot.

In the middle of the morning our post arrived, with a thud, on the hall mat. A couple of circulars, a bill, and oh joy, the seed catalogue. This welcome arrival meant many hours could be whiled away in pleasurable anticipation of the delights of spring planting, oblivious to the miserable weather outside. Norman liked to get things in early, forgetting that 800 foot above sea level on Exmoor is very different from 400 feet in Devon. Though many years retired from farming, he still thought like a farmer and relied on the old countrywise sayings.

I had an inkling how these sayings evolved through the seasons of the year and down the centuries. No matter what date the calendar on the wall said, we always got a strong wind in this garden when the daffodils were in full bloom and as the big buds on my peonies burst into flower. Whether they opened early or late, along came the wind, buffeting the heavy flower heads in all directions and, unless carefully staked, breaking them to the ground. Each year in the garden was marginally different from the last, and each year was governed by Nature's calendar. People's observations, down the years, have led to the amassing of a wide range of weather predictions. Norman always watched March closely. Unpredictable in its own weather habits, it yet gives us two good indications for the coming months: "misty mornings in March mean frosty mornings in May". Many an anxious evening in May was spent debating whether to cover up the rows of young plants or risk a touch of frost.

Covering up is a fiddly, time-consuming exercise and, more often than not, the risk was taken and they were left uncovered. One year Norman was seen to cover the young potato plants with straw. This certainly kept the frost from doing any damage, but it also encouraged an enormous growth which was weak and straggly and susceptible to wind! Although no longer farming, we still needed hay for Tangle and the behaviour of the sheep in the middle of a warm March day was worthy of note: "sheep that go to shade in March will go to shelter in June". We hated to see sheep lying panting in whatever shade they could find during March as we then feared for a wet hay harvest.

I had no time for browsing through the seed catalogue, but it was something of interest for Norman to get stuck into. Apart from the one flare up, he was being very kind to me over this cat, humouring me and not making waves about the mounting cost, even though he was convinced 'it' had a tumour and 'it' was going to die. At every new crisis when, yet again, I headed for Minehead and the comforting aura of the veterinary clinic, I had to clamber over the hump of his scepticism.

Chapter 32
IS THERE NO END TO THIS?

At midday I was fearing for Martha again. She had gone back to lying braced and stiff, though not as rigid as during the night. Just as I was finishing the lunchtime dishes she gave a despairing cry and the kitchen was invaded by a terrible smell. Clamping my hand over my nose, in fear and trepidation, I looked into the cage. The most vile stuff was pouring from Martha's bowels, but she wasn't dead. At great speed, gagging as I worked, I placed Martha on a blanket with her back against the Aga and rushed outside with the cage. Having dumped everything into a sack for burning and washed the cage, I stood in the courtyard taking great gulps of fresh air and gradually felt a little less sick. Cold and shaky, but no longer in imminent danger of throwing up.

With Martha once again warmly ensconced in the cage, I phoned the veterinary clinic. Afternoon surgery was finished and the vets had left, so instead I had a tearful talk with Maggie, the surgery assistant. I was awash with feelings of helplessness. I seemed to be getting nowhere. Maggie, with a hundred and one jobs waiting for her attention, heard me out. It was such a relief to talk to someone outside the home, moreover someone who understood the trauma of caring for a sick animal. Maggie was calm, practical and matter of fact. Just what I needed. She said: 'Where there is life there is hope. I suggest you bring her in for evening surgery.' I came off the phone if not exactly whistling a happy tune, at least a little lighter in spirits.

Mother, who was keeping in touch constantly by phone, heard of this latest catastrophe and suggested that she come down to watch over Martha while I grabbed a couple of hours sleep. Norman was in the sitting room totally absorbed in the promised glory of giant onions, prize winning carrots and eternal colour in the flower beds, all found predicted between the glossy pages of the seed catalogue. I could tell that Mother, while generous with her offer of keeping an eye on Martha for me, didn't relish doing just that in the kitchen. Never one to waste a good fire, she came up with the brilliant idea that Martha, who was looking much brighter since her appalling turnout, needed stimulating! I had my doubts but bowed to her unspoken desire to be beside the fire in a chair. Visions of two hours in bed rapidly fading, I hunted around for some makeshift draught excluders which I arranged at the foot of each door, finally placing Martha on a thick square of blanket on top of the hearthrug. Something told me it would be unwise to leave them to it, and I reluctantly collapsed into my recliner.

Well, we stimulated Martha to the detriment of any rest I had hoped to have.

She lay and observed the room for approximately ten minutes before moving off the blanket to wander around. She decided to lie at the back of the room where I couldn't easily see her. Worried she would have an accident on the carpet, I placed a blanket under her. Immediately she no longer wanted to lie just there. Anyway, she was tired of blankets. I expect that the carpet felt cool and refreshing to her body, so began a procession around the room – a few steps, a flop down, a few steps and a flop down. After about an hour she had ambled around the whole room, and I decided enough was enough and returned her to the kitchen.

After this unintended exercise in the sitting room, she seemed content to lie with her back to the comforting warmth of the Aga, looking around from a different angle, although, except at night, she had not been shut in the cage. The top had always been kept open so that she could jump out if she felt so inclined. Right from the beginning I had thought it important to keep up her interest, fearing her becoming introspective, giving up and dying.

At our mealtime, when we should have been thinking of leaving for Minehead, down came the fog. Martha seemed no worse, she was still on antibiotics, of course, I was getting liquid and chicken soup down her, so we decided to stay at home.

Early Saturday morning, at that awful 2am slot of the night when, I am convinced, life is at its lowest ebb, Martha was in worse trouble. She suddenly seemed to go almost lifeless. By this time I had some beef jelly organized and I got as much down as she would swallow, followed by another go at 4am and by 8.45am I was sitting in my car right at the surgery door. No one was going to queue jump my right to be seen first!

Morning surgery was taken by Mr Denham's partner, Mr Gibbins, and by 9.05 he was examining Martha. He studied Mr Denham's notes and asked me some detailed questions. I was feeling on the defensive for not braving the fog the previous evening, but he only commented, quite mildly, on her extreme state of dehydration. It was now the seventh day since I first noticed she was becoming unwell. Mr Gibbins thought the disease had most likely run its course and with some additional help from him and attentive nursing from me we might pull her through.

His suggestion that I go away and do some shopping fell on deaf ears. My purse was clean shopped out, never before this had I made so many six trips to town in a one week period. I elected to wait. He warned me that it might be a long wait, depending on the number of other patients he had to see. He wanted to give Martha an intravenous injection and needed absolute quiet, which of course couldn't be guaranteed until surgery had finished. I toyed with the idea of driving uptown for a coffee, but decided the energy required in finding a parking space was not worth the effort. I settled myself on their hard chairs – no chance of a nap, and watched the procession of dogs, cats and a rabbit pass through the waiting room.

To while away the time I tried guessing the severity of the animals' conditions by the looks on the owners' faces. Even the dogs' attitudes gave much away. The Alsatian, sitting bolt upright beside its owner, was obviously terribly worried and would far rather not have been there. A collie lay quietly, shaking like a leaf, at its owner's feet and the far corner of the room was occupied by a terrier, full of bounce and curiosity. The cat owners, though their pets were safely hunkered down in carrying crates, tended to choose seats far removed from the dogs. The owner of the rabbit, a young boy, fearing for his pet's peace of mind while waiting their turn, hovered in the narrow space between the door and the reception desk, effectively creating a minor traffic block.

It is amazing how uncomfortable a veterinary waiting room can be if one has to spend any length of time there. Although bright and airy, it usually lacks the social comforts of other professionals' waiting rooms. There are no comfortable chairs with a small table within easy reach loaded with those glorious glossy magazines so beloved by interior decorators. Here everything is inclined towards the utility of the requirements. Chairs are of basic wood or plastic and the floor is tiled or covered with linoleum for ease of maintenance and cleaning. Reading matter is confined to small information booklets relating to the care and feeding of animals. The sort of thing that is easily stuffed into a pocket if one's dog suddenly bounds across the room to investigate the strange noises emanating from the blanket being so closely clutched on a tense lap.

To stretch my legs, I stood and studied the notice board occupying a large space on one wall. Here a motley collection of advertisements jostled for space among the more mundane notices about prompt payments of accounts and reminders of the necessity of regular worming and vaccinations. If the receptionist is of a methodical turn of mind, the advertisements will follow a logical sequence and one is able to map out a pattern for survival throughout the experience of being owned by a pet.

Firstly, we might be encouraged to take out Health Care Insurance to cover the bills that were surely coming our way. While my animals remained healthy and saw the vet once a year for their inoculations, I never gave it a thought. But being caught out over this matter of Martha's illness had set me thinking. Maybe it is no bad thing to be prepared in advance for unexpected expenses. The housekeeping purse will only stretch so far. Paying the vet's bill instead of buying that juicy piece of prime rib roast so beloved of one's hubby for Sunday lunch is not the most popular of moves.

Frequently the local Dog Obedience Club is advertising classes for beginners, intermediate and advanced. Arriving for the first session of a beginner's class with a young dog can be an event fraught with anxiety. Jason, in our case, was in full control, with feet slipping in all directions on the polished wooden floor, he towed me around the hall, aiming to make friends with everyone there in the shortest possible time. His rather overwhelming overtures of friendship drove one shy little dog to seek sanctuary under a bench from which she refused to budge. Dragged forth to take part in the class, she crept along with her head hanging at one end and her tail at the other. Thankfully, by the end of the course this particular participant was enjoying herself hugely and doing rather better than Jason at the various exercises. Enrolling in obedience classes is a must for gaining that mutual respect and obedience so necessary for trouble free walking with a dog.

Cats love walks too. At the beginning they dash along, tails erect, doing feather-light sideways forays as they bat at pebbles or pounce among the fallen leaves. Unfortunately they have an annoying habit of yowling and lagging behind once they are into territory strange to them, or, even worse, of climbing a tree at the point furthest from home. Both activities are designed to cause maximum worry to the owner, not to mention the embarrassment of she who buys the food and pays the bills. Standing under a well-leafed tree in the middle of nowhere beseeching your favourite moggy to stop parading up and down on a sturdy branch just out of reach and to return to Mother Earth can be a discomforting experience, especially if caught in the act by a troop of sturdy ramblers.

A small notice tucked away in a corner of the notice board informed us that animals which have to be put down or otherwise die while in the care of the clinic will be disposed of by cremation according to today's stringent regulations. For those wishing a more lasting memorial a Companions' Garden of Rest is indicated. There was a choice to be found in this commodity, from the large burial ground with acres of immaculately mown lawns and plots with headstones to the small, intimate type of country garden.

All, in its own way, a source of comfort and reassurance to the pet owner and hopefully providing a buffer between the veterinary surgeon and the raw emotions so often experienced by people who choose to make a four footed creature part of their lives.

Gradually the waiting room emptied and quiet descended. Mr Gibbins disappeared into the back, emerging five minutes later with Martha in her cage. Almost, but not quite, ready for home. Firstly I had to be instructed in my role for the ensuing period of convalescence. I was loaded with new supplies, a tin of Liquivite cat food, a sachet of Lectade, some more syringes and fresh instructions. 5ml of the Liquivite, an easily digestible, extremely nourishing, form of food for ill or very old cats, were to be fed every hour. The Lectade, to be dissolved in a pint of water and stored in the fridge, would replace essential nutrients lost during the illness, and she was to have 5ml of this every half an hour. In effect, ministering to her every half an hour except at night when we could both do with some rest, so every two hours during the night. I was to take her back to the surgery on Tuesday.

I reeled out of the surgery aghast at the thought of syringes every half an hour, albeit feeling I'd now really got something to work with. I couldn't wait to get home and start. Even the look of disbelief on Norman's face when I arrived home couldn't dampen my renewed hope for Martha's survival.

Mother offered to take over the cooking of our main meal of the day, which would leave me freer to concentrate on Martha and, of doubtful benefit, an unforeseen worry about all the Christmassy things which were not getting done. Christmas cards had been arriving, seemingly, for weeks, a daily reminder that most of mine were still to do. Luckily the overseas ones had been sent off in November, long before the advent of Martha. There was a surprise card from an old Canadian friend with a letter asking for advice and ideas about an impending visit to England the following April. Most years Canadian friends or relatives of friends passed through or maybe stayed a night or two, a pleasing legacy of the twenty two enjoyable years which I spent in that large country.

Resolutely putting all thoughts of visitors aside and consigning anything to do with Christmas to the back burner, I prepared to devote myself to Martha.

Chapter 33
DAYLIGHT AT THE END OF THE TUNNEL?

For twenty-four hours there was not much improvement in Martha's condition. Although she had no energy and was weak and lethargic, she clearly resented the increased attention necessitated by the instructions to water or feed her every half hour. Her determination to hang on to life had brought her this far, but she found the methods we employed to help her to do so rather undignified. However carefully I inserted the syringe into the side of her mouth and however slowly I depressed the plunger, some food still came dribbling out. Her neck and chest fur were becoming matted and sticky.

Martha could have faded away if we had waited for her to start wanting food again. As lovingly as possible, I kept determinedly to the routine prescribed by the vet.

On Sunday Mother, an inveterate early riser, arrived as we were finishing breakfast. I hate being caught eating a meal. This morning we were late and she was more than a little early. I'd been up every two hours during the night and had gone back to bed at 6.30 am with a large mug of hot, sweet tea. Knowing that Norman would wake me eventually, I relaxed into a deep sleep. Two and a half hours later I came to in response to an insistent voice: "Gay, it's nine o'clock!" Hence the rather belated breakfast.

Mother, with the briefest of greetings to us, went immediately to look into the cage. After a few moments of silent study she announced that Martha was looking a trifle 'less tense'. I had yet to spot any great change, but often those closest to a sick being are the last to spot any improvement, however hard they look.

We busied ourselves with our allotted tasks. Mother's early arrival, plus her dog Roanne, meant that Norman could walk both dogs whilst lunch was being cooked. He went down to the old mill, now converted into a dwelling. This is a reasonably level walk beside the remains of the leet which carried the water to drive the millwheel. The river from which the leet was taken runs along one side of some meadows, and on the other side are hillocks and little valleys of the old lime workings, still as they were left at the end of the last century, though now covered with grass and providing shelter to numerous foxes, badgers and rabbits. How neat it is, in winter, to identify the occupied warrens. The ring of green in an otherwise white sea of frosted grass betrays the rabbit's underground existence as warm air, rising from his body, holds the frost at bay at the front door to the burrow.

The right of way followed the route taken by the lime carts all those years ago. For a mile or so it was easy going, which suited Norman with his gammy knee. I tended to range over this small area, happily with the owner's consent. The dogs got lots of exercise as they ran up and down the slopes, often retrieving a ball I'd thrown from the highest mounds. Bounding up the slopes was such good exercise for the muscles of their hindquarters and it helped in keeping their wind clear, too.

If there was snow on the ground we were able to track, with ease, the wildlife of the area. Sometimes we came face to face with a fox, probably hungry and on its way to raid our chicken house. Jason had no idea of chasing them, he'd like to play, but no self respecting fox was going to hang around to find that out. One summer we lost eighteen fowl in two afternoon raids, to foxes. The first time the hens were loose and the fox caught and killed twelve, some of them old favourites. The place looked like a battlefield and Norman was so upset. The second raid took place some six weeks later. We had bought new pullets, Norman having spent hours reorganising the run, and we genuinely thought it to be fox-proof. Six foot netting, well secured to the ground. The fox went in over the netting and, after running amok and killing six fowl, went out over the netting carrying one of the pullets. We disturbed his meal as he sat under the neighbour's hedge eating our pullet. Foxes are an absolute menace.

Over our elevenses Mother chided me for being rather silent. In truth, I was off in a dreamlike state picturing Norman with the dogs and imagining what he might be seeing. As I had rather stout wellie boots, I often walked the length of the river, hoping to spot dippers. Although I knew they were there, I seldom saw one. I expect Jason running on ahead and constantly in and out of the water sent them flying swiftly off upstream. Walking along the bank one day, after a torrential rainfall, and marvelling at the strength of our usually placid river, as, swollen with flood water, it raged at the banks restricting its course, I saw him – the dipper.

No longer able to trot along the stony bed of the river looking for food, the dipper was perched on a rock, morosely surveying the turgid brown waters swirling past his feet. He was a picture of utter dejection, too unhappy, even, to fly away at my approach. We stared at each other, communing our feelings across the swollen waters. He shifted his feet and, with a mighty shrug, loosed a fine spray of water from his plumage. I hastened on, lest Jason, sprinting back to see what was keeping me, frightened him from his chosen perch.

I returned to the present with a mental jerk. By Martha's lunchtime feed I could feel a difference in her body. It was more relaxed and malleable. She wasn't so resentful of being moved for the regular change of bedding. Her bowel movements were thickening up and no longer showing signs of blood, and she hadn't vomited all morning. After her syringes, she attempted a little song as I gently stroked the top of her head.

It was a wonderful sound and I began to feel hopeful for her recovery. Norman, coming in from his walk, reported snipe in the marshy areas and ice on all the puddles.

Enjoying our traditional Sunday afternoon by the fire with the papers, and after lunchtime coffee I went sound asleep with Martha on my lap. Mother and Norman, in a rare moment of silent communication, decided my need for sleep was greater than Martha's for food and let me sleep on. Martha, easing herself onto the floor after her longest time ever on my lap, woke me up. Time for syringes again and a refreshing cup of tea.

Tangle, my horse, slept in every night. Longing for some fresh air I decided to fetch her myself. The dogs thought this a great idea and, to make sure I realized how full of energy they were, rushed off down the drive.

Using this as a good excuse to lengthen the task, I followed them to go the long way round, which was really not very long at all. It was down the drive, up the land and down the field above ours, and I picked up Tangle as we came back across our field. Twelve minutes at the most, a satisfying little leg stretch for the end of the day. By this time on a winter's afternoon Tangle was waiting within sight of the gate, anxious to be taken in. It was the only time of year that she asked to be caught.

Once the new grass started to grow in the spring, she no longer felt hungry enough to come to us – we had to go to her when we wanted her. She was usually at the farthest, highest point of the field and, even then, if she was feeling fractious she would avoid capture for up to twenty minutes. This really annoyed Norman who stomped back without her, and threatened never to fetch her again.

I enjoyed Tangle's antics when she occasionally indulged in these fits of independence. She ran circles around me, sometimes coming quite close, with her ears flat back and her eyes rolling, and she would jump and kick as she went past. Once she came very close, she looked as if she had every intention of running me over and I threw the headcollar at her. This uncharacteristic act of mine served to remind her to keep her distance.

I stool and watched, maybe making a move towards her which set her off again, circling and high kicking. I waited for her to run out of steam or get bored with the game. I could tell by her change of expression when I was going to be successful in catching her. Her eyes ceased to flash and roll, a peaceful look came over them and I was able to walk up to her with ease.

She dropped her head into the proffered headcollar and led in like a lamb. Such a change from the previous wild exhibition.

This cold December afternoon was rapidly drawing to a close. It had already been dusk when I left the yard and now, in the gathering gloom, there was the welcome shape of a horse by the fence. Fastening the headrope, we surged through and closed the gate. The dogs ran on ahead and we hurried towards the warm beam of light streaming from the stable doorway.

Chapter 34
BACK, YET AGAIN TO THE VETS

I felt pleasantly invigorated for my short walk in the frosty air, and found myself humming a tune as I fed the animals and then made our tea. Later in the evening, Martha did not seem able to settle. She would not lie quietly on my lap. She was restless and seemed uncomfortable, but in a different sort of way. Suddenly she came to a decision and hurried to the back to the sitting room and proceeded to clean herself. It took her ages. Norman asked "where's the cat?" and I replied "still washing". How happy I was to see her making such an effort to improve herself. Surely this was a good sign?

Mother stayed at home on Monday. We had plenty of leftovers for lunch and Martha was brightening up so rapidly that I could, to a degree, relax our rigid regime. I poached a piece of fish for her, as I thought perhaps she might soon start accepting some solid food. I did so want her to be eating properly by her check up. There was only one dark cloud on the horizon – sometime on Monday night her breathing started to quicken.

On Tuesday morning she fed herself a morsel of fish and drank some stock. At surgery I was told to stop the antibiotic and not to worry about the breathing. Mr Gibbins thought there might be some fluid around her lungs and it would be a good idea to X-ray them in January when she was to be spayed. We came home. No meanderings over the moor. It was now nine days to Christmas and there was a lot of catching up to do. I had a grand old tidy up, put away the cage and gave the floor a final disinfectant swab.

Determined to do something towards Christmas, I got out the boxes of cards and the previous year's list and made a start. Fortunately the ones for Canada, New Zealand and Australia had already been completed and sent off before the advent of Martha. I was so tired from the ten days of physical and mental stress that all I wanted to do was to curl up with a good book and let time drift by. This was a longed-for luxury which was seldom available. Paradoxically I dreaded the time when I might have too few tasks to do, or I be so infirm that reading a book becomes something to do to while away the time.

Martha ate three small meals and either dozed by the Aga or sat on the mat by the back door. At some point it dawned on me that she might be wanting to do her business. I didn't want to let her out in case she became frightened and ran off, yet she seemed to have forgotten how to use the dirt box. This is an old cattle feed tub and the sides are rather high. She had been walking past it on her way to the back door and had used it in the early days of her illness. All clean and sweet-smelling from the fresh sawdust, she didn't remember its purpose or recognise it. By keeping an eye on her and plonking her in the box when she started to wander around looking worried, we reached an understanding.

All day I had been looking forward to a complete night's sleep. I was out of the habit, and within half an hour of dropping off I was wide awake again. I tossed and turned for hours, not wanting to put on the light for fear of disturbing Norman. At three o'clock I could stand it no longer and went down to the kitchen to make tea. As good an excuse as any to check on Martha. She was happy to see me, but her breathing was definitely faster than it had been at bedtime. She slowly lapped at the saucer of stock I offered and sang to me, but things didn't look right. Returning to bed, I set the alarm and willed myself to sleep.

At breakfast Martha would not eat and was listless, although still singing. By mid morning things were no better, and I was beginning to panic. Jason kept trying to talk to Martha and lick her face, and was yelled at as my head was enveloped in the most appalling tension headache. I phoned the vets and left a long, involved message with the receptionist. Both vets were out on call, so we arranged to take Martha in for the 2pm surgery. By lunchtime she was lying stretched out and panting so fast I was unable to count her breaths per minute. She was very frightened. Time for the cage, blankets and hot water bottle. Same routine as previously.

Norman came with me into Minehead. In fact, I think he drove as I was in a very twittery state. For some reason Martha meant more to me than the other three cats put together. I was desperately afraid that this would be the end of her road. Although dreading her loss, I assured Norman that I would insist on her being put down if her pitiful state of distress could not be relieved.

Mr Gibbins was taking surgery, and was quite flummoxed by her state of breathlessness. To X-ray was imperative. He could not treat her by guesswork. I, of course, agreed with this, remembering my conversation with Norman on the way in. Martha was placed in a heated cage to wait until the other patients had been treated.

Wearing one of the incredibly heavy lead lined protection aprons, I helped to hold Martha absolutely still for the X-ray. it only took a few minutes for Maggie to develop the picture, and I was called back in. Mr Gibbins sounded very relieved and said immediately that he could treat her. There was no trachea problem nor any sign of tumours, just a woolly looking area on part of the lung. This was most likely the cause of the original symptoms. Was I prepared to dose her with antibiotics and diuretic pills? Rather a silly question, what else had I done but dose her for the past ten days?

Norman and I made a good team when dosing the cats for their regular worming. The counter behind the Aga was the ideal height. Norman picked up a cat and placed it on the counter. He then gently, but firmly, gripped the front legs.

The cat's body was enclosed between Norman's forearms and his tummy region. I tilted the cat's head back with my left hand and, with the pill held between thumb and first finger of my right hand, I prised open the cat's mouth at the front with my middle finger and dropped the pill onto the back of the throat. Closing the mouth and stroking the throat on the outside, to encourage the animal to swallow, completed the exercise. Most cats tended to struggle for the first couple of times, but dosing this way was so quick and easy that they soon get used to it.

Agreeing to whatever Mr Gibbins thought necessary if it was really going to make her better, I suggested that he give her the first dose right then. For some reason vets are always reluctant to do this, preferring to send you on your way clutching your little packet of pills, with their instructions ringing in your ears. With home over half an hour away and her breathing so laboured, I insisted on her having her first dose there and then. Humouring me, Mr Gibbins popped two pills down her throat, omitting to tell me how rapidly the diuretics worked. We arrived home with the blankets soaked in urine, I guess you could say I got my just deserts.

Martha now needed to be out of draughts, but where she could stretch out and make herself comfortable. Norman's captain-style kitchen chair suggested itself. I covered the seat with a sheet of plastic and squares of blanket and hung blankets on the arms. I placed a hot water bottle under the blankets near the front in such a way that, lying across it, Martha's chest was somewhat elevated. She spent hours lying in this fashion, watching my every move and then, as her breathing eased, she actually curled up and went to sleep. Seeing her sleeping thus bought home to me the fact that during the peak of her illness she never actually slept, she endured, to what depth I will never know.

Chapter 35
CONVALESCENCE: RE-ESTABLISHING OUR MORE NORMAL ROUTINE

Martha started wanting food again after a few hours of starting the new medication, but she was very fussy. Mr Gibbins, anticipating this situation, had suggested that I buy in a couple of tins of pilchards or sardines in tomato sauce. These often prove tempting to a convalescing cat. I opened a tin and waved it under her nose, which excited her but she quickly lost interest when some was placed on a saucer in front of her. I suppose childhood memories prompted the idea that she might eat if fed with a fork. This worked. She would eat if I held the food close to her chin with one hand and presented bits of fish to her off the fork with the other hand. Alternatively, placing the food on the floor and feeding her with the fork whilst stroking her lightly between her shoulder blades proved most stimulating. And so we progressed.

We were still not out of the woods, but things were steadily improving. Three quarters of an hour after each diuretic pill, she flooded her blankets but otherwise was making it to the dirt tray without accident. Her breathing pattern was softer and less laboured. I took to giving her little promenades around the house. Lying along my forearm she fitted nicely between my elbow and my wrist, with her head on my hand. This was no burden as she weighed very little. She enjoyed being carried like this and from the dining room we could watch the birds coming to feed at the tube of nuts and the homemade tin of fat hanging in the branches of the plum tree on the lawn.

The tin of fat was hung upside down to thwart the magpies and starlings. It lasted the little birds about a week, but would be gone in a day if the bigger birds, who are such bullies, were able to eat it too. As it was, we had one particularly agile magpie who learned to jump from the ground, give a twist, much as a basketball player twists to make a net, and grab a billfull of fat before his body weight took him back to terra firma.

Blue tits and chaffinches were our most numerous customers, followed by great tits. Occasionally I saw a coal tit and once in a while a marsh tit. These are difficult to distinguish, and, being rather shy, are easily intimidated by the other birds. Two pairs of greenfinches were frequent feeders and, if all was very quiet in the garden, a pair of nuthatches came to feed, upside down. Again, if all was quiet, one or other of the bullfinches came, flitting from branch to branch in search of tasty young buds. Blackbirds, thrushes and robins completed the tally of birds to be seen from our front room windows during the winter months. And let us not forget the humble sparrow, although they were most often seen around the stables and in the hen house.

The chaffinches loved the nuts but were unable to feed, as did the tits, from the nut container. However, they could hover beneath the tin of fat long enough to grab one or two beakfulls that fell to the ground when other birds were feeding. Once the fat was halfway reduced, this was no longer possible, although one enterprising male has taught himself to hang in the tin, giving a rather precarious imitation of a tit. They bobbed around at the base of the tree, snacking on all the bits that fell to the ground. They all looked perky and well fed.

A turkey carcass hung high in the tree, out of reach of cats, caused great excitement. Being large, the small birds could hang on it whilst picking it clean.

The garden opposite had many brooding, towering, evergreen trees which I found rather oppressive, especially in periods of prolonged wet or persistent fog. At such times I longed for the absentee owner to come along and go wild, as men are sometimes wont to do, with a chain saw and cut the whole lot down. But to do so would have destroyed the habitat of these birds which do so much good in the garden and provide such pleasing winter entertainment.

Carrying Martha around like this was most rewarding, albeit rather time consuming. As I watched her awakening interest and her enjoyment of all our little chats, I was very aware that she appreciated all I was doing for her. There was a rapport building between us, a thread of feeling such as I never envisaged between a cat and human. I had never visualised cats, being such independent creatures, as ever letting down their guard sufficiently to open a line of real communication. I felt awed and honoured by the confidence which she had placed in me.

Preparations for Christmas came and went in a haze. Fortunately it was my sister's turn to entertain on Christmas Day, as I doubt there would have been a meal in our house. The last of our cards were posted on the 22nd, with a prayer on the wind that everyone else had posted theirs early, thereby letting mine through at the last minute.

On Friday night we went to a party. Arriving home at midnight, we divided the chores between us. I ran upstairs to turn on the electric blankets before feeding Martha. Norman supervised Jason's little run out before putting him to bed in his stable. He gave Tangle her late night feed and skipped out her box so she had somewhere clean to lie.

We stood around the kitchen table drinking mugs of tea and discussing our getting up time for the morning. I would lie in if there wasn't any need to feed Martha. We decided to leave food down for her, which meant we had to evict the other cats from the kitchen. Sadly lacking in charity they would have had her snack eaten before we were up the stairs. There was nothing for it but to give them the added run of the sitting room. As far as they were concerned, their standard of living was on the up and up, from the comfortable chairs in the dining room to the very comfortable chairs in the sitting room!

We went to bed and I slept for eight hours. For the first time in nearly two weeks Norman went down for our early morning tea. He reported that Martha had eaten her snack and was asking for more. She had stayed in her cosy chair by the Aga, looked up at him and sung and sung. Every mealtime now she fed herself, looking up at me and going 'Brrurp, brrurp' before starting to eat, as she had when she first arrived. She turned against the fish in tomato sauce and started accepting tinned cat food alternated with steamed cod. Still very weak, she was content to spend hours in Norman's seat, lying, stretched out, watching my every move or curled up in a ball asleep.

On Monday I took her for her check up and she was declared fit I experienced an enormous sense of self satisfaction. Her lungs still sounded wheezy, but she was to continue on the diuretic pills but no more antibiotics. We came home and I put the cage away. You would have thought that now I could relax. The pressure was off, Martha was returned to good health. But not so! It was almost as if I had to have something to worry about. My paranoia settled on the possibility of losing her. I became convinced that she was going to give us the slip, either by an oversight on our part, or by design on hers.

In the open space of the courtyard Martha assumed a feral attitude and crept nervously around the base of the walls, holding her body close to the ground. She ignored any attempts at reassurance. This performance made me extremely uneasy. The slightest noise sent her scurrying for the narrow gap under the door leading into our neighbour's field, and I certainly did not want her out there. Once this escape route was blocked she sought refuge under the car in the garage, much safer.

On Christmas Eve I planned to leave home for a couple of hours to give a riding lesson – getting back to normal, but there was the problem of Martha's security and my peace of mind during my absence. Norman assured me that he was not born in a barn, and having seen the house where he was born, a sizeable Devon farmhouse, I believed him, but, oh dear, I wish he remembered to close the back door each time he passed through it! He was courteous and mindful of the cats' wishes, but they, in true feline fashion, had only to see a door closed against them to want to go through it. At least, that is the excuse he offered up in the face of my frequent annoyance: so often returning cold and tired from giving riding lessons I found the usually warm, cosy kitchen as cold as charity and Norman hugging a fire he had just lit in the sitting room – so illogical!

Obviously I was not going to leave home until I was reassured that Martha was safely indoors and going to stay there. I placed a large notice at eye level on the back door. This read, in a mixture of bold red and black strokes:

    TO ALL WHO ENTER HERE
    THE CALICO CAT INSIDE
    MUST NOT BE LET OUT (and in smaller writing at the bottom:)
    WHOEVER LETS HER OUT PAYS THE VET'S BILLS.

This, unpredictably, scared my neighbours to such an extent that they took to telephoning me before coming up for eggs and left my family, at whom it was aimed, totally unimpressed.

I enjoyed the half hour drive to St Audries for Catherine's riding lesson. She was ready and eager to get started, as there had been a long gap since her last lesson at the end of the summer holidays. I was tempted to cut and run at the end, but the offer of refreshment was too good to pass up. Over the welcome cup of hot coffee and mince pies I regaled everyone with the saga of my traumatic experience of the preceding two weeks. Being animal lovers, everyone showed a pleasing interest.

Norman had been very good whilst I had been away, and had kept the back door shut all the time. Martha was on her chair and lost no time in jumping down to greet me and demand lunch. All in all, a most satisfactory morning.

Chapter 36
THE MERRY-GO-ROUND CONTINUES

Christmas Day dawned soft and warm. After breakfast I saddled Tangle, much to Jason's joy, and we went for a ride. We startled a lone pheasant searching industriously among the leaf mould at the base of a sheltering beech hedge and it whirred away through the bare branches at our approach. Tangle, who had been wandering along half asleep, no doubt reliving the taste of Christmas goodies for breakfast, woke up with a bang, almost projecting me into space as she shot sideways and rapidly forwards. Further on, a covey of partridge was similarly employed in the undergrowth of a small copse. Forewarned is forearmed and, not wanting a repeat of our previous shake up, I kicked Tangle forward into a smart trot.

Dunkery Beacon was standing out sharp and clear. I paused a moment, looking across to the Codsend Moor Allotments, and pondering on the folly of man's devising. The allotments are large, enclosed areas of former common land, which was affected by the Enclosures Act of 1773. Twenty per cent, or thereabouts, of the commons to be enclosed went to the Lord of the Manor, with the remainder being allocated to those farmers or smallholders who held grazing rights on the commons. Many allocations, Codsend among them, took the form of long, narrow strips. On Codsend they were extremely long as well as narrow, and they ran from the high moorland to the river bottom. Why this was, we do not know, it can't have been a need for water as there are natural springs all over. Maybe it was for ease of access. Whatever the reason, the cost of fencing here and the short length of time given for this to be done, and I suspect elsewhere, proved prohibitive to most people and the more well-to do quickly stepped in. For the price of the fencing they bought up many of the lots adjoining their own, thereby circumventing the original concept of creating more landowners.

The mare was glad to be out and trotted along brightly with her head up and ears pricked. I sang carols at the top of my voice to the sheep in the fields I passed along the way. Jason thought I was quite mad and kept coming back to see what this awful noise meant. Was it a new way of giving commands? Tangle didn't think much of my singing either, but was too polite to comment. I arrived home feeling very exhilarated, and bustled around settling the animals before changing for lunch. Tangle was let into the field, Jason given a large bone in his house and Martha fed.

Families grow up and scatter and at no time is this more keenly felt than at Christmas. Our family party was missing three key members. Present were my sister Liz, her husband Peter and son Ben, Norman and myself and Mother. Absent was Liz's daughter – trying out Australia, and both of my girls, one in Alberta and the other in Cambridgeshire. We determined to be cheerful, drank toasts to absent loved ones and ate a gorgeous goose dinner. When we were children the day always followed a set pattern to facilitate the care of the animals, and my sister and I adhered to this pattern in our own families. On Christmas Eve there was a choice of services for us to attend. A Christingle in the evening or a midnight communion. Christmas Day itself was a leisurely affair now that there only were our domestic animals to care for, no large herds of cattle or flocks of sheep to attend. Lunch was started around one o'clock, to be finished in time for the Queen's speech. Presents were then exchanged and the sitting room became a welter of torn and crumpled wrapping paper, half finished drinks and congealing mugs of coffee. It was always a wrench to leave this cosy clutter, but there were animals at home waiting for their tea.

We spent an hour over our chores, making sure the sheep had enough hay, catching Tangle and settling her in her night box, giving Jason a leg stretch in the failing light before feeding him and the cats and shutting in the hens.

We returned to my sister's and spent a comfortable evening in front of the fire eating yet more food! This was the longest Martha had been left since her illness. She seemed none the worse for it, except being very demanding with her affections when we finally arrived home for the night.

In spite of the gaps in our ranks, Christmas had been a happy day, but Boxing Day dawned flat and rather uninteresting. Home alone with Norman I found I was more than ever missing the comings and goings of the young people. The cheerful chatter of their voices and their air of purpose. Even their extreme untidiness began to look attractive during this period of protracted separation. The perennial problem of what to eat had to be addressed. Even the thought of producing a meal was nauseating after the overindulgences of the previous day. Why have we let ourselves turn Christmas into such a gastronomic orgy? Each year I say "never again", and each year, as November gets under way, out come the cake tins, the pudding bowls and the mixer with the resulting extra trip to the supermarket for all those packets of fruit and pounds of butter necessary for the production of delectable puddings, cakes and pies. Not to mention the bottle of brandy!

As Boxing Day dragged to a close I found myself watching Martha rather more closely again and counting her respirations. They were quickening up and by bedtime she was looking distressed and didn't want her usual snack. I gave her an extra diuretic and planned to be in Minehead for the morning's surgery. Were we ever going to get this cat right? The surgery staff were surprised to see us back. Mr Denham was on duty. He hadn't seen Martha since the middle of the crisis and complimented me on her improved appearance. This was all very well, but her breathing was still not right. In fact, it was proving to be a very stubborn problem. Mr Denham surmised that there was a deep pocket of infection on her lung, and she must go back on to antibiotics. She was to stay on diuretics, but only once a day. This time, on reaching home, I did not put away the cage. I'd done that twice and decided that it would be tempting fate to put it away for a third time. I left it in a corner of the utility room where it immediately became a receptacle for indoor shoes and wellies. I filled the hot water bottle and made up Norman's chair as before and settled Martha there with her chest elevated over the bulge of the bottle. Norman, coming in for a cup of coffee with me before I left for Catherine's lesson, gave her a despairing look and took one of the other chairs.

Coming home rather late, I was met by Martha demanding lunch. It was twenty four hours since she had last eaten, and she made it clear just how hungry she was by getting under my feet and yowling. I hastened to feed her before getting something for ourselves. This was when Martha started bringing up her meals. Was there to be no end to the problems this cat was able to produce?

I had my back to her as I worked at the counter when the pattern for the next few days started. In a most distressing fashion, with a choking cry, she started retching and heaving until she coughed up a sausage-like wedge of food plus gobs of mucous and a froth-looking substance. For twenty four hours any food I offered was returned in this way. She was desperately hungry because nothing was staying down. I put it down to the new antibiotics, but this was disproved when I talked to Mr Gibbins the following day. He really couldn't offer an explanation as to why this was happening, but did explain that the food was not getting to the stomach. The aperture at the bottom of the throat must have become inflamed and swollen and it might never return to normal. I was speechless. We'd come so far and now she was going to die because she couldn't eat! That couldn't be so, could it? Mr Gibbins patiently waited for me to reply to him. Pulling myself together, I listened to his suggestions. I was to place her feeding dish at such a level that she had to eat standing up, thereby ensuring a smooth, downward passage into her stomach, and everything she ate was to be reduced to a liquid form.

This dreadful upchucking of anything solid really threw me for a loop. Martha seemed intent on stretching my powers of adaptability to the limit. I had no experience to guide me. What to feed her was my main concern. She was constantly hungry, yet, being very fussy over what she would eat. Tinned cat food mashed to a lappable consistency with hot water proved unappetising. To achieve a variety, pounds of liver, chicken and fish were cooked in the bottom of the Aga overnight. The solids went through the mincer twice over and were then remixed with their stocks and frozen in small containers, one or two meals in each container for easy defrosting and serving.

Poor Martha's insides were taking their time to heal. Her tummy was swelling alarmingly after each meal. We pretended not to hear Norman's description of "a rugger ball on legs". She was too uncomfortable to laugh at herself, and I wouldn't dare for fear of hurting her feelings. She was making repeated trips to the dirt box with little or no result. The reason for these frequent visits finally registered with me: she was constipated.

From one source or another we acquired ten brace of pheasant that winter. Usually the cooked carcasses were hung in the plum tree for the birds to pick over, but now they, too, went into the stock pot. Martha went wild with desire on first scenting the resulting liquid. Luckily we didn't share the same taste in foods as I thought that it smelled dreadful! Homemade brown bread made into very fine crumbs and mixed with some of this stock and fed once a day helped ease things gently through. Problem solved by trial and error.

Slowly, with much throwing up, she learned to eat in a manner completely foreign to cats: standing up and taking it slowly. She soon realized that if she gulped the first few mouthfuls it would all come up. She hated it when this happened and often would not return to that food. For a while it seemed we just had to go through this performance to get rid of the accumulated mucous or phlegm. By reducing everything to a suitable consistency, Martha was eating four small, nutritious, meals a day. She started putting on weight and shedding her coat.

Chapter 37
HAPPY NEW YEAR

New Year's Eve bought an unexpected and delightful surprise. My daughter Bridget arrived with her future husband Dorian for a week's holiday. Bridget, full of excitement at coming home, ran into the house with the steel tips of her heels making a rattling tattoo on the floor. Dorian followed more slowly, his rather large feet in heavy boots must have sounded ominous to Martha. She panicked and fled. She shot into the courtyard, saw the strange car, turned tail and bolted under our car. And stayed there. Nothing would induce her to come out. At tea time, with Bridget and Dorian out of the way in the sitting room, Martha responded to the deliberately loud clattering of the feed dishes and ventured back indoors.

She spent the greater part of their holiday hiding, usually on the dining room chairs which are always pushed well in under the table. I spent the greater part of their holiday bent double checking that that was where she was. As for eating, well, she wouldn't eat if those feet were anywhere around. Breakfast was easy. Bridget and Dorian were not the earliest of risers, particularly when on holiday. Lunch was a little more dicey, but they had usually left by then. Tea time I could never get right as I never knew when they would be returning. As soon as they drove in, Martha would lift her head from her food, tense up and listen, poised to run. I would stand at the kitchen window making frantic signs to them to tiptoe and to use the front door. It was sad because Bridget had heard so much about this cat and wanted to make friends.

Thursday 2nd January was quite a turning point in Martha becoming one of the family. Bridget and Dorian had taken themselves off for twenty four hours to visit friends and peace had returned. I happened upon Smarty talking to Martha in the afternoon and that evening, for the first time, she really relaxed whilst on my lap in the sitting room. She was lying with her head hanging down between my knees and I was gently rubbing up and down the length of her tummy. I thought she was asleep when, wham, she grabbed one of my fingers in her teeth and started vigorously kicking at my hand with her back legs. Norman, alerted by my gasp of pain, was grinning from ear to ear. We both felt great joy at this manifestation of her well being.

On Friday I saw Tom having a conversation with Martha, and he gave her a lick under her right ear! All the time that she had been so gravely ill Tom, Smarty and Suzy had totally ignored her. She might as well not have been in the house. With Smarty, and now Tom, acknowledging her presence in the home I put to rest my last niggling doubts of her survival.

On 6th January we were signed off by Mr Denham. The eating, although costing me a bomb, was under control. Her lungs were still wheezy and she was to stay on diuretics, but I was to gradually lengthen the interval between tablets. Mr Denham in his quiet, almost offhand, way said that it was my nursing which had brought her through her terrible illness. How astounding that I, who hate all forms of nursing, had pulled this cat back from the brink of death.

As I was paying the bill at Reception, Maggie commented "not many people would have gone to the lengths you have over a cat". I thought to myself: this wasn't over a cat, this was Martha, a person in her own right. My mind rebelled against trying to explain my complicated feelings about a being who had stretched my resources to the limit and, in return, had given me renewed faith in my own abilities.

It is a continual source of wonderment to me that such a small creature can so influence one's life and can, without a single spoken word, command the attention it requires and return that affection with unlimited affection. Can turn the process of 'caring' into an exercise lovingly carried out, no matter the cost. We give and we receive. How true. Unless we give of ourselves how can we be open to receive? To give of ourselves for the benefit of those around us is to reap the riches of fulfilment. To receive in return the twin blessings of inner satisfaction and contentment is to sip at the cup of tranquillity.

Martha became the joy of my life. She grew, certainly lengthwise and the funny hump before her tail levelled off, giving her a proper straight top line. Her body felt more alive, more supple, and her skin moved freely on her frame. She grew a glossy new coat which she was forever washing. She became full of energy and took to playing with the end of Jason's tail as he sat begging for toast crusts which usually fell his way. He seemed oblivious of the attention his tail was receiving as he concentrated on willing Norman to remember he was there.

Martha made tentative efforts to play with the other cats and, it being many years since they had played games, they took umbrage at her advances. Tom tried bullying, he seemed to reckon a swift clout to her head would put her in her place, but she retaliated. She hissed and spat at him and gave him the same back again. Gathering the remains of his shattered ego like a cloak around him, he leapt for the psychological advantage of the height of the Aga to stare balefully down at her where, with complete unconcern for his discomfort, she was belting one of her toys across the kitchen floor.

Suzy, unfortunately, would not stand up for herself, and it didn't take long for Martha to discover this weakness. She delighted in perching on the arm of the chair chosen by Suzy for her afternoon nap, thus preventing Suzy from relaxing into a restful sleep. Not knowing if you are to be washed or walloped can be trying on the nerves of an elderly lady. Suzy's efforts to steel herself against the threatening menace were admirable to behold. Curled up extra tight with one wary eye on Martha she attempted to defy interference.

Although reluctant to intervene, I was not going to let Suzy be bullied by yet another cat. Scolding Martha was a waste of breath, and I resorted to giving her a couple of light taps with a rolled up newspaper. To hit her with my hand would have been to seriously damage our rapport, the newspaper served as an intermediate form of chastisement which, along with a strong "No", was recognised by Martha as a reprimand. After a few attempts at getting Suzy on the run and being told off, she gave up, at least when I was around.

This left Smarty on the receiving end of her restless energy, and here she found her soulmate. He was always prone to skittish moods when he would tear through the house at great speed. Now Martha joined in, two feline bullets in top gear, great fun. When he had enough or Martha tried for some all-in wrestling, he demanded to be let out of the back door, knowing that Martha wouldn't follow him.

She tried all ways to show her affection for me. Sitting on my lap was not demonstrative enough for her. She wanted to be up by my head and attempted to drape herself around my neck. This I gently discouraged, but she was a persistent cat and tried curling up on my shoulder once I was relaxed in my recliner in the evenings. Now I am not one of your big, broad-shouldered women, even small and thin as she was, there simply wasn't room, plus her fur tickling my nose was liable to make me sneeze. Years of blocked airway passages and sinus trouble have taught me to let a sneeze fly and the ensuing eruption is enough to topple Mount Olympus. Martha had no chance at all.

We reached an amicable compromise. She was allowed to stretch up over my chest with her head on my shoulder, ensuring that I received the full benefit of her continuous, contented purring. If Norman was the recipient of the evening's affection, she chose to curl into the crook of his elbow from whence she could lift her head to stare into his eyes or raise a paw towards his chin, a picture of pure contentment.

Notes
- We paid nine visits to the vets with the ill cat Martha – totalling 180 miles.
- Martha spent 25 days on antibiotics.
- Martha spent 51 days on diuretics.
- The extra food and petrol must have brought the cost up to at least £100.00
- Martha will always be known as "the hundred-pound cat". This was 1987. The RSPCA heard about this and, as she was a genuine stray, offered to pay one third of the vet bill, for which I was very grateful.

Chapter 38
OUR FAVOURITE PASTIME – WATCHING THE RED DEER OF EXMOOR

We loved travelling over the moors and watching the big red deer. With Martha recovered, we picked up this routine once again. Many an afternoon in winter or evening in summer was spent driving over Dunkery, up past Cloutsham and through Stoke Pero and Wilmersham or up to Luccombe Post and down towards Nutscale Reservoir. We had our favourite viewing places. We liked to park on the seaward flank of Dunkery Hill, pulling into the side of the road after the first dip down. There was a plank bench there, the eroded ground at its base testifying to its frequent use by the many people resting there to glory in this unique panorama of Exmoor: my favourite view in all the world.

The vast sweep of the moorland drops, fold by fold, from Dunkery Beacon to Webbers Post and onwards into the "barley renowned" vale of Porlock. Before us lies the ancient farmstead of Cloutsham, situated snugly below a brow of the hill and again the moorland, climbing this time, rises to Stoke Pero Plain and the high expanses of Exford Common and Lucott Moor. The thickly treed slopes of Horner Woods fill the valley below and surge to the heather-covered dome of Ley Hill.

Letting our eyes swing right handed, we followed the flow of the trees into Porlock Bay and thence to the sea. The bank of shingle from Porlock Weir to Bossington Beach defines the divide between land and water. Hurlstone Point juts sharply into the bay and the bulk of Bossington Hill rises to the lofty heights of Selworthy Beacon. The straggling line of Bossington village is barely discernible at the base of the hill along the far side of the vale.

Wildlife abounds. Foxes lie up in dry hollows at the head of the combes, sheep dot the landscape and deer are often seen. Buzzards, kestrels, crows and the odd raven fly overhead, and numerous are the numbers of smaller birds who come to breed here each year.

The changing seasons, from the browns of winter to the greens and purples of high summer, the ever-moving patterns of sunlight and shadow as clouds chase across the sky keeps this a view of never-ending fascination and delight.

Jason was often with us on these excursions and knew he got walked from here to Webbers Post. He started to whine and moan in anticipation as soon as the handbrake was applied, and the longer we looked at the view the stronger become the protests from the back of the car. With strong commands to "sit" and "stay" I opened the boot. This was good training for him, and once released from bondage he had to sit outside the car while I tightened my shoe laces and generally fiddled around, emphasizing the need for obedience before we set off. As we progressed down the stony track Selworthy church, standing out stark and white from the wooded hillside behind, came into view. Green fields lay, as a carpet, at its base and the village itself was difficult to pick out so closely did it fit into the narrow cleft between the fields.

Norman waited for us in the car park at Webbers Post. Any student of aromatherapy should take a walk here in the spring. The cloying sent of the gorse in bloom hangs heavily on the senses and early bees are busy among the bright yellow flowers. I longed to bottle some of this rich almond scent to release on a dull winter's afternoon.

Leaving Webbers Post the road took us into the East Water valley, across the water splash and up a couple of tortuous bends through Cloutsham Farm. The road is very narrow with steep drops on the lower side and needs to be driven with care. Arriving at our viewing point above Cloutsham we were looking south over the fields bordering Bagley Combe towards Dunkery Beacon. Directly in front of us across the valley were the remains of an Iron Age hill slope enclosure.

We stopped to count the "tame deer" grazing in the fields. These were not tame at all, they were free to come and go at will. Norman insisted on calling them tame as they appeared to be enclosed. One evening we watched two foxes working their way on converging lines across these fields. One came from the old enclosure and the other one appeared from the deep combe in front of us. They trotted across the fields pausing here and there to investigate a molehill or overturn a stone in their search for supper. Eventually they came upon each other by the fallen tree. There was a brief greeting, nose to nose, and they continued on their separate ways.

From here to Cloutsham Gate the conversation went something like this: "Which way at the cattle grid?" "I don't mind, you choose." "No, I chose last time, which way do you think?" I drove slower and slower as we tossed around the relative merits of going straight ahead on the more open and wider road or choosing the narrow, enclosed one through Stoke Pero with the steep drop into Stoke Combe and the resulting climb through Wilmersham with the disadvantage of, possibly, two or more gates to open and close.

The direction of the wind played a prominent role in our deliberations, too. It is pointless looking for deer on a north facing moor if the wind is blowing from the north, the north-west or the north-east. During prolonged periods of wet, windy weather they retreat to lower ground, preferring the shelter of the trees in the deeper combes to the exposed open moorland. Dry sunny conditions will find them lying up or feeding on the leeward side of the hills and here they are visible, even to the naked eye, if their chosen location is close to one of the roads that cross the moor.

It is interesting to note, through the year, the changing composition of the herds. Over the winter there are groups of stags and groups of hinds with calves and one or two young stags still in attendance from the rut; the autumn breeding season which starts near the end of September and runs, with varying degrees of intensity, for five or six weeks. A winter's drive over the moor is much enhanced by observing a herd of thirty or forty stags browsing on the open common or lying in some sheltered depression in the undulating moor; only the weak winter sunlight glinting on their antlers betraying their camouflaged presence.

Into April the segregation of the sexes appears complete. The deer stay very much apart until the start of the rutting season. The stags, singly or in small groups, are deep in the woods, while their annual change of antlers takes place. The young deer, the previous year's calves, are under the watchful eyes of older, barren hinds. The in-calf hinds wander away to choose lonely, sheltered combes on the higher moorland for giving birth and raising their young.

We learned to recognise other regular deer watchers by the binoculars lying on the dashboards and the knowing way they swung their cars into just the right position for good viewing. Deer watching can be a lengthy business, for they don't appear on command. They are roamers, browsing and picking as they go with weather and vegetation playing an important part in their choice of location. A good pair of binoculars and loads of patience are the main requirements for this enjoyable pastime.

Deer are most readily seen during the rutting season. The population is in a general state of flux, the stags are travelling to collect hinds for breeding and an air of restlessness and movement prevails across the moor. We once went out at such a time of year. It was an afternoon of clear light and very little wind, although cold once we were out of the car.

We drove to a secluded area which had come up trumps once before. Leaving the car, we walked in and finding a sheltered spot in the lee of a beech hedge we settled down to wait.

We were looking across a sparsely wooded combe to a large acreage of previously cultivated moorland now going back, with bracken and heather encroaching around the edges and up the gullies. The middle section of bog and wetland was getting ever bigger as the drains filled in and ceased to work, allowing the swamp and bog grasses freedom to spread. Only the deer and sheep were light enough to travel safely here. There were clumps of pine trees and rhododendrons for shelter and always the combe for retreat in times of danger. An ideal habitat for deer and a difficult place to cross for the unwary.

We swept the hillside with our binoculars. We were in luck, it was alive with deer. We counted thirty five in that first quick survey and the numbers fluctuated during the hour we were there as they moved in and out of our vision. Twelve hinds with some calves grazed peacefully to the left of a stand of pine; their Lord and Master, a mature stag with a fine spread of antlers, lying among them. He didn't stay down for long. He seemed happier pacing nervously among the hinds, pausing occasionally to strike at the ground with a foreleg or throw back his head to roar forth a challenge to any would-be marauder.

Two younger stags, together on the lower side of the main bunch, interrupted their grazing with some mild head-to-head confrontation. We heard the clash as their antlers met, but the performance lacked conviction and they soon returned to their grazing. Yet another stag was working off his rutting frustrations by thrashing at a dead branch of an elderberry bush with his horns, much to the detriment of the bush. The eventual uprooting of the luckless bush seemed likely, such was his determined assault on it!

A Nott stag, an abnormal deer who does not grow antlers, hovered on the perimeter behaving obnoxiously among the single hinds dotted around. Having selected a quarry, he made repeated rushes at her, striking viciously with his front feet. Having forced her to move on, he savaged the ground where she had been standing by digging at it and kneeling down to thrust his head again and again into the ground. A beast of more than usual uncertain temper for this time of year: one to be avoided at all costs.

The cold, creeping insidiously into my body, went largely unnoticed, so absorbed was I by this busy scene. Norman was the first to cry quits. Such was the frozen state of my feet I almost fell over when I came to stand in response to his wishes to be gone. Clutching at his arm, I hobbled painfully around restoring circulation to my cramped and cold limbs before we climbed back to the car and the flask of hot coffee awaiting us there.

Chapter 39
JANUARY WITH FURTHER UPS AND DOWNS

January dragged its weary way forward, foggy, cold and miserable. The low ebb of the year for us, its only saving grace being that, once over, we didn't have to suffer it again until next year. Even the snowdrops, sensible things, wait until February to put in an appearance in this part of the world. How appreciative of the occasional day of sunshine we are. It lifts our spirits, puts a lilt into our voices and a sparkle into our eyes, and we laugh more readily. It was on one of these days, a day stolen from summer, that Tangle injured herself.

Coming home from one of our moorland expeditions, we caught sight of her gavotting around the field. A spirited gallop from end to end, rearing into halt at the uppermost point, the wind in her tail, head high, nostrils flaring. Then off again, with a buck and a jump, to repeat the performance. I went to bring her in. She must have seen me coming, for I arrived in time to witness her headlong dash for the gate and the calamitous end to her glorious expression of freedom.

The field funnelled down to the gate with a wire fence on one side and a sloping earth bank on the other. Tangle, who never, ever, came to the gate to be caught was, today, galloping straight for it. Realizing that she could neither jump the gate nor stop before crashing into it, she turned sharply left and attempted to jump up the bank. Here she met her Waterloo, her chest hit the bank with a sickening thud and she slid back, in a jumble of legs, to lie winded by the gate. I was frozen to the spot with horror.

Yelling for Norman, which I did, was a waste of breath, he was far too far away to hear, but it must have penetrated to the mare as she lifted her head and gazed at me with a dazed look. Throwing open the gate for fear that in her efforts to get up she would become entangled in it, I dropped my voice to a soothing murmur and slowly attached the leadrope to her headcollar. She struggled to her feet and stood up. With her heaving sides and dejectedly hanging head she was a sorry sight indeed. This was a sad ending to her wild evening fling around the pasture.

Worse was to reveal itself. Her offside foreleg was dangling. She would not put any weight on it. I tried a couple more yells for Norman, but no reassuring presence appeared around the side of the barn. I was on my own. What to do? Leave Tangle there and go for Norman? I tied her to the gatepost and started to walk away. She was not having any of this. "Abandon her in her hour of need. No thank you. She was coming with me!" She tried hopping around and neighed. I deemed it wiser to see if she could come with me. We started down the steep. Amazing how dextrous a horse can be on three legs. We were making good, but slow, progress when Norman met us on his way to the henhouse.

He didn't say anything, he stood and looked, and I could see the thoughts chasing through his mind. "What disaster now? Looks bad. Broken shoulder, perhaps? Have to shoot it." He came closer. "No, not a broken shoulder, but bound to cost money, more vet's bills." I could read him like a book, probably because his thoughts were mirroring my own. Silent communication has its uses. Fewer recriminations and no accusations flying around. Tangle and I continued on our painful way, giving Norman time to think about it while shutting up his poultry. We made it into the yard and up the steps into the grooming box. This was a bare floor of non-slip brick and I chose it in preference to her night box with its thick bed of straw.

It was most perplexing. There was no blood and she didn't mind being poked and prodded. She just would not put that leg to the ground. She stood unconcernedly pulling at a net of hay while we waited for Norman's return. Thankfully, the area of injury soon became apparent. Norman was quick to notice a small swelling at the top of the splint bone under the back of the knee. Could she have struck into herself, the front of a back shoe hitting the splint bone area causing immediate excruciating pain which prevented her from completing the jump? How else to account for the fall as the bank is hardly worthy of the name, being more of an incline than an actual vertical barrier. The leg swelled visibly, the larger it became the more weight she was prepared to put on it. Within half an hour she was able to walk, fairly soundly, to her night box and by the following morning, with her leg the same size from knee to coronet, she was, incredibly, sound.

We were now to spend many weeks poulticing and cold water hosing as it proved a most stubborn injury. Tied up in the grooming box with a net of hay, Tangle spent many hours with a hosepipe dripping cold water into a thick leg wrap bandaged over the injury. To prevent the hosepipe being trodden on, it was threaded through a bandage around Tangle's neck and tied, with a quick release knot, above the knee. It worked a treat. There has to be no more boring job in the stable than standing for hours on end directing a hose at a horse's leg. Tangle wasn't lame, but every night the leg swelled and each day, once I started turning her out again the swelling went down. There was considerable heat present to begin with, this gradually lessened as the degree of swelling decreased, until we were left with one small area that stayed persistently warm and slightly swollen. It is said that time is the greatest healer, and so it proved in this case. Eight whole weeks to heal an injury acquired in the blink of an eye!

Keeping a watching brief over Tangle and the hosepipe presented an ideal opportunity for introducing Martha to the great outdoors. My halfhearted attempts to encourage her to go out had not been successful. She was reluctant and I was suffering from an irrational fear that she would leave once she was offered freedom. Coward-like, I had not pushed the issue.

Now I hardened my resolve and actively assisted her into the courtyard. Her extreme nervousness was very worrying. She crept along the bottom of the walls holding her body close to the ground, stopping here and there to sniff, sometimes at ground level, sometimes rearing up onto her hind legs to catch a scent left on a flower or bush by other cats. The slightest sound sent her scurrying for refuge under the car in the garage. Five minutes was about all either of us could take. We were both relieved when I opened the kitchen door and let her back inside!

Martha definitely had more confidence if I followed her as she explored. Gradually, depending on my schedule and the weather, five minutes lengthened into ten and the immediate area around the house, the courtyard and stable yard and even the front garden became familiar to her. She began to walk more uprightly, and with increased confidence she dashed up and down the lilac tree or danced sideways across the yard after fallen leaves.

One fine sunny afternoon, I decided that Martha really had to stay out by herself. Letting her know I was going yet making no attempt to take her with me, I returned indoors. Not many minutes later I heard an awful cry and feet running in the gravel under the kitchen window. Martha shot around the corner into the utility room and stood clawing at the glass door, demanding entrance. So much for my fears that she was going to run away and leave me!

What a state she was in, shaking and crying, there was nothing for it but to pick her up and wander through the house with her in my arms until she calmed down. Having settled her I went out to find out what had upset her. Norman hadn't seen anything untoward, but he thought he'd seen her going up towards the hen house. Maybe she'd been too adventurous and become frightened by the space around her and panicked. I will never know, but I do know it was an extraordinary example of her dependence on me She was frightened and she came to me for comfort, to still her pounding heart and restore her trembling spirit to calmness and quiet.

I found myself longing for the arrival of spring, so I could throw open all the doors and windows and Martha could have freedom to come and go when it felt right for her to do so.

Chapter 40
MARTHA BACK TO HEALTH

Martha had her last diuretic pill on February 6th. At one point I thought I would be forever dropping pills down her throat and now we were finished with it. This didn't stop me watching her anxiously when she was asleep, counting the speed of her respirations to ensure that they were not increasing or becoming laboured. She had been at the forefront of my every waking hour for such a long time that it was difficult, suddenly, to discontinue the watching brief.

We weren't to be left long in doubt as to her well-being. She came into season. In my experience cats are either spayed or neutered, and don't get up to the antics now exhibited by Martha. No one and nothing was safe. She thoroughly embarrassed Tom and Smarty and if the kitchen table could have up sticks and left I am sure it would have. Even Jason came in for his share of sexual harassment.

Each morning started with a great show of affection for Norman as he made our early tea. Then she worked her way through Tom and Smarty, who really did not know what all this loving was about and didn't want to know, either! She even cuddled up to Suzy, who sat, with a mesmerized look on her face, expecting the worst. When abandoned by the boys, she wrapped herself around the table leg, choosing the one between Norman and myself and usually at mealtimes. Crooning, mewing, giving little cries, it was enough to put one off one's food. By teatime Jason was the only four legged one with any patience left. She settled between his front legs, alternately washing them and herself. She wasn't above giving him a love bite, too. He retaliated by pinning her down with a leg placed over her middle and washing her ears!

And now, when least convenient, she wanted out. She became adept at slipping through Norman's legs and escaping; to bolt under the door into the neighbour's field or down the drive into the overgrown garden opposite, with me in close pursuit. With varying degrees of intensity, this went on for ten days. Ten days of keeping all the doors and windows shut. Ten days of acute anxiety on my part and frantic worry on Jason's as he strove to hold the tide of invading tom cats at bay.

We were now to go through a full-blown false pregnancy. I knew she could not be pregnant, never once had she been out of my sight or loose for long enough for anything to have happened. My extreme vigilance and fast running feet had ensured no adverse event taking place. Nevertheless, she was convinced she was pregnant. I borrowed a book on cats from the library. Martha's supposed condition followed the information exactly, even to the "pinking up" of her nipples during the third week. She developed a huge appetite and an enormous tummy and began demanding milk in the middle of the morning at elevenses time. She believed in communication before birth, too. She spent many hours lying by the Aga purring to her imaginary young, a deep, satisfying rumble of sound that must have been heard throughout her body. At the end of the usual gestation period, there were a couple of damp spots on the rug one morning and Martha's tummy went down like a slow puncture. Poor Martha!

Time now hung heavily on my hands. Tangle was still laid up and it was not possible to work in the garden except for some general tidying up after the winter gales. Saving Martha had taken me out of myself. With time to think, the nagging worries about my health resurfaced. The symptoms I had been putting up with for a long time now brought themselves to my attention with renewed vigour: the sore throats each morning, the sleeplessness, the physical difficulty in getting out of bed each morning and the facility of being able to fall asleep anywhere and anytime, as early as ten o'clock in the morning, all added up to an abnormal condition but no one seemed to know what. Arthritis drugs offered relief for brief periods, but the benefits soon wore off, leaving me wishing that I had never had a respite as each time the symptoms returned they seemed worse than ever. I needed an absorbing challenge to take my mind off myself. I decided to write Martha's story.

How to begin? I have haunting schoolday memories of facing a blank sheet of paper and being expected to fill it during the hour given over to "composition", and failing miserably. I started jotting down remembered things on odd scraps of paper, backs of envelopes, old point-to-point programmes, jamming the glove compartment of the car until I had a sizeable pile of miscellaneous information and a couple of steno pads full of random thoughts. The need for a typewriter became evident, and a trusty old Olympia was found through the "For Sale" column of the local paper.

Martha found the typewriter fascinating. She decided to sit on it, the better to watch the keys going up and down. Of course, nothing worked when she was trying to do this, all it achieved was a typewriter full of cat hair. The more healthy she became, the more difficult it was to get down to work each morning. She took to making flying leaps from the windowsill onto the table, landing with her head well down between her front paws. Diving across the table in this fashion sent all the neat piles of paper notes flying in a most satisfactory manner. She would sit on the edge of the table watching them float to the ground before picking up all the small objects such as the eraser or the stapler and dropping them overboard. Some days I shut her in the kitchen before starting, but it didn't seem right, somehow, to deny her this ten minutes of pleasure which was all the time it took before she ran out of steam and retired for a nap.

February drifted into March, the weather improved and Martha began to lead a more normal life. She supervised the digging of the vegetable garden and discovered the delights of going to the field to catch Tangle. Jason considered it his duty each afternoon to count the sheep, look for rabbits and, incidentally, have a leg stretching run. Martha inspected anything that Jason sniffed at, she even ventured into the middle of the field. All went well until the day Tangle started one of her games. Martha bolted for the safety of the lower hedge, horrified by this thing galloping crazy circles around "her mum". Once Tangle was caught we all arrived at the gate. Tangle was led through first and we hold the gate wide open for Jason, who usually came at a gallop. Martha brought up the rear, tripping daintily around the muddy patches with a little run and a meow, meow, thank you.

She was a very talkative cat. She used her voice, usually on a rising note, along with her tail, to communicate. Her voice said "Hello, Thank You, Gosh, I'm pleased to see you." Her tail, carried aloft, with the tip curled over, signified well being or pleasure. She would scoot in through a door, opened specially for her with a Br-urp, Br-urp, then halt and look around, her little square end with the question mark flying expressing pleasure at being let in and "what shall I do now?" written all over her.

We were invited by friends in Staffordshire to visit, and felt very reluctant to go because of Martha. Mother offered to "cat mind" if we would take Jason with us. This was a first for Jason, going away on holiday, and he must have found the speed on the motorway rather frightening as he curled up tight in his basket and never lifted his head until he felt us slowing down at our exit. He behaved beautifully and quickly learned that the house was out of bounds. He had his bed in their utility room. He disgraced himself once when he went swimming in the canal after some ducks, and had a struggle to get up the vertical side out of the canal. He had been stupid and I told him so, and he didn't go in again.

We were away for a week and I wondered how Martha had taken my desertion. Cats are such odd creatures, and I thought she might act strangely when we came home, but not a bit of it. I put her along my forearm, where she liked to be carried, and she looked up at my face and sang such a lovely song.

After supper she became completely wound up, like an over-excited child. It started mildly enough as I relaxed in my recliner. She moved from my lap to lie on my chest, then she just had to rub her cheek against mine, over and over again. She worked herself into an ecstasy of loving, became carried away and almost bit me. I smacked her bottom and she leapt onto the floor and had a good wash where the smack had landed. Norman's chair came in for her attention next. She crawled up the side of the chair underneath the cover. She lay on the floor on her back and dragged herself along the base. She grabbed great mouthfuls of the cover as she lay on her back kicking vigorously with her hind legs. Norman could not resist dabbling his fingers over the side of the chair teasing her, until, with one swift swipe of her paw, she drew blood from his middle finger. In the rush to mop up the blood and get a bandage, Martha retired to the kitchen, fully aware that she had gone over the top with her demonstrations of happiness at our return.

Chapter 41
TRAVEL ACROSS EXMOOR
EXMOOR – MY PLAYGROUND

Tangle's leg had fully recovered before we went on holiday and I came home looking forward to riding again. Our first rides were gentle affairs, our weakened muscles not able to cope with anything too strenuous. Jason, always very fit, was thrilled at our resumption of riding out. He ran ahead and leaped up and down the high banks of the lane likes a mountain goat. To every mile that Tangle and I did, Jason must have done three or four!

One day, sitting in a gateway on Tangle with Jason flopped out beside us, tongue lolling and chest heaving from the exertions of the ride, I tried to define my feelings. I often stood in gateways when walking, but how much greater was my appreciation from the back of a horse. The views are the same, the weather presents its usual unpredictable face, but there is a heightened awareness, a thrill which plummets deep into the well of pleasure and comes up dripping with love, appreciation and that semi-sweet haunting feeling of potential loss.

It is akin in a way to going to Evensong. The familiar chanting of the Magnificat and the Nunc Dimittis, the singing of the heavenly evening hymns. It calls deep to one's soul and tugs at the heartstrings.

This view from this gateway might never be the same again. Those cattle tearing strongly at the lush, green grass could be gone tomorrow. That flock of sheep skilfully herded by a man and his dog from one pasture to the next presents change before my eyes. It is Man's lot to feel emotion too deep for comfort, to scheme, to plan, to be forever changing. Lucky the sheep and cattle, leading their day to day lives with no thought or imagination for tomorrow. Yet would I have change my lot for theirs? I think not.

April arrived with its teasing mixture of sunshine and showers. Also, my long-awaited visitors from Canada. Norman and myself derived great pleasure from taking our overseas guests on scenic tours of Exmoor. We delighted in their amazement at our sweeping open spaces, our hidden valleys and dramatic coastline.

One of those tours might start close to home at St John's church, Cutcombe. There is a feeling of strength here, an aura of time enduring embodied in this sturdy monument to Man's survival and conquering of this harsh environment down the centuries. I liked to breathe deeply of the keen, fresh air as we stood before the church, drinking in the far-reaching views of hills and woods and valleys. This, the second highest church on Exmoor, saw us for many years, when I was a child, occupying the front left-hand pew. Here, on raw winter evenings, Mother surreptitiously wrapped a car rug around her legs in an endeavour to keep her teeth from chattering. Father read the lessons and the handful of people in the congregation bravely lifted their voices into the lofty space of the high-arched roof. The poem to wayfarers to be found by the visitors' book says it all, so much better than I could hope ever to do.

Timberscombe church, with its rather austere whitewashed interior and magnificent screen could be next on our list, then onwards to Dunster. We parked on the outskirts and allowed a couple of hours or more to explore this interesting village.

With a sense of anticipation we pushed open the gates leading into the walled garden beside the church. We discovered anew the delights of the wrought iron gates and appreciated the peace of this and the adjacent memorial garden, the dovecote and tythe barn. To complete the circle, we walked down the High Street, past the Yarn Market to find ourselves drawn towards the castle, standing, like a sentinel, on the hill overlooking the village.

Maybe we strolled up the hill and poked our noses into the castle stables where the long-lasting aroma of horse, the sweet smell of sweat and muck, hay and straw, lingered on in the echoing vastness. It was many empty years though, since the last line of horses stood patiently waiting for the early morning footfalls heralding breakfast and the start of another working day. Then all would have been noise, the soft whisker, the flared nostril searching among the chaff for a last, elusive oat, the sharp crack of shoe against cobble and the jingle of buckles as the harness was slapped into place. All building to a final ringing crash of sound as the horses turned and left. Now, not even the swish of a broom breaks the silence of this once-busy place.

Shaking off our feelings of, possibly inappropriate, nostalgia things never having been as rosy as we like to picture them we headed for Allerford and Bossington. It is chocolate-box pretty through here. A packhorse bridge spans the river beside the ford and ducks paddle lazily back and forth beneath the arches, occasionally upending in the shallows to dredge the muddy bottom. Many cottages have beehive-like bulges on the outside of their walls. These denote bread ovens within and generated much discussion on the living conditions of times past.

If this was an evening tour, we would hope to find the tide "on the make" at Porlock Weir and sip a drink there while watching the fishing boats come home. The sun setting behind the hills would throw the harbour into deep shadow and a chill settled on the water. It was time to go. We headed for home, passing through Porlock and Horner and up Chapel Steep, hurrying on to catch the lingering, myriad hues of purples, pinks and reds left in the darkening sky by the sun as it sank to the west beyond the serried ridges of the higher moorland.

Only recently have I learned that if the red in the evening sky stretches well south of the westering sun it will, before nightfall of the following day, rain! So much for "Red sky at night, shepherd's delight." "Red sky in the morning, shepherd's warning" works well, though, for those of us up early enough to see it.

The rising moon emphasised the coming of nightfall; the soft dusk deepened and enfolded the hills in refreshing sleep. There could be a glimpse of deer on the move, their silhouettes outlined briefly above the horizon by the moonlight. An owl might skim silently past the car, heightening the air of mystery that envelopes the moor with the coming of darkness. If it was spring, a fox hunting for a mate broke the silence with a series of short, sharp barks.

Sitting in the dark in a car with the windows down on top of an often windy moor is not everyone's cup of tea. Visitors, too polite to demur when I said "Just five minutes here!" gave tangible sighs of relief when Norman announced, in no uncertain tone, "enough of this, I'm for home". And home we went.

A picnic at Weir Water was a must. I have fond memories of this place before all the wire fencing went up. We went out by way of Exford and up the Wellshead road to park at Alderman's Barrow and walked across to the Stone Circle at Almsworthy Common. I am a sucker for local history lectures. I can listen to the same topic over and over; the subject matter flowing in at one ear and out at the other, but some facts do eventually lodge in between. Our local historians tell us the barrows are Bronze Age burial mounds dating from 2300 BC. The stone circles and rows of standing stones dotted around the moors date from the same period. The stone circles are usually to be found near a source of water, positioned to receive the rays of the sun at midday in the mid winter. Their use is uncertain, their standpoints suggest a ritualistic or religious significance.

Driving on, we passed close to the stone circle at Lucott Moor. This particular circle used to have a round sign on a metal pole: "Ancient Monument", but the sheep have long since rubbed it to the ground and the vast majority of visitors, not realising it is there, drive straight past.

We continued on, pulling into the Whitstones car park to look across the Bristol Channel deep into Wales. Then down the tortuous twisting old coach road to Robbers Bridge and our picnic lunch beside the sparkling river that is Weir Water. I liked to sit and dabble my toes in the clear, cold water and look for flints from the Stone Age among the stones. A forlorn search as I never found any, but I am sure they could be there, washed down from the uplands on either side of the river.

The valley winds on to Malmsmead with its large car park for those wishing to walk up Badgworthy Water, the Doone Valley of R. D. Blackmore's classic tale *Lorna Doone*. Passing Oare church on the way, we popped in. I never tire of reading the wording on the memorial tablet to that notable country squire, Nicholas Snow. Readers of *Lorna Doone* are thrilled to be visiting this little church.

As the road twists and turns after Malmsmead, we caught glimpses of the tumbling East Lynn River making its way to Lynmouth and the sea. We entered an area of sparse woodland where the sun filtered through the open canopy of leaves, dappling the sheep-cropped grass in the little glades.

How this road rejoices as it swoops and dives, into the valleys and up again, around the bends and over the heights. We usually opted for turning right in Brendon village to climb to the high road and turn left for Countisbury and Lynmouth. The views are superb and visitors always wanted to see Lynmouth. From here it was anybody's choice, we usually retraced our steps, maybe taking a different route over the moors in the hope of seeing deer.

Chapter 42
LEARNING TO COPE WITH POLYMYALGIA RHEUMATICA

I struggled on, healthwise, all summer. Putting my symptoms down to how hard, physically, I had worked all my life; the intermittent back pain, sore muscles, the general stiffness, the riding (I started riding when I was five) the breaking in of horses, the falls, the ultra long days, the mucking out, the heaving of too many heavy saddles onto too many large horses, digging the garden etc. A busy, active life which I relished. Having passed the fifty mark I figured I was well into middle age and must expect more of the same. The symptoms I was now experiencing somehow did not fit into any known pattern.

The doctor listened but I don't think he heard what I was saying. He seemed to think all my aches and pains, the depressions, acute anxiety attacks and persistent nagging headaches were commonplace in one who had an active and somewhat stressful lifestyle. He put them down to the Change of Life. I considered I'd weathered that condition most successfully, thanks, in a large part to a homeopathic medicine recommended by a friend. I enjoyed three blissful months free of those symptoms before I started this lot.

Riding became a non event, at least competitively. Looking back I can see the pattern emerging with the horse I had before Tangle. She was difficult to ride forward into her bridle and for a while I sought help from a dressage instructor, Betty Howett. Increasingly, during the lessons, I was having to ask for rest periods as I felt my legs were turning to jelly and I was feeling insecure and feeble, stupid too. After all I'd been riding all my life. I knew how to do the movements. I taught riding, had done for many years. Why was I now unable to sustain forward impulsion and complete the exercises?

Tangle was easier to ride from that point of view; more onward going and very safe in traffic. Her specialities were dropping behind the bit or grabbing it and running away in trot. The efforts required to properly work in a horse and ride a dressage test are considerable. I began using pain killers. Even stuffed with them the remarks at the bottom of the test sheets were, with desponding regularity stating "this horse is capable of a better test. The rider needs to use her legs more, the rider is stiff" etc, etc. My heart was no longer in it, I gave up.

Norman was doing his usual splendid job in the vegetable garden. I dragged myself around in a parody of my former lifestyle. Yes, the flower beds were weeded after a fashion, the dog was exercised from the back of the horse; twenty minutes to half an hour being all I could comfortably cope with, food was cooked and the house cleaned. Three thirty each afternoon was the high point of the day. Everything eased up about this time and from then until bedtime I was halfway to being in a normal, mobile, state and this was when I did my work.

I dreaded going to bed. The chills and fevers all night long plus the pain in my backside and legs virtually making sleep impossible. I couldn't bear being touched. Norman moved into a single bed beside the double one. Never mind wall to wall carpeting, we had wall to wall beds! All night long I thrashed from one side of the double bed to the other, alternately hugging a hot water bottle to warm up or throwing off layers of blankets to cool down. The duvet was useless under these conditions and was banished to the spare bedroom.

Breakfast time was tricky. Normally Norman and I were not ones to have rows, now this time of day produced endless bickerings which sometimes developed into real upsets. I can laugh about it now but at the time it was horrible. We had one terrible, terrible row. I took umbrage at something Norman said, I expect it was an implied criticism which Norman would not retract. He sat there stolidly eating his way through his breakfast whilst I tried to win my point. I was beside myself. I grabbed the nearest moveable object and heaved it at him. It happened to be the butter dish. Thankfully the dish missed his head, the butter, flying loose, scored a bulls-eye by landing in the middle of his forehead and dropped, via his nose, onto his breakfast plate. I couldn't stop crying. I couldn't get through to him. I left.

Minus hat, minus boots, minus coat. I threw the tack onto Tangle mounted and galloped out of the yard. My sister was driving out of her driveway, she stopped, lowered her window and asked me what on earth I was doing then she closed the window and drove off! No comfort there then. When Tangle ran out of breath I slowed her up and realized it was raining. Still we went on getting wetter and wetter and further from home. Eventually, whilst the driving rain mingled with the tears still pouring down my cheeks and Tangle's head drooped lower and lower as the misery of the situation overcame that first wild exhilaration of our mad gallop up the road, common sense returned. We turned for home. Norman and I trod warily around each other for the rest of the day and then, without reference to the breakfast incident, resumed our normal relationship. I resolved, privately, to keep a tighter rein on my emotions in the future.

Yet with all this I looked so well. Mother kept asking me to explain what I thought was wrong. All I could say was I hurt. I hurt all the time, sometime all over. I can't tell you more than that. The pain was constant and forever moving. My shoulders one day, my bottom the next, my arms, my legs, in fact any area of muscle could be affected. There was a pain that went up my spine into my head and settled like a close-fitting cap on my scalp. I had a constant headache.

We put the house on the market and the horse up for sale. Things eventually came to a head. Each year I designed the jump courses for our local horse show and ran the jumping classes on the day of the show. The show is held in June in a field well exposed to the west winds. Usually this show is lucky with the weather, this particular year it chose to blow and rain. My circulation, never good since the start of my mysterious symptoms, now appeared to be completely on the blink. I could not keep warm, the day was one long agony.

Once the jumping started at 11 am until we finished at 5.50 pm I was constantly in and out of the judges caravan, constantly in and out of the ring rebuilding knocked down jumps and altering courses. Never was the end of a day so eagerly awaited.

I shivered and shook all that evening finally giving up the unequal struggle to warm up and took myself off to bed. I slept. I must have because the next thing I knew I was awake in the early hours of the morning. I was intensely cold, in a chill the like of which I never experienced before nor wish to again. The chill was so penetrating and so frightening that I said to myself as I sat on the edge of the bed "Good God, it's a good thing I woke up or I would be dead by now." And I am convinced it was so. I can still hear my voice as I said those words out loud.

I staggered to the loo and afterwards collected a couple of pillows from the spare room. These I added to the two I already had to create a high sloping effect that I could rest against without sleeping. Going back to sleep was not on my agenda for the rest of the night for I was feeling very frightened. And I settled down, clutching the hot water bottle to while away the remaining hours of the night.

Over our early morning cup of tea I told Norman some of my night-time experiences without mentioning my fright about dying. It was many months before I could bring myself to explore the meaning of that experience. I find comfort now when I think of it, obviously there was still work to do here, my time was not yet come.

The events of this past night determined me to demand action, whatever form that might take from the doctor. I marched into his office and was confronted by a 'locum'. That set me back on my heels and scattered my wits before I'd even started. Marshalling my thoughts I explained as clearly and concisely as possible my many symptoms. I was asked to remove my outer clothes and lie upon the couch for an examination.

I lay there feeling foolish as he manipulated my joints, they all moved freely and obediently into whatever position he required. The muscles came next. Excrutiating pain best describes the feeling as he applied pressure between his thumb and fingers on my upper arms and thighs. He took a step backwards. "I know what is wrong with you. Please get dressed and I will explain it to you." After all these months with just a five minute examination I was to know my problem. "You have Polymyalgia Rheumatica". I wasn't much the wiser as I had never heard of it. He quickly assured me that it wasn't life threatening. It is an autoimmune disease you pick-up rather like catching a cold and eventually, if you are lucky, it will leave you. The answer is steroids. My knowledge of steroids was sketchy. I had memories of a friend in Canada going on them and becoming very fat and moonfaced. I didn't want to be moonfaced or fat either! The poor doctor had a job persuading me to at least try them for forty eight hours. He knew that once I was on them I wouldn't want to come off as the relief is fantastic, but I did not know that at that point so allowed myself to be persuaded to try them. Within twenty four hours I felt I had been born again. I celebrated the forty eight hours with getting up before breakfast to go riding.

Later that day I returned to see the doctor. I agreed to stay on the steroids as he did such a good job of explaining how steroids worked. A large dose to begin with, slowly being reduced over the coming weeks as the disease ran its course. It was anybody's guess how long this would take. His advice sounded sensible to me especially as I appear to have a cast iron stomach and thought I could tolerate the drug.

My quality of life improved immediately although it did take a while to find the correct dose. Norman certainly appreciated the new me. I realize now how worried he must have been.

So began a roller coaster of treatment; a high dose of steroids followed by a lowering of the dose then it all became painful again so back onto a high dose. Why? Then I learnt through a friend of a support group in Porlock and I went along to meet them. They were all in differing stages of recovery and so kind and helpful. Basically I needed to see a doctor who specialised in this disease. There was a Doctor Judy Davis at The Royal Rheumatic Hospital in Bath who they thoroughly recommended. A long journey to make, made easier by using the Park and Ride scheme as parking in Bath so difficult. I duly got myself referred to her and we made the long journey.

I was to be there an hour before the actual appointment so blood could be taken which left us time for a welcome coffee and snack before returning to the hospital. In to see Dr Davis who had a student doctor with her and I was asked and agreed to the student being present throughout the examination and consultation. It was interesting about the blood taken earlier. Put simply, the blood had been taken early to allow the sediment in the blood to settle in the test tube which it does in people with this disease; this mimics what happens to the blood in our bodies whilst we are asleep, the sediment in our blood settles into our muscle masses which is what causes the pain.

I was ushered into a second room and asked to undress and Dr Davis did much the same as the locum in Dunster and, afterwards, asked me to get dressed again and come back into the other room. As they left I heard Dr Davis say to the student "this is a classic case of polymyalgia". My relief was immeasurable; I really did have this painful disease, the doubters would have to accept it, I was not malingering!

So began two years of learning to manage the steroids. Initially we made the journey to Bath once a month for blood tests and support, then every second month. The whole point of the treatment was to get the disease stabilised, to stop the roller coaster I had been on. By the beginning of the second year Dr Davis considered it had run its course, now I had to learn how to manage the withdrawal of the steroids. I was given a programme to follow and Dr Davis was always available at the end of the phone for advice. She said this could take up to a year and she was correct. Slow and sure was the way to go and it is thanks to her excellent care and understanding that I fully recovered.

Chapter 43
FESTA, THE BENGAL EAGLE OWL TAKES UP RESIDENCE

Now free of the constant pain of Polymyalgia Rheumatica I was enjoying life again. My much loved, patient and long-suffering husband was much happier too; the twinkle returned to his eyes and his general equilibrium once again surfaced. At times I am sure he felt he was bottom of the totem pole so surrounded was I with various other forms of living flesh and blood (livestock?). Until recently these had been your general run-of-the-mill jobs as previously described – cats, dogs, hens, sheep and the odd horse or two. But then we entered the realm of the exotic. A disabled Bengal eagle owl came to stay.

We first met Festa when he was just five weeks old. He arrived, in a cardboard box, with his newly acquired owners, Bridget and Dorian for Sunday lunch. An uglier babe I have yet to see. He was a voracious bundle of down, all eyes, beak and feet. He was still being fed every two hours and was not of a patient disposition if his food was late. We had barely finished our lunch before he set up a clamour for his own, which could not be ignored.

The idea that he should be loose in the kitchen while he ate made me very nervous. Any one of the four cats and even Jason would, I felt, find this expensive bird a tasty mouthful. I don't know why I was worrying. Tom, who weighed in at sixteen pounds, was the first to venture close. Festa immediately went into a threat display: he puffed himself up to twice his normal size, hissed and clacked his beak and chased Tom right out of his own kitchen. Consternation all round. The cats could not believe such a puny thing could become so menacing. Jason was fascinated, but luckily his training held good, and he observed from a distance.

Festa grew rapidly. My infrequent trips to Minehead usually ended with a visit to Bridget and Dorian's flat above the butcher's on Park Street. Enjoying a well-earned cup of coffee, I would become aware that I was being watched. On looking around, I'd locate a pair of huge eyes peering at me from a dark corner or regarding me from the edge of the curtains which partially obscured the wide windowsill.

Festa was about ten weeks old before Bridget noticed that one of his wings was weak and hanging down. The vet could find no reason for this deformity and could offer no hope that it would right itself, as indeed it didn't. He could not fly properly, but this did not stop him in the early days from trying. He would practice standing in front of the big picture window of the flat. A passerby noticed this and rang up the local branch of the RSPCA. One day there was a knock on the door, and it was an inspector from the RSPCA standing there. Bridget let him in so he could meet Festa and assess the situation. Festa, obligingly gave a demonstration and the inspector realised that everything was OK and there was no need to take any action. Festa hated being carried and would not ride on a wrist. He walked everywhere or rather he ambled like a little old man, with his head thrust forward and his wings held akimbo, very Churchillian. If excited or happy he did short, circling, low level flights, always ending up facing the way he started as the stronger wing swept him around.

Bridget and Dorian decided to move house. Bridget and Festa came to stay, using our home as a sort of halfway house. Things came and went but not Festa. It was "Mum, could you keep Festa for a few more days?" "Mum, we are still at sixes and sevens here. How is Festa?" I began to suspect a master plan that hadn't been brought into the open.

Festa had been occupying the utility room, much to the annoyance of the cats whose free access in and out was now denied them. Norman wasn't too keen on this addition to our menagerie, either! One of the things that really bothered Norman was that Festa had jessies on his legs. Festa stayed, on condition that I could move him into the spare loose box, and we could take the jessies off. Easier said than done. Taking him by surprise one morning I quickly wrapped a towel around him, yelled for Norman to come and, with great difficulty, as he never gave up struggling, managed to remove the jessies. I made the loose box into a home from home, carpeting some of the floor, building a roost, etc. and he was allowed the freedom of the yard or garden whenever possible.

I found him a fascinating creature to watch, the greatest time waster since television was invented. The incredible swivel of the head, the natural desire to be camouflaged at all times when in the garden, whether beside the trunk of a tree or under a bush or on an old stump at the bottom of the garden; he melted into the background of his chosen perch. One morning Festa was close to the side of the house as the postman walked past to deliver the post. He walked right by Festa without noticing him on his way to the front door. Coming back around the corner Festa hissed at him, the poor man nearly jumped out of his skin with fright. Used as I became to this preference didn't prevent mild panic attacks when I looked out at a seemingly empty garden, and I had to rush out frequently to reassure myself as to his safety.

Whether it was the banishment to the stable (and we are talking early September here, not cold midwinter) or he was finding four cats and a large dog more stressful than I realized I will never know, but Festa came down with a respiratory infection. Expert advice seemed indicated. Standing the cat crate on its end to accommodate Festa's height, I shoved him inside – he was furious, he hadn't been so confined since his baby days – and took him to the vet.

Expecting a cat to emerge she was rather surprised when Festa hopped out and did his circling fly act around the surgery. Talk about self-possessed! He stood on the examination table and allowed her to listen to his chest, although he found the stethoscope a little chilly. Once that was done, he hopped onto a pile of books that were on a corner of the table and relieved himself over the edge! Having made himself comfortable, he accepted being returned to the cage quite calmly.

It appeared he had the bird equivalent of pneumonia (he did not have lungs as such, he had air sacs) and must go on to antibiotics. We came home with a five-day course, to be administered twice a day. How to persuade Festa to take his medication was now the problem. He wasn't voluntarily going to open his beak, and I had no idea how to persuade him to accept the syringe full of medication. Time to hand the problem over to his owners. I phoned Dorian who came down that evening and showed me. To be fair, Dorian offered to take Festa home with him, but that would have produced yet more stress and really, once I knew how, I found dosing Festa quite easy. It is amazing what one can do if one has to. I've now added Dosing Birds of Prey to the long list of off-beat skills I could offer up to prospective employers if, heaven forbid, the need ever arose again to seek a job.

The antibiotic worked and was followed on veterinary advice, by a worming dose, but things were obviously not right in Festa's world. He was again enjoying his free time, in the yard or the garden, particularly finding warm corners for sunbathing and he was eating, but only enough to stay alive. His weight dropped by four and a half ounces when he was ill, which is a lot when you only weight three pounds after a good feed! He wasn't putting any weight back on. Very worrying.

I decided that he was lonely and pining away. Dorian and Bridget pooh poohed this theory as, in the wild, eagle owls are very solitary birds. But I kept returning to my theory. He had warmth and food and every mod con a bird could desire, but he lacked the constant noise of people's voices, the ringing telephone, the TV and the radio. I, again, summoned Dorian for a consultation, but as it happened, I made my decision before their arrival.

We had been away all day and on our return I went immediately to check on Festa. He had not moved all day and had not eaten. He was still in the corner which he had been occupying when I had looked in before leaving. I bought him into the house, covered the windowsill in the dining room with newspaper, and set him down there and prepared to evict the cats from the utility room, at least during the night. Dorian and Bridget both turned up and Dorian who is experienced with birds, gave Festa a thorough going-over and couldn't find anything amiss except for his lack of weight. This was Friday evening and that night, although in the utility, he only picked at his food. We decided that if he wasn't better by Monday we should take him back to the vets. Saturday night, secure in the utility room, again, he ate properly for the first time in two weeks. Monday came and went, there was no need for a trip to the vets, Festa just plumped up before my eyes. My theory had been right (much to Norman's dismay)!

House training a bird of prey is a joke. It can't be done. The best you can do, if you decide to give one house room, is to cover up your best furniture, place newspaper under its favourite perches and hope to catch half of the droppings. And as for imposing discipline, well, forget it, although, being of a rather determined nature, I hadn't totally given up on that one. Festa became totally at home and very territorial of the two rooms into which he was allowed, occasionally swooping down to attack any passing cat. He then jumped to the high back of his favourite chair and crowed triumphantly. It was difficult to be cross, but I wouldn't have my beautiful cats terrorized, and I tried a series of short, sharp "no's" if I caught him about to have a go in the forlorn hope that something would connect. There has to be room for all.

He loved spending time in the garden, especially by the rockery, which was at the top of the, slightly, sloping lawn. By the rockery he felt camouflaged, and it was a good starting point for trying to fly. Many times, I watched him running down the slope trying to take off only to fail yet again and despondently head back up the lawn. Once I saw him scramble onto the rockery and hide amongst the plants. I had heard there was a Golden Eagle in the area, escaped from a Bird of Prey display. I rushed outside in time to witness this large bird heading our way from Wheddon Cross. It passed over the garden. What extra keen eyesight Festa must have had to have spotted it from such a distance and to recognise it was a danger to him; a bird born in an aviary outside London. Amazing!

Indoors, he had his favourite occupations. He regularly beat up the dining room hearth rug and then hopped to his perch to crow. Another entertainment was sending piles of typing paper drifting to the floor. He stood on the edge of the table and watched the result of his reshuffling with an enquiring look on his face: "Did I really do that?" For some reason my feet in shoes were acceptable. My feet in slippers were subject to sneaky attacks when my back was turned.

He showed great affection for his toys and enjoyed playing with them. His favourite companion was Hamish, a large grey and white stuffed toy which Dorian met Bridget with at Heathrow in the early days of their courtship. Festa used Hamish much as a child uses a favourite teddy bear, sometimes fighting with him but more often cuddling up to him or sitting, brooding, on top of him. The little round hearth brush by the wood burner got firmly clasped in one claw while he preened down the bristles with his beak. He had a sock stuffed with soft material and tied into a knot at the open end. Sometimes he brooded this, squatting on the hearth rug with the sock cradled between his feet and his chest. At other times he carried the sock from perch to perch or left it lying on the worktable so I knew he had been up there poking around.

Festa had an enchanting repertoire of sounds. The triumphant crowing mentioned earlier, guttural chuckling and a general hoarse croak which seemed to be used as a greeting. He didn't exactly come when called, but would, with a series of his circling flight, arrive at an indicated doorway when I was fetching him in from the garden.

His basic diet came from roadside casualties. We often found mysterious parcels by our back door as the word had spread far and wide among our friends who were happy, as we were, to keep a couple of plastic bags in the boot of the car and pick up what they found. I was in the middle of supper preparations once when the phone rang. "There is a freshly killed rabbit, not mangled, on that dangerous corner not far from you. Sorry, I couldn't stop, but if you are quick you could salvage it!" I dashed into the sitting room where Norman was patiently awaiting my call to eat: "won't be long, dear, dead rabbit up on the road". And off I went at a smart trot, even remembering to put on a light-coloured coat and take the torch.

Having retrieved the corpse, I debated with myself whether to paunch and butcher it whilst still warm or leave it until we had eaten our meal. Sounds of merriment from the sitting room where Norman had the TV on at full blast made the decision for me, and I immediately got out the knives, the newspaper and the chopping block, and five minutes later four more tasty meals for Festa were being thrown back into the freezer. Any delectable goodies brought in by the cats were swiftly seized and handed over, unfair, I feel, but that's how things were now at home. When Festa was six years old she laid an egg. Up till then we had not known which sex she was. I went to let her out one morning and her room (she was back to sleeping in the stable as she spent all day out and about) looked like a hurricane had hit it. Every sheet of paper had been ripped into shreds like confetti and, under the perch was a white egg. The whole event must have been so traumatic for her, and I was not even there to offer her comfort.

Laying eggs caused Festa to become quite broody and, therefore, cuddly. I had talked to a chap at Dunster Show, who had a Bird of Prey display there including a Bengal eagle owl, about Fetsa and the egg laying. He explained to me that I should curtail this activity by making a nest and, once I had three eggs collected (she laid an egg every third day) put these eggs onto the nest and settle Festa there. It was amazing, I could actually cuddle her whilst she sat on the eggs. Swiftly taking advantage of this situation I found I could withdraw one leg at a time and trim her talons which were becoming rather too long. Living in the wild these would have worn back naturally. Then there was her beak to think about: this had a crack up one side and needed trimming off to stop it getting too high up the beak. Once egg laying was over she went back to using her perch. I started running the nail clippers up and down her beak until she accepted this then, one day, taking careful aim I would snip the end off the top beak. She would shriek and throw herself backwards off the perch. Job done for another six month!

And so the weeks and months rolled by. Always busy, sometimes fraught and stressful, seldom boring. I no longer had to think about the gap in my life Festa's leaving would make. Bridget and Dorian moved again to a place even less suitable for a spoiled, undersized, eagle owl who enjoyed his semi-free life in this quiet backwater. He remained with us for keeps: one more friend to fit under our Exmoor umbrella.

Epilogue

This writing is a tricky business or it was back then when I started doing some serious work. I have such admiration for writers who turn out book after book but, I wonder, were they running a small holding, exercising a horse or two, walking a dog, doing the house work and producing three meals a day?

At Gunns Farm I used to write at the dining room table with the life of the house going on around me as the dining room was used as the main route between the kitchen and the sitting room. The dog, the cats, the eagle owl all chose to keep me company; I think they liked to hear the tap of the keys as I rattled words down on the old typewriter bought through an advert in the *West Somerset Free Press*. And Norman and Mother frequently passing through also. I eventually acquired a computer; what a struggle it was to get to grips with this new way of putting words into print, I think I missed the tapping away of the keys too.

With Martha fit and well I picked up various other activities: the WI, some teaching for Pony Club and private lessons in my small arena at home, some dressage competitions, teaching with our local branch of Riding for the Disabled, and Public Speaking. I won the Somerset WI competition to attend a course at Denman College and followed this through by attending two WI weekend courses on Public Speaking in Taunton at the end of which we all took The City And Guilds exam in Advanced Spoken English which I passed, gaining the second grade. I think to gain the top one had to be a trained actor. I also did a few broadcasts on Musgrove Hospital Radio and became Secretary to our newly formed Local History Society although not all at once I must point out.

I spent many enjoyable years taking my talks on Exmoor, Life in The Yukon, in northern Canada and Festa all over Somerset and even to the WI in both islands in New Zealand. Great fun.

Then things had to slow down, as both Mother and Norman were not getting any younger. Poor Mother. She had such a hard time accepting a son-in-law just a year and a half younger than she was. We all rubbed along so well though until age caught up with her and she died just short of her 90th birthday. Her last couple of weeks were spent in Williton hospital receiving such tender care; we, my brother, sister, sister-in-law and brother-in-law spent all her last day with her and I alone returned to be her through the night and was there as she gently passed just before midnight, with myself and three nurses holding hands in a circle, with Mother.

Norman died, after a short stay in Minehead hospital, aged ninety-three years and two months. Dr Currie phoned whilst I was eating breakfast. I hurriedly phoned Norman's daughter in Devon, changed my clothes and headed to Minehead, breaking speed limits as I went I am sure, and was able to spend the last fifteen minutes or so of his life holding his hand and chatting. End of an era.

But life does go on even though it felt, suddenly, without purpose. I kept riding until I was seventy-two and just recently resigned from Labrador Rescue where, over some twenty-odd years I helped re-home 36 Labradors in the West Somerset region.

Meeting Derek twelve years ago was a real bonus. He is such a good friend and companion. He so enjoyed coming with me three times to visit family in western Canada and The Yukon where he was kind enough not to complain as I indulged myself with my love of long road trips; the last one was 5000 miles!

And, finally becoming a published author at the age of eighty-five in the *Exmoor* magazine which, in turn led to the publication of this autobiography. May I continue to ruin yet another rack of bread for a while yet.

The leaves are gone
The bare bones of the land visible
Once more to our discerning eye

The winding road
Which, driven in summer,
A series of hidden twists and turns
Reveals its secrets now

A glimpse of meadow
A distant water, hidden wall, disused well,
Deer grazing in a secluded field
All these and more enrich the winter scene